Compensation

COMPENSATION
Fair Pay for Executives and Employees

A Harvard Business Review Paperback

Harvard Business Review paperback No. 90071

The *Harvard Business Review* articles in this collection are available as individual reprints, with the exception of "Management, Labor, and the Golden Goose." Discounts apply to quantity purchases. For information and ordering contact Operations Department, Harvard Business School Publishing Division, Boston, MA 02163. Telephone: (617) 495-6192, 9 a.m. to 5 p.m. EST. Fax: (617) 495-6985, 24 hours a day.

© 1978, 1983, 1985, 1986, 1987, 1988, 1989, 1990, 1991 by the President and Fellows of Harvard College.

Editor's Note: Some articles in this book may have been written before authors and editors began to take into consideration the role of women in management. We hope the archaic usage representing all managers as male does not detract from the usefulness of the collection.

All rights reserved. No part of this book may be reproduced, stored in a retrieval system, or transmitted, in any form or by any means, electronic, mechanical, photocopying, recording, or otherwise without the prior written permission of the copyright holder.
Printed in the United States of America.
93 92 91   5 4 3 2 1

Contents

Executive Compensation

**CEO Incentives—
It's Not How Much You Pay, But How**
Michael C. Jensen and Kevin J. Murphy
3

Cash compensation of CEOs is not going through the roof, according to the results of an extensive field study. The problem is the tenuous link between the compensation of top executives and company performance.

Four Ways to Overpay Yourself Enough
Kenneth Mason
19

The logic of many executive compensation plans is that pay improves when performance does—and when it doesn't. The author, a former president of Quaker Oats, offers some unorthodox ideas for stiffening the sweetheart deals.

Top Executives Are Worth Every Nickel They Get
Kevin J. Murphy
25

At large companies compensation and performance *are* positively related, according to the author. Claims to the contrary are contradicted by his ten-year analysis of over 1,000 large U.S. corporations.

Fold Up Those Golden Parachutes
Peter G. Scotese
33

Some parachutes are so golden that they would make a king or queen blush. The author gives sensible guidelines for balancing fairness to executives and to shareholders.

Compensation and Benefits for Startup Companies
Joseph S. Tibbetts, Jr. and Edmund T. Donovan
37

You've decided to start a company. The basics are sound, but you need top-quality managers. How do you recruit them from secure positions at larger companies without exhausting your finances?

Employee Compensation

The Attack on Pay
Rosabeth Moss Kanter
45

Pay systems that value status instead of contribution are ineffective. Employers are now changing their policies to forge better links between compensation and performance. But when they do, they have to be prepared for a stream of consequences such as the attenuation of hierarchy.

Management, Labor, and the Golden Goose
William E. Fruhan, Jr.
53

When wages and fringe benefits are negotiated upward without regard to industry economics, companies can be bled of the capital they need to modernize or adapt. And if non-wage-related liabilities grow, companies may have no reasonable exit option when a mature industry enters a crisis period.

Teamwork for Today's Selling
Frank V. Cespedes, Stephen X. Doyle, and Robert J. Freedman
65

How do you encourage teamwork in selling industrial goods but reward individual performance? The solution demands a clear but more complex compensation formula than standard packages.

How to Pay Your Sales Force
John P. Steinbrink
73

How do you decide among the three basic options for paying salespeople: salary, commission, or a combination? The author lays out criteria for tailoring the decision to the needs of your company.

Tie Salesmen's Bonuses to Their Forecasts
Jacob Gonik
85

The dilemma is common: the sales force receives performance incentives but their territories differ widely in potential. Here is a way to accommodate the differences without undermining effectiveness.

Confronting Comparable Worth

Coping with Comparable Worth
George P. Sape
95

The issue is inflamatory, but the underlying problem will not go away. The best solution resides in an honest review of all company compensation and employment practices to look for unsuspected discrimination.

Compensation, Jobs, and Gender
Benson Rosen, Sara Rynes, and Thomas A. Mahoney
103

The authors present a set of strategic options for reviewing and taking action on the question of comparable worth.

Executive Compensation

Paying top executives "better" would eventually mean paying them more.

CEO Incentives—It's Not How Much You Pay, But How

by Michael C. Jensen and Kevin J. Murphy

The arrival of spring means yet another round in the national debate over executive compensation. Soon the business press will trumpet answers to the questions it asks every year: Who were the highest paid CEOs? How many executives made more than a million dollars? Who received the biggest raises? Political figures, union leaders, and consumer activists will issue now-familiar denunciations of executive salaries and urge that directors curb top-level pay in the interests of social equity and statesmanship.

The critics have it wrong. There are serious problems with CEO compensation, but "excessive" pay is not the biggest issue. The relentless focus on *how much* CEOs are paid diverts public attention from the real problem—*how* CEOs are paid. In most publicly held companies, the compensation of top executives is virtually independent of performance. On average, corporate America pays its most important

Michael C. Jensen is the Edsel Bryant Ford Professor of Business Administration at the Harvard Business School. His most recent HBR article, "Eclipse of the Public Corporation" (September-October 1989), won a McKinsey Award. Kevin J. Murphy is an associate professor at the University of Rochester's William E. Simon Graduate School of Business Administration. His earlier HBR article on executive compensation, "Top Executives Are Worth Every Nickel They Get," appeared in the March-April 1986 issue.

leaders like bureaucrats. Is it any wonder then that so many CEOs act like bureaucrats rather than the value-maximizing entrepreneurs companies need to enhance their standing in world markets?

We recently completed an in-depth statistical analysis of executive compensation. Our study incorporates data on thousands of CEOs spanning five decades. The base sample consists of information on salaries and bonuses for 2,505 CEOs in 1,400 publicly held companies from 1974 through 1988. We also collected data on stock options and stock ownership for

 Despite the headlines, top executives are not receiving record salaries and bonuses.

CEOs of the 430 largest publicly held companies in 1988. In addition, we drew on compensation data for executives at more than 700 public companies for the period 1934 through 1938.

Our analysis leads us to conclusions that are at odds with the prevailing wisdom on CEO compensation:

Despite the headlines, top executives are not receiving record salaries and bonuses. Salaries and bonuses have increased over the last 15 years, but

CEO pay levels are just now catching up to where they were 50 years ago. During the period 1934 through 1938, for example, the average salary and bonus for CEOs of leading companies on the New York Stock Exchange was $882,000 (in 1988 dollars). For the period 1982 through 1988, the average salary and bonus for CEOs of comparable companies was $843,000.

Annual changes in executive compensation do not reflect changes in corporate performance. Our statistical analysis posed a simple but important question: For every $1,000 change in the market value of a company, how much does the wealth of that company's CEO change? The answer varied widely across our 1,400-company sample. But for the median CEO in the 250 largest companies, a $1,000 change in corporate value corresponds to a change of just 6.7 cents in salary and bonus over two years. Accounting for all monetary sources of CEO incentives—salary and bonus, stock options, shares owned, and the changing likelihood of dismissal—a $1,000 change in corporate value corresponds to a change in CEO compensation of just $2.59.

Compensation for CEOs is no more variable than compensation for hourly and salaried employees. On average, CEOs receive about 50% of their base pay in the form of bonuses. Yet these "bonuses" don't generate big fluctuations in CEO compensation. A comparison of annual inflation-adjusted pay changes for CEOs from 1975 through 1988 and pay changes for 20,000 randomly selected hourly and salaried workers shows remarkably similar distributions. Moreover, a much lower percentage of CEOs took real pay cuts over this period than did production workers.

With respect to pay for performance, CEO compensation is getting worse rather than better. The most powerful link between shareholder wealth and executive wealth is direct stock ownership by the CEO. Yet CEO stock ownership for large public companies (measured as a percentage of total shares outstanding) was *ten times* greater in the 1930s than in the 1980s. Even over the last 15 years, CEO holdings as a percentage of corporate value have declined.

Compensation policy is one of the most important factors in an organization's success. Not only does it shape how top executives behave but it also helps determine what kinds of executives an organization attracts. This is what makes the vocal protests over CEO pay so damaging. By aiming their protests at compensation *levels*, uninvited but influential guests at the managerial bargaining table (the business press, labor unions, political figures) intimidate board members and constrain the types of contracts that are written between managers and shareholders. As a result of public pressure, directors become reluctant to reward CEOs with substantial (and therefore highly visible) financial gains for superior performance. Naturally, they also become reluctant to impose meaningful financial penalties for poor performance. The long-term effect of this risk-averse orientation is to erode the relation between pay and performance and entrench bureaucratic compensation systems.

Are we arguing that CEOs are underpaid? If by this we mean "Would average levels of CEO pay be higher if the relation between pay and performance were stronger?" the answer is yes. More aggressive pay-for-performance systems (and a higher probability of dismissal for poor performance) would produce sharply lower compensation for less talented managers. Over time, these managers would be replaced by more able and more highly motivated executives who would, on average, perform better and earn higher levels of pay. Existing managers would have greater incentives to find creative ways to enhance corporate performance, and their pay would rise as well.

These increases in compensation—driven by improved business performance—would not represent a transfer of wealth from shareholders to executives. Rather, they would reward managers for the increased success fostered by greater risk taking, effort, and ability. Paying CEOs "better" would eventually mean paying the average CEO more. Because the stakes are so high, the potential increase in corporate performance and the potential gains to shareholders are great.

How Compensation Measures Up

Shareholders rely on CEOs to adopt policies that maximize the value of their shares. Like other human beings, however, CEOs tend to engage in activities that increase their own well-being. One of the most critical roles of the board of directors is to create incentives that make it in the CEO's best interest to do what's in the shareholders' best interests. Conceptually this is not a difficult challenge. Some combination of three basic policies will create the right monetary incentives for CEOs to maximize the value of their companies:

1. Boards can require that CEOs become substantial owners of company stock.

2. Salaries, bonuses, and stock options can be structured so as to provide big rewards for superior performance and big penalties for poor performance.

3. The threat of dismissal for poor performance can be made real.

Unfortunately, as our study documents, the realities of executive compensation are at odds with these principles. Our statistical analysis departs from most studies of executive compensation. Unlike the annual surveys in the business press, for example, we do not focus on this year's levels of cash compensation or cash compensation plus stock options exercised. Instead, we apply regression analysis to 15 years' worth of data and estimate how changes in corporate performance affect CEO compensation and wealth over all relevant dimensions.

We ask the following questions: How does a change in performance affect current cash compensation, defined as changes in salary and bonus over two years? What is the "wealth effect" (the present value) of those changes in salary and bonus? How does a change in corporate performance affect the likelihood of the CEO being dismissed, and what is the financial impact of this new dismissal probability? Finally, how does a change in corporate performance affect the value of CEO stock options and shares, whether or not the CEO exercised the options or sold the shares? (For a discussion of our methodology, see the insert, "How We Estimate Pay for Performance.")

The table "The Weak State of Pay for Performance" provides a detailed review of our main findings for a subsample of CEOs in the 250 largest publicly held companies. Together, these CEOs run enterprises that generate revenues in excess of $2.2 trillion and employ more than 14 million people. The results are both striking and troubling. A $1,000 change in corporate market value (defined as share price appreciation plus dividends) corresponds to a two-year change in CEO salary and bonus of less than a dime; the long-term effects of that change add less than 45 cents to the CEO's wealth. A $1,000 change in corporate value translates into an estimated median change of a nickel in CEO wealth by affecting dismissal prospects. At the median, stock options add another 58 cents worth of incentives. Finally, the value of shares owned by the median CEO changes by 66 cents for every $1,000 increase in corporate value. All told, for the median executive in this subsample, a $1,000 change in corporate performance translates into a $2.59 change in CEO wealth. The table also reports estimates for CEOs at the lower and upper bounds of the middle two quartiles of the sample. (For an extensive review and comparison of the pay-for-performance relation for individual CEOs, see "A New Survey of Executive Compensation" that follows this article.)

This degree of pay-for-performance sensitivity for cash compensation does not create adequate incentives for executives to maximize corporate value. Consider a corporate leader whose creative strategic plan increases a company's market value by $100 million. Based on our study, the median CEO can expect a two-year increase in salary and bonus of $6,700—hardly a meaningful reward for such outstanding performance. His lifetime wealth would increase by $260,000—less than 4% of the present value of the median CEO's shareholdings and remaining lifetime salary and bonus payments.[1]

Or consider instead a CEO who makes a wasteful investment—new aircraft for the executive fleet, say, or a spanking addition to the headquarters building—that benefits him but diminishes the market value of the company by $10 million. The total wealth of this CEO, if he is representative of our sample, will decline by only $25,900 as a result of this misguided investment—not much of a disincentive for someone who earns on average $20,000 per week.

One way to explore the realities of CEO compensation is

The Weak State of Pay for Performance

A $1,000 Change in Shareholder Wealth Corresponds to...	Estimates for CEOs in the 250 Largest Companies	
	Median	Middle 50%
Change in this year's and next year's salary and bonus	$0.067	$0.01 to $0.18
Present value of the two-year change in salary and bonus	0.44	0.05 to 1.19
Change in the value of stock options	0.58	0.16 to 1.19
Wealth effect for change in likelihood of dismissal	0.05	0.02 to 0.14
Total change in all pay-related wealth	$1.29	$0.43 to $2.66
Change in value of direct stockholdings	0.66	0.25 to 1.98
Total change in CEO wealth	$2.59	$0.99 to $5.87

Note: The median individual components do not add to the median total change in CEO wealth since sums of medians do not in general equal the median of sums.

to compare current practices with the three principles that we outlined earlier. Let's address them one at a time.

CEOs should own substantial amounts of company stock. The most powerful link between shareholder wealth and executive wealth is direct ownership of shares by the CEO. Most commentators look at CEO stock ownership from one of two perspectives—the dollar value of the CEO's holdings or the value of his shares as a percentage of his annual cash compensation. But when trying to understand the incentive consequences of stock ownership, neither of these measures counts for much. What really matters is *the percentage of the company's outstanding shares the CEO owns.* By controlling a meaningful percentage of total corporate equity, senior managers experience a direct and powerful "feedback effect" from changes in market value.

Think again about the CEO adding jets to the corporate fleet. The stock-related "feedback effect" of this value-destroying investment—about $6,600—is small because this executive is typical of our sample, in which the median CEO controls only .066% of the company's outstanding shares. Moreover, this wealth loss (about two days' pay for the average CEO in a top-250 company) is the same whether the stockholdings represent a big or small fraction of the CEO's total wealth.

But what if this CEO held shares in the company comparable to, say, Warren Buffett's stake in the Berkshire Hathaway conglomerate? Buffett controls, directly and indirectly, about 45% of Berkshire Hathaway's equity. Under these circumstances, the stock-related feedback effect of a $10 million decline in market value is nearly $4.5 million—a much more powerful incentive to resist wasteful spending.

Moreover, these differences in CEO compensation are associated with substantial differences in corporate performance. From 1970 through 1988, the average annual compound stock return on the 25 companies with the best CEO incentives (out of the largest 250 companies examined in our survey) was 14.5%, more than one-third higher than the average return on the 25 companies with the worst CEO incentives. A $100 investment in the top 25 companies in 1970 would have grown to $1,310 by 1988, as compared with $702 for a similar investment in the bottom 25 companies.

As a percentage of total corporate value, CEO share ownership has never been very high. The median CEO of one of the nation's 250 largest public companies owns shares worth just over $2.4 million—again, less than 0.07% of the company's market value. Also, 9 out of 10 CEOs own less than 1% of their company's stock, while fewer than 1 in 20 owns more than 5% of the company's outstanding shares.

It is unreasonable to expect all public-company CEOs to own as large a percentage of their company's equity as Warren Buffett's share of Berkshire Hathaway. Still, the basic lesson holds. The larger the share of company stock controlled by the CEO and senior management, the more substantial the linkage between shareholder wealth and executive wealth. A few companies have taken steps to increase the share of corporate equity owned by senior management. Employees of Morgan Stanley now own 55% of the firm's outstanding equity. Companies such as FMC and Holiday have used leveraged recapitalizations to reduce the amount of outstanding equity by repurchasing public shares, and thus allow their managers to control a bigger percentage of the company. After FMC adopted its recapitalization plan, for example, employee ownership increased from 12% to 40% of outstanding equity. These recapitalizations allow managers to own a bigger share of their company's equity without necessarily increasing their dollar investment.

Truly giant companies like IBM, General Motors, or General Electric will never be able to grant their senior executives a meaningful share of outstanding equity. These and other giant companies should understand that this limitation on executive incentives is a real cost associated with bigness.

Cash compensation should be structured to provide big rewards for outstanding performance and meaningful penalties for poor performance. A two-year cash reward of less than 7 cents for each $1,000 increase in corporate value (or, conversely, a two-year penalty of less than 7 cents for each $1,000 decline in corporate value) does not create effective managerial incentives to maximize value. In most large companies, cash compensation for CEOs is treated like an entitlement program.

There are some notable exceptions to this entitlement pattern. The cash compensation of Walt Disney CEO Michael Eisner, whose pay has generated such attention in recent years, is more than ten times more sensitive to corporate performance than the median CEO in our sample. Yet the small number of CEOs for whom cash compensation changes in any meaningful way in response to corporate performance shows how far corporate America must travel if pay is to become an effective incentive.

Creating better incentives for CEOs almost necessarily means increasing the financial risk CEOs face. In this respect, cash compensation has certain ad-

---

1. The median CEO in our sample holds stock worth $2.4 million. The average 1988 salary and bonus for the CEOs in our sample was roughly $1 million. At a real interest rate of 3%, the present value of the salary and bonus for the next five years to retirement (the average for the sample) is $4.6 million. Thus total lifetime wealth from the company is $7 million.

vantages over stock and stock options. Stock-based incentives subject CEOs to vagaries of the stock market that are clearly beyond their control. Compensation contracts based on company performance relative to comparable companies could provide sound incentives while insulating the CEO from factors such as the October 1987 crash. Although there is some evidence that directors make implicit adjustments for market trends when they set CEO pay, we are surprised that compensation plans based explicitly on relative performance are so rare.[2]

The generally weak link between cash compensation and corporate performance would be less troubling if CEOs owned a large percentage of corporate equity. In fact, it would make sense for CEOs with big chunks of equity to have their cash compensation less sensitive to performance than CEOs with small stockholdings. (For example, Warren Buffett's two-year cash compensation changes by only a penny for every $1,000 increase in market value.) In some cases, it might even make sense for pay to go up in bad years to serve as a financial "shock absorber" for losses the CEO is taking in the stock market. Yet our statistical analysis found no correlation between CEO stock ownership and pay-for-performance sensitivity in cash compensation. In other words, boards of directors ignore CEO stock ownership when structuring incentive compensation plans. We find this result surprising – and symptomatic of the ills afflicting compensation policy.

> **Baseball managers often get fired after one losing season. CEOs stay on the job despite years of underperformance.**

Make real the threat of dismissal. The prospect of being fired as a result of poor performance can provide powerful monetary and nonmonetary incentives for CEOs to maximize company value. Because much of an executive's "human capital" (and thus his or her value in the job market) is specific to the company, CEOs who are fired from their jobs are unlikely to find new jobs that pay as well. In addition, the public humiliation associated with a high-visibility dismissal should cause managers to carefully weigh the consequences of taking actions that increase the probability of being dismissed.

Here too, however, the evidence is clear: the CEO position is not a very risky job. Sports fans are accustomed to baseball managers being fired after one losing season. Few CEOs experience a similar fate after years of underperformance. There are many reasons why we would expect CEOs to be treated differently from baseball managers. CEOs have greater organization-specific capital; it is harder for an outsider to come in and run a giant company than it is for a new manager to take over a ball club. There are differences in the lag between input and output. The measure of a baseball manager's success is the team's won-lost record this year; the measure of a corporate manager is the company's long-term competitiveness and value. For these and other reasons, it is not surprising that turnover rates are lower for CEOs than for baseball managers. It is surprising that the magnitude of the discrepancy is so large.

On average, CEOs in our base sample (2,505 executives) hold their jobs for more than ten years before stepping down, and most give up their title (but not their seat on the board) only after reaching normal retirement age. Two recent studies, spanning 20 years and more than 500 management changes, found only 20 cases where CEOs left their jobs because of poor performance.[3] To be sure, directors have little to gain from publicly announcing that a CEO is leaving because of failure – many underperforming CEOs leave amidst face-saving explanations and even public congratulations. But this culture of politeness does not explain why so few underperforming CEOs leave in the first place. University of Rochester's Michael Weisbach found that CEOs of companies that rank in the bottom 10% of the performance distribution (measured by stock returns) are roughly twice as likely to leave their jobs as CEOs whose companies rank in the top 10% of the performance distribution. Yet the differences that Weisbach quantifies – a 3% chance of getting fired for top performers versus a 6% chance of getting fired for laggards – are unlikely to have meaningful motivational consequences for CEOs.

Our own research confirms these and other findings. CEOs of large public companies are only slightly more likely to step down after very poor performance (which we define as company earnings 50% below market averages for two consecutive years) than after average performance. For the entire 1,400-company sample, our analysis estimates that the poor-performing CEOs are roughly 6% more likely to leave their jobs than CEOs of companies with average returns. Even assuming that a dismissed CEO never works again, the personal wealth consequences of this increased likelihood of dis-

---

2. See Robert Gibbons and Kevin J. Murphy, "Relative Performance Evaluation for Chief Executive Officers," *Industrial and Labor Relations Review*, February 1990, p. 30-S.

3. See Jerold B. Warner, Ross L. Watts, and Karen H. Wruck, "Stock Prices and Top Management Changes," *Journal of Financial Economics*, January-March 1988, p.461; and Michael S. Weisbach, "Outside Directors and CEO Turnover," *Journal of Financial Economics*, January-March 1988, p.431.

missal amounts to just 5 cents for every $1,000 loss of shareholder value.

With respect to pay for performance, there's no denying that the results of our study tell a bleak story. Then again, perhaps corporate directors are providing CEOs with substantial rewards and penalties based on performance, but they are measuring performance with metrics other than long-run stock market value. We tested this possibility and reached the same conclusion as in our original analysis. Whatever the metric, CEO compensation is independent of business performance.

For example, we tested whether companies rewarded CEOs on the basis of sales growth or accounting profits rather than on direct changes in shareholder wealth. We found that while more of the variation in CEO pay could be explained by changes in accounting profits than stock market value, the pay-for-performance sensitivity was economically just as insignificant as in our original model. Sales growth had little explanatory power once we controlled for accounting profits.[4]

Of course, incentives based on other measures will be captured by our methodology only to the extent that they ultimately correlate with changes in shareholder wealth. But if they don't—that is, if directors are rewarding CEOs based on variables other than those that affect corporate market value—why use such measures in the first place?

Moreover, if directors varied CEO compensation substantially from year to year based on performance measures not observable to us, this policy would show up as high raw variability in CEO compensation. But over the past 15 years, compensation for CEOs has been about as variable as cash compensation for a random sample of hourly and salaried workers—dramatic evidence of compensation's modest role in generating executive incentives.[5] "Common Variability: CEO and Worker Wages" compares the distribution of annual raises and pay cuts of our CEO sample with national data on hourly and salaried workers from 1975 through 1986. A larger percentage of workers took real pay cuts at some time over this period than did CEOs. Overall, the standard deviation of annual changes in CEO pay was only slightly greater than for hourly and salaried employees (32.7% versus 29.7%).

Looking Backward: Pay for Performance in the 1930s

CEO compensation policies look especially unsatisfactory when compared with the situation 50 years ago. All told, CEO compensation in the 1980s was lower, less variable, and less sensitive to corporate performance than in the 1930s. To compare the current situation with the past, we constructed a longitudinal sample of executives from the 1930s using data collected by the Works Projects Administration. The WPA data, covering fiscal years 1934 through 1938, include salary and bonus for the highest paid executive (whom we designate as the CEO) in 748 large U.S. corporations in a wide range of industries. Nearly 400 of the WPA sample companies were listed on the New York Stock Exchange, and market values for these companies are available on the CRSP Monthly Stock Returns Tape. In order to compare

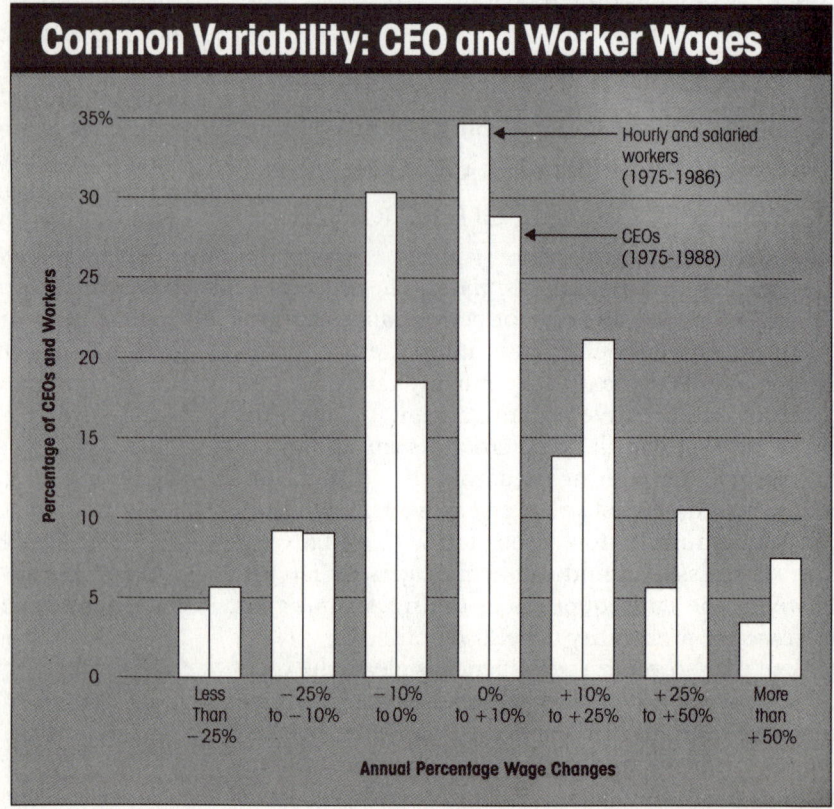

4. For more detail on these tests, see our article, "Performance Pay and Top-Management Incentives," *Journal of Political Economy*, April 1990.

5. Data on hourly and salaried workers come from the Michigan Panel Study on Income Dynamics. The sample includes 21,895 workers aged 21 to 65 reporting wages in consecutive periods. See Kenneth J. McLaughlin, "Rigid Wages?" University of Rochester Working Paper, 1989.

similar companies over the two time periods, we restricted our analysis to companies in the top 25% of the NYSE, ranked by market value. WPA compensation data are available for 60% of this top quartile group (averaging 112 companies per year), while data for more recent times are available for 90% of the top quartile companies (averaging 345 companies per year).

The results are striking. Measured in 1988 constant dollars, CEOs in top quartile public companies earned an average salary and bonus of $882,000 in the 1930s—more than the 1982 through 1988 average of $843,000 and significantly more than the 1974 through 1981 average of $642,000. Over this same time period, there has been a tripling (after inflation) of the market value of top quartile companies—from $1.7 billion in the 1930s to $5.9 billion in 1982 through 1988. Coupled with the decline in salaries, the ratio of CEO pay to total company value has fallen significantly—from 0.11% in the 1930s to 0.03% in the 1980s. Compensation was more variable in the 1930s as well. The average standard deviation of the annual pay changes—the best statistical measure of the year-to-year variability of compensation—was $504,000 in the 1930s compared with $263,500 in the 1980s.

The incentives generated by CEO stock ownership have also declined substantially over the past 50 years. To test this trend, we reviewed stock ownership data for CEOs in the 120 largest companies (ranked by market value) in 1938, 1974, and 1988. "Whatever Happened to CEO Stock Ownership?" reports our findings. The percentage of outstanding shares owned by CEOs (including shares held by family members) in the top 120 companies fell by a factor of nearly ten from 1938 to 1988. The trend is unmistakable: as a percentage of total market value, CEO stock ownership has declined substantially over the last 50 years and is continuing to fall.

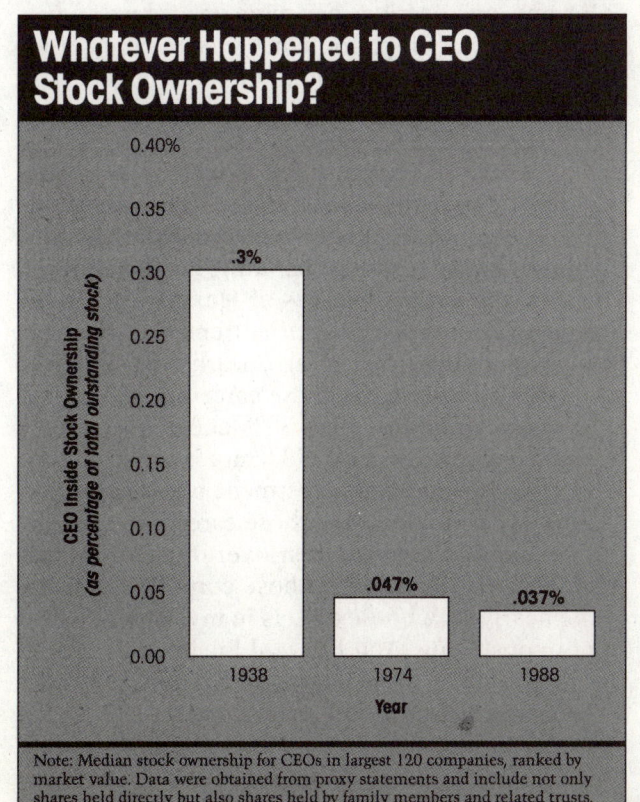

The Costs of Disclosure

Why don't boards of directors link pay more closely to performance? Commentators offer many explanations, but nearly every analysis we've seen overlooks one powerful ingredient—the costs imposed by making executive salaries public. Government disclosure rules ensure that executive pay remains a visible and controversial topic. The benefits of disclosure are obvious; it provides safeguards against "looting" by managers in collusion with "captive" directors. The costs of disclosure are less well appreciated but may well exceed the benefits.

Managerial labor contracts are not a private matter between employers and employees. Third parties play an important role in the contracting process, and strong political forces operate inside and outside companies to shape executive pay. Moreover, authority over compensation decisions rests not with the shareholders but with compensation committees generally composed of outside directors. These committees are elected by shareholders but are not perfect agents for them. Public disclosure of "what the boss makes" gives ammunition to outside constituencies with their own special-interest agendas. Compensation committees typically react to the agitation over pay levels by capping—explicitly or implicitly—the amount of money the CEO earns.

How often do shareholder activists or union leaders denounce a corporate board for *under*paying the CEO? Not very often—and that's precisely the problem. Most critics of executive pay want it both ways. They want companies to link pay to performance, yet they also want to limit compensation to arbitrary amounts or some fuzzy sense of "what's fair." That won't work. Imposing a ceiling on salaries for outstanding performers inevitably means creating a floor for poor performers. Over time, by cutting off the upper and lower tails of the distribution, the entire pay-for-performance relation erodes. When mediocre outfielders earn a million dollars a year, and New York law partners earn about the same, influen-

Whatever Happened to CEO Stock Ownership?

Year	CEO Inside Stock Ownership (as percentage of total outstanding stock)
1938	.3%
1974	.047%
1988	.037%

Note: Median stock ownership for CEOs in largest 120 companies, ranked by market value. Data were obtained from proxy statements and include not only shares held directly but also shares held by family members and related trusts.

tial critics who begrudge comparable salaries to the men and women running billion-dollar enterprises help guarantee that these companies will attract mediocre leaders who turn in mediocre performances.

Admittedly, it is difficult to document the effect of public disclosure on executive pay. Yet there have been a few prominent examples. Bear, Stearns, the successful investment bank, went public in 1985 and had to submit to disclosure requirements for the first time. CEO Alan Greenberg's $2.9 million salary and bonus was the nation's fourth highest that year, and his ranking drew attention to the firm's compensation system. Under private ownership, compensation of the firm's managing directors was set at a modest $150,000 base plus a bonus pool tied to earnings – a tight link between pay and performance. Because the firm was so profitable in 1986, the bonus pool swelled to $80 million, an average of $842,000 for each of the firm's 95 managing directors. A public outcry ensued. Six months after going public, Bear, Stearns announced it was lowering the bonus pool from 40% to 25% of the firm's adjusted pretax earnings in excess of $200 million. According to one account, the firm's business success had "yielded an embarrassment of riches for top executives."[6]

More recently, we interviewed the president of a subsidiary of a thriving publicly traded conglomerate. This president is compensated with a straight fraction of his subsidiary's earnings above a minimum threshold, with no upper bound. Today he makes roughly five times what he made before his operation was acquired by the conglomerate, and corporate headquarters recognizes him as one of the company's outstanding executives. Why doesn't he want to be an officer of the conglomerate? For one, because his salary would have to be made public – a disclosure both he and the CEO consider a needless invitation to internal and external criticism.

We are not arguing for the elimination of salary disclosure. (Indeed, without disclosure we could not have conducted this study.) But it's time compensation committees stood up to outside criticism and stopped adopting policies that make their companies' incentive problem worse. The costs of negative publicity and political criticism are less severe than the costs to shareholder wealth created by misguided compensation systems.

Corporate Brain Drain

The level of pay has very little to do with whether or not CEOs have incentives to run companies in the shareholders' interests – incentives are a function of how pay, whatever the level, changes in response to corporate performance. But the level of pay does affect the quality of managers an organization can attract. Companies that are willing to pay more will, in general, attract more highly talented individuals.

> **Are current levels of CEO compensation high enough to attract the best and the brightest? Probably not.**

So if the critics insist on focusing on levels of executive pay, they should at least ask the right question: Are current levels of CEO compensation high enough to attract the best and brightest individuals to careers in corporate management? The answer is, probably not.

Who can disagree with these propositions?
☐ It is good when our most talented men and women are attracted to the organizations that produce the goods and deliver the services at the heart of the economy.
☐ People evaluate alternative careers at least in part on the basis of lifetime monetary rewards.
☐ People prefer to make more money than less, and talented, self-confident people prefer to be rewarded based on performance rather than independent of it.
☐ If some organizations pay more on average and offer stronger pay-for-performance systems than other organizations, talent will migrate to the higher paying organizations.

These simple propositions are at the heart of a phenomenon that has inspired much handwringing and despair over the last decade – the stream of talented, energetic, articulate young professionals into business law, investment banking, and consulting. Data on the career choices of Harvard Business School graduates document the trend that troubles so many pundits. Ten years ago, nearly 55% of newly graduated HBS students chose careers in the corporate sector, while less than 30% chose investment banking or consulting. By 1987, more than half of all HBS graduates entered investment banking or consulting, while under 30% chose careers in the corporate sector. Last year, just over one-third of all graduating HBS students chose corporate careers, while nearly 40% chose careers in investment banking or consulting. And Harvard Business School is not alone; we gathered data on other highly rated MBA programs and found similar trends.

We don't understand why commentators find this trend so mysterious. A highly sensitive pay-for-

---
6. *Wall Street Journal,* March 21, 1986.

How We Estimate Pay for Performance

Our analysis draws primarily on two sources of data: annual executive compensation surveys published in *Forbes* magazine from 1975 through 1988 and Standard & Poor's Compustat file. The base sample includes information on 2,505 CEOs from 1,400 companies. We estimated pay-for-performance sensitivities for each CEO using a variety of statistical techniques. The findings reported in the table "The Weak State of Pay for Performance" represent the median and "middle 50%" CEOs in a sample of the 250 largest companies.

Perhaps the best way to illustrate our methodology is to review pay-for-performance calculations for a single CEO – for example, David H. Murdock of Castle & Cooke, Inc., who tops our list of large-company CEOs with the best incentives. For each element of Mr. Murdock's compensation, we estimated answers to the same question: How does that compensation element change in response to a $1,000 change in corporate value, as measured by annual share price appreciation and dividends?

Two-Year Change in Salary and Bonus. We used least squares regression to calculate the relation between the dollar change in salary and bonus and the dollar change in shareholder wealth for all companies with at least seven years of pay-change data from 1975 through 1988. We estimate a single pay-for-performance sensitivity for each company, therefore our estimates for Castle & Cooke use data on both Murdock and his predecessor Donald Kirchhoff. We did not use data on three other former CEOs – Robert Cook, Ian Wilson, and Henry Clark, Jr. – because they each served as CEO for less than two years and we could therefore not calculate pay changes. The regression equation uses last year's performance in addition to this year's performance as explanatory variables. The result was:

$$\text{(change in salary and bonus)} = \$32,300 \\ + .000986 \text{ (change in this year's shareholder wealth)} \\ - .000219 \text{ (change in last year's shareholder wealth)}$$

The pay-for-performance sensitivity is defined as the estimated slope coefficient in the regression equation. For this regression, the sum of the estimated coefficients implies that each $1,000 increase in the wealth of Castle & Cooke shareholders corresponds to an increase of 98.6 cents in this year's salary and bonus for Murdock, and a decrease of 21.9 cents in next year's salary and bonus.

Thus the total expected increase in salary and bonus over two years is 77 cents per $1,000 change in value.

We estimated 430 separate regressions like the one for Murdock, having eliminated 740 companies due to incomplete information and 230 companies that were no longer in the sample in 1988. The pattern of t-statistics for the individual regressions implies that the average pay-performance coefficients are positive and statistically different from zero at confidence levels exceeding 99%.

Pay-Related Wealth. The estimate of 77 cents is an accurate measure of how David Murdock's and Donald Kirchhoff's salary and bonus change due to a $1,000 change in shareholder value. But it underestimates the change in their wealth. Since part of the change is permanent, they will earn it for the rest of their careers. In addition, Murdock and Kirchhoff received "other" income as fringe benefits and payoffs from long-term performance plans. We measure the change in their total wealth as the discounted present value of the permanent component of the change in compensation plus other income for the year.

To estimate the wealth change, we make three assumptions: (1) all changes in salary and bonus are permanent, while other forms of pay are transitory; (2) the CEO receives the change in salary and bonus until age 66; and (3) the wage increase to age 66 is discounted at the real interest rate of 3%. The resulting regression equation for Castle & Cooke, based on these assumptions, is:

$$\text{(other income + present value of change in salary and bonus)} = \\ \$150,000 + .00310 \text{ (change in this year's shareholder wealth)} \\ + .00060 \text{ (change in last year's shareholder wealth)}$$

The sum of the estimated coefficients in this regression implies that Murdock's and Kirchhoff's wealth (as a result of changes in salary and bonus) changes an average of $3.70 for every $1,000 change in the market value of Castle & Cooke.

Stock Options. Stock options are an increasingly important component of executive compensation packages, and their value relates directly to changes in share price. However, holding a stock option does not provide the same incentives as owning a share of stock – a distinction sometimes overlooked by compensation practitioners. For example, stock ownership rewards both price appreciation and dividends, while options reward only appreciation.

Moreover, the value of an option changes by less than $1 when the stock price changes by $1. How much less depends on factors such as interest rates, dividend yields, and whether the option is in or out of the money. Our simulation results show that 60 cents is a good approximation for the value change of at-the-money options for a company with a (sample average) dividend yield of 5%. This holds for a reasonable range of maturities, variance of stock returns, and interest rates.

We collected data on total stock options held by each of the sample CEOs from the proxy statements issued in advance of the company's 1989 annual meeting. Unfortunately, outstanding options are not always reported on proxy statements. So we estimated Murdock's outstanding options as options granted in 1988 (50,000 shares) plus options exercisable within 60 days (300,000 shares). Castle & Cooke had 59.3 million shares outstanding. A $1,000 change in shareholder wealth corresponds to the following change in the value of Murdock's options:

$$\left(\frac{60\text{¢ change in value of option}}{\$1 \text{ change in stock price}}\right) \times \left(\frac{350{,}000 \text{ Options}}{59{,}250{,}000 \text{ Total Shares}}\right) \times \$1{,}000 = \$3.54$$

Thus Murdock's option-related wealth changes by $3.54 for every $1,000 change in shareholder wealth. This estimate understates the change in the value of his options to the extent that he holds options granted prior to 1988 that are not exercisable within 60 days. We also underestimate the option-value change if his outstanding options are in the money, while we overstate the value change of out-of-the-money options.

Dismissal Incentives. The threat of being fired for poor performance provides monetary as well as nonmonetary incentives for CEOs to maximize value. We estimate the financial incentives associated with dismissal through a four-stage process. First, using nonlinear "logistic" regression techniques on our 1974 through 1988 sample of 2,505 CEOs, we estimate the probability that a CEO will leave the job as a function of industry, company size, CEO age, market-relative performance, and lagged market-relative performance. Second, we compute point estimates of the departure probabilities when the company earns the market rate of return for two years versus when the company realizes share-price returns 50% below the market in two consecutive years. Third, we multiply the difference in these two "dismissal probabilities" by the discounted value of the CEO's potential lost wages, assuming that the CEO would have received the current salary until age 66, and, if dismissed, never works again. Fourth, we calculate the dismissal performance sensitivity by dividing the CEO's potential wealth loss by the shareholder loss associated with earning 50% below-market returns for two years.

In Murdock's case, the probability that a 65-year-old CEO in a smaller-than-median-size company leaves his job is 20.7% in years when the company earns the market return and 23.9% when his company earns 50% below the market return for two straight years. The probability that Murdock will be fired (or encouraged to leave) for poor performance is 3.2%. Murdock's dismissal-related loss is his $1.5 million 1988 pay multiplied by the turnover-probability difference, or about $48,000. (If Murdock had been younger than 65, we would have calculated the present value of his 1988 pay until he reached 66.) Castle & Cooke shareholders, on the other hand, would lose about $1.25 billion of their $1.67 billion equity from two straight years of 50% below-market performance. Thus Murdock's potential wealth loss is about 3.8 cents per $1,000 lost by shareholders.

It is important to note that while our estimates of other CEO incentive sources use data for the individual CEO's company, our estimates of CEO-dismissal performance sensitivities are based on the entire sample. It is generally impossible to make company-specific estimates of the wealth effects of dismissal threats.

Stock Ownership. The most important component of CEO incentives is also the easiest to measure. As of March 1989, Murdock held directly 13,203,932 shares of Castle & Cooke. In addition, his children hold 80,870 shares in trusts. All told, his family holds 13,284,802 shares, or 22.42% of Castle & Cooke's outstanding stock. His total stock-related incentives are roughly $224.24 per $1,000 change in market value.

Putting It All Together. David Murdock's total pay-for-performance sensitivity is simply the sum of the sensitivities of each compensation element, or $231.53 per $1,000 change in shareholder value. This makes Murdock the CEO with the best incentives in the 250 largest companies.

performance system will cause high-quality people to self-select into a company. Creative risk takers who perceive they will be in the upper tail of the performance and pay distribution are more likely to join companies who pay for performance. Low-ability and risk-averse candidates will be attracted to companies with bureaucratic compensation systems that ignore performance.

Compensation systems in professions like investment banking and consulting are heavily weighted toward the contributions made by individuals and the performance of their work groups and companies. Compensation systems in the corporate world are often independent of individual, group, or overall corporate performance. Moreover, average levels of top-executive compensation on Wall Street or in corporate law are considerably higher than in corporate America. Financially speaking, if you are a bright, eager 26-year-old with enough confidence to want to be paid based on your contribution, why would you choose a career at General Motors or Procter & Gamble over Morgan Stanley or McKinsey & Company?

Most careers, including corporate management, require lifetime investments. Individuals must choose their occupation long before their ultimate success or failure becomes a reality. For potential CEOs, this means that individuals seeking careers in corporate management must join their companies at an early age in entry-level jobs. The CEOs in our sample spent an average of 16 years in their companies before assuming the top job. Of course, many people who reach the highest ranks of the corporate hierarchy could also expect to be successful in professional partnerships such as law or investment banking, as proprietors of their own businesses, or as CEOs of privately held companies. It is instructive, therefore, to compare levels of CEO compensation with the compensation of similarly skilled individuals who have reached leadership positions in other occupations.

The compensation of top-level partners in law firms is one relevant comparison. These numbers are closely guarded secrets, but some idea of the rewards to top partners can be gleaned from data on average partner income reported each year in a widely read industry survey. The table "Salaries for Top Lawyers

Salaries for Top Lawyers Are High...

Rank	Firm	Average Income per Partner	Number of Partners
1	Cravath, Swaine, & Moore	$1,595,000	67
2	Cahill Gordon & Reindel	$1,420,000	57
3	Sullivan & Cromwell	$1,375,000	91
4	Wachtell, Lipton, Rosen & Katz	$1,350,000	46
5	Skadden, Arps, Slate, Meagher & Flom	$1,155,000	177

Source: *The American Lawyer*, July-August 1989, p. 34.

Are High..." reports 1988 estimated average incomes earned by partners in the highest paying corporate law firms. These five firms paid their 438 partners *average* incomes ranging from $1.35 million to nearly $1.6 million. Partners at the very top of these firms earned substantially more. When comparing these results with corporate compensation, the appropriate question to ask is "How many public companies paid their top 67 or 177 executives average salaries of $1.6 million or $1.2 million in 1989?" The answer is, few or none. How surprising is it, then, that law school classes are bulging with some of the country's brightest students?

Compensation for the most successful corporate managers is also modest in comparison with compensation for the most successful Wall Street players. Here too it is difficult to get definitive numbers for a large sample of top executives. But the most recent annual survey, as reported in the table "...So Are Salaries on Wall Street," documents the kinds of rewards available to top investment bankers. At Goldman, Sachs, for example, 18 partners earned more than $3 million in 1988, and the average income for those partners was more than

...So Are Salaries on Wall Street

Firm	Number of Partners Earning More Than $3 Million in 1988	Average Earnings for Partners Earning More Than $3 Million in 1988
Drexel Burnham Lambert	20	$18,000,000
Goldman, Sachs	18	$ 9,100,000
Morgan Stanley	11	$ 4,300,000
Sterling Group	6	$36,700,000
Kohlberg Kravis Roberts	5	$59,000,000
Lazard Freres	5	$17,200,000
Salomon Brothers	5	$ 4,700,000
Neuberger & Berman	5	$ 4,700,000

Source: *Financial World*, July 11, 1989. Average earnings are based on *Financial World's* lower bound earnings estimate, p. 32.

$9 million. Only nine public-company CEOs had incomes in excess of $9 million in 1988 (mostly through exercising stock options), and no public company paid its top 18 executives more than $3 million each. The Wall Street surveys for 1989 are not yet available, but consistent with high pay-for-performance systems, they will likely show sharp declines in bonuses reflecting lower 1989 industry performance.

The compensation figures for law and investment banking look high because they reflect only the most highly paid individuals in each occupation. Average levels of compensation for lawyers or investment bankers may not be any higher than average pay levels for executives. But that's not the relevant comparison. The very best lawyers or investment bankers can earn substantially more than the very best corporate executives. Highly talented people who would succeed in any field are likely to shun the corporate sector, where pay and performance are weakly related, in favor of organizations where pay is more strongly related to performance – and the prospect of big financial rewards more favorable.

Money Isn't Everything

Some may object to our focus on monetary incentives as the central motivator of CEO behavior. Are there not important nonmonetary rewards associated with running a large organization? Benefits such as power, prestige, and public visibility certainly do affect the level of monetary compensation necessary to attract highly qualified people to the corporate sector. But unless nonmonetary rewards vary positively with company value, they are no more effective than cash compensation in motivating CEOs to act in the shareholders' interests. Moreover, because nonmonetary benefits tend to be a function of position or rank, it is difficult to vary them from period to period based on performance.

> **Money isn't everything, but nonmonetary rewards often create the wrong incentives for CEOs.**

Indeed, nonmonetary rewards typically motivate top managers to take actions that *reduce* productivity and harm shareholders. Executives are invariably tempted to acquire other companies and expand the diversity of the empire, even though acquisitions often reduce shareholder wealth. As prominent members of their community, CEOs face pressures to keep open uneconomic factories, to keep the peace with labor unions despite the impact on competitiveness, and to satisfy intense special-interest pressures.

Monetary compensation and stock ownership remain the most effective tools for aligning executive and shareholder interests. Until directors recognize the importance of incentives – and adopt compensation systems that truly link pay and performance – large companies and their shareholders will continue to suffer from poor performance.

Authors' note: A more technical and comprehensive analysis of our findings – based on slightly different methodology and less recent data – appears in the April 1990 issue of the Journal of Political Economy. *We are indebted to Brian Barry for help in compiling the options data.*

Reprint 90308

"A New Survey of Executive Compensation,"
an extensive review and comparison of the pay-for-performance
relation for individual CEOs, begins on the next page.

A New Survey of Executive Compensation

Routinely misused and abused, surveys contribute to the common ills of corporate compensation policy. Surveys that report average compensation across industries help inflate salaries, as everyone tries to be above average (but not in front of the pack). Surveys that relate pay to company sales encourage systems that tie compensation to size and growth, not performance and value. Surveys that rank the country's highest paid executives stir public outrage, raise legislative eyebrows, and provide emotional justification for increased demands in labor negotiations.

The basic problem with existing compensation surveys is that they focus exclusively on *how much* CEOs are paid instead of *how* they are paid. Our focus on incentives rather than levels leads naturally to a new and different kind of survey. Instead of reporting who's paid the most, our survey reports who's paid the best—that is, whose incentives are most closely aligned with the interests of their shareholders.

Our survey considers incentives from a variety of sources—including salary and bonus, stock options, stock ownership, and the threat of getting fired for poor performance. It includes only companies listed in the *Forbes* executive compensation surveys for at least eight years from 1975 through 1989, since we require at least seven years of pay change to estimate the relation between pay and performance. Our methodology is described in the insert "How We Estimate Pay for Performance."

Compensation surveys in the business press, such as those published by *Fortune* and *Business Week*, are really about levels of pay and not about pay for performance. Yet they often include an analysis or ranking of the appropriateness of a particular CEO's pay by relating it to company performance in some fashion. The methods adopted by *Fortune* and *Business Week* share a common flaw. CEOs earning low fixed salaries while delivering mediocre performance look like stars; on the flip side, CEOs with genuinely strong pay-for-per-

The 25 CEOs of Large Companies with the Best Incentives

Total Effects (over Two Years) on CEO Wealth Corresponding to Each $1,000 Change in Shareholder Wealth

Rank	Company	CEO	Change in All Pay-Related Wealth	Change in the Value of Stock Owned	Change in Total CEO Wealth
1	Castle & Cooke	David H. Murdock	$7.29	$224.24	$231.53
2	Amerada Hess	Leon Hess*	$0.02	$152.71	$152.73
3	Wang Laboratories	An Wang*	$0.84	$137.83	$138.68
4	Aon Corp.	Patrick G. Ryan	$0.76	$137.46	$138.22
5	Loews	Laurence A. Tisch	$0.00	$126.40	$126.40
6	Ethyl	Floyd D. Gottwald, Jr.	−$0.25	$90.73	$90.48
7	Marriott	J. Willard Marriott, Jr.*	$1.55	$72.58	$74.14
8	MCA	Lew R. Wasserman	$0.05	$70.10	$70.15
9	Paine Webber Group	Donald B. Marron	$55.59	$11.44	$67.03
10	Paccar	Charles M. Pigott	$2.25	$50.86	$53.12
11	Times Mirror	Robert F. Erburu	$3.29	$45.39	$48.67
12	Coastal Corp.	Oscar S. Wyatt, Jr.*	$0.43	$44.33	$44.75
13	Archer-Daniels-Midland	Dwayne O. Andreas	−$0.15	$41.23	$41.07
14	Carter Hawley Hale	Philip M. Hawley*	$23.36	$16.25	$39.60
15	McDonnell Douglas	John F. McDonnell*	$0.09	$33.79	$33.88
16	CBS	Laurence A. Tisch	$1.79	$31.58	$33.37
17	Humana	David A. Jones*	$1.34	$25.88	$27.22
18	Winn-Dixie Stores	A. Dano Davis	$2.72	$23.22	$25.95
19	Masco	Richard A. Manoogian	$8.78	$14.08	$22.86
20	American Int'l Group	Maurice R. Greenberg	$0.50	$21.72	$22.22
21	Digital Equipment	Kenneth H. Olsen*	$1.00	$19.06	$20.07
22	MCI Communications	William G. McGowan*	$1.77	$17.95	$19.73
23	Cummins Engine	Henry B. Schacht	$18.46	$0.87	$19.33
24	Walt Disney	Michael D. Eisner	$15.62	$2.88	$18.50
25	FMC	Robert H. Malott	$8.43	$7.04	$15.47

Note: Sample consists of CEOs in the 250 largest companies, ranked by 1988 sales. *Denotes founder or founding-family CEO.

formance practices rank poorly. For example, *Business Week*'s 1989 survey calculates the ratio of the change in shareholder wealth to the CEO's total compensation, both measured over three years. Executives with the highest ratios are labeled the "CEOs Who Gave the Most for Their Pay." Low-ratio CEOs purportedly gave shareholders the least. *Fortune*'s 1989 compensation issue uses a regression model to estimate how compensation varies with factors such as the CEO's age and tenure, company size, location, industry, and performance. Although the author cautions against taking the results too literally, CEOs earning more than predicted are implicitly designated as "overpaid," while those earning less than predicted are "underpaid."

Consider the case of Disney's Michael Eisner. By all accounts, Mr. Eisner's pay is wedded to company performance—in addition to loads of stock options, he gets 2% of all profits above an annually increasing threshold. Shareholders have prospered under Eisner, and few have complained that his compensation is unreasonable in light of the $7 billion in shareholder wealth he has helped create since joining the company in 1984. But *Business Week* ranks Eisner second on the list of CEOs who gave their shareholders the least (right behind option-laden Lee Iacocca, who over the past decade helped create $6 billion in wealth for Chrysler shareholders), while *Fortune* flags Eisner as the nation's third most overpaid CEO. Surveys ranking Eisner and Iacocca low are clearly not measuring incentives. In contrast, our survey ranks Eisner and Iacocca as the nation's fourth and ninth respectively "best paid" CEOs measured on the basis of pay-related wealth alone.

We estimated the pay-for-performance relation for each of the 430 companies for which we have sufficient data. The results are summarized in the four nearby tables. Three of the tables include results for the 250 largest companies ranked by 1988 sales. The 25 CEOs with the best and worst overall incentives, as reflected by the rela-

The 25 CEOs of Large Companies with the Worst Incentives

Total Effects (over Two Years) on CEO Wealth Corresponding to Each $1,000 Change in Shareholder Wealth

Rank	Company	CEO	Change in All Pay-Related Wealth	Change in the Value of Stock Owned	Change in Total CEO Wealth
226	Central & South West	Merle L. Borchelt	$0.14	$0.32	$0.46
227	Campbell Soup	R. Gordon McGovern	$0.07	$0.38	$0.44
228	3M	Allen F. Jacobson	$0.28	$0.11	$0.39
229	Sears Roebuck	Edward A. Brennan	$0.17	$0.20	$0.37
230	AMP	Walter F. Raab	-$0.03	$0.39	$0.36
231	Consolidated Edison	Arthur Hauspurg	$0.22	$0.12	$0.34
232	Detroit Edison	Walter J. McCarthy, Jr.	$0.24	$0.07	$0.31
233	Commonwealth Edison	James J. O'Connor	$0.24	$0.06	$0.30
234	Texas Utilities	Jerry S. Farrington	$0.23	$0.07	$0.29
235	Exxon	Lawrence G. Rawl	$0.14	$0.11	$0.25
236	AT&T	Robert E. Allen	$0.19	$0.04	$0.24
237	ARCO	Lodwrick M. Cook	-$0.10	$0.33	$0.23
238	IBM	John F. Akers	$0.13	$0.06	$0.19
239	Borden	Romeo J. Ventres	-$0.20	$0.38	$0.18
240	Eastman Kodak	Colby H. Chandler	$0.09	$0.08	$0.17
241	R.R. Donnelley & Sons	John R. Walter	-$0.18	$0.34	$0.16
242	Johnson & Johnson	Ralph S. Larsen	$0.11	$0.05	$0.15
243	Chevron Corp.	Kenneth T. Derr	-$0.04	$0.15	$0.11
244	GTE	James L. Johnson	$0.04	$0.07	$0.11
245	Pacific Gas & Electric	Richard A. Clarke	$0.06	$0.04	$0.10
246	Philadelphia Electric	Joseph F. Paquette, Jr.	$0.07	$0.01	$0.08
247	PacifiCorp	Al M. Gleason	-$0.04	$0.08	$0.04
248	Honeywell	James J. Renier	-$0.51	$0.40	-$0.10
249	Carolina Power & Light	Sherwood H. Smith, Jr.	-$0.61	$0.45	-$0.16
250	Navistar International	James C. Cotting	-$1.61	$0.20	-$1.41

Note: Sample consists of CEOs in the 250 largest companies, ranked by 1988 sales.

tion between their total compensation (composed of all pay-related wealth changes and the change in the value of stock owned), are summarized in the first two tables. Castle & Cooke, whose current CEO is David Murdock, ranks first with a total change in CEO wealth of $231.53 for every $1,000 change in shareholder wealth. His stockholdings contribute $224.24 of this amount, while the change in all pay-related wealth adds another $7.29.

With a few exceptions, it is clear that the best incentives are determined primarily by large CEO stockholdings. Donald Marron of Paine Webber is such an exception, with more than $55 of his total of $67 coming from changes in pay-related wealth. So too are Philip Hawley of Carter Hawley Hale, Henry Schacht of Cummins Engine, and Disney's Eisner.

The 25 companies providing their CEOs with the worst total incentives are led by Navistar International whose CEO James Cotting on average receives a $1.41 *increase* in wealth for every $1,000 *decrease* in shareholder value.

Carolina Power & Light's Sherwood Smith, Jr. receives a 16-cent increase for every $1,000 decrease in shareholder wealth. Other well-known corporations whose CEOs appear on the worst-incentives list include Chevron, Johnson & Johnson, Eastman Kodak, and IBM.

Although one has to recognize that there is statistical uncertainty surrounding our estimates of pay-related wealth sensitivity, no CEO with substantial equity holdings (measured as a fraction of the total outstanding equity) makes our list of low-incentive CEOs. As we point out in the accompanying article, an important disadvantage of corporate size is that it is extremely difficult for the CEO to hold a substantial fraction of corporate equity.

The inverse relation between size and stockholdings (and therefore the negative effect of size on incentives) is readily visible in the much higher sensitivities shown for the top 25 CEOs in smaller companies, those ranking from 251 to 430 in 1988 sales. (See the table "The Best of the Rest: CEO Incentives in Smaller Companies.") Warren

The Best of the Rest: CEO Incentives in Smaller Companies

Total Effects (over Two Years) on CEO Wealth Corresponding to Each $1,000 Change in Shareholder Wealth

Rank	Company	CEO	Change in All Pay-Related Wealth	Change in the Value of Stock Owned	Change in Total CEO Wealth
1	Berkshire Hathaway	Warren E. Buffett	$0.06	$446.77	$446.83
2	Williamette Industries	William Swindells, Jr.	$0.64	$427.10	$427.75
3	Riggs National	Joe L. Allbritton	$1.22	$358.19	$359.40
4	Hilton Hotels	Barron Hilton*	$0.85	$245.90	$246.75
5	Timken	William R. Timken, Jr.*	$5.20	$142.46	$147.66
6	United Missouri Bancshares	R. Crosby Kemper	$1.08	$118.65	$119.73
7	Zions Bancorporation	Roy W. Simmons	$2.76	$89.17	$91.93
8	First Empire State	Robert G. Wilmers	$18.72	$71.63	$90.36
9	Florida National Banks	John D. Uible	$1.85	$87.66	$89.51
10	Equimark	Alan S. Fellheimer	$15.53	$72.28	$87.81
11	W.W. Grainger	David W. Grainger*	$0.21	$79.13	$79.34
12	Fin'l Corp. of Santa Barbara	Philip R. Brinkerhoff	$54.68	$21.41	$76.09
13	Golden West Financial	Herbert M. Sandler*	$4.48	$67.36	$71.83
14	Merchants National	Otto N. Frenzel III	$9.59	$60.19	$69.79
15	First City Bancorp of Texas	A. Robert Abboud	–$0.21	$58.75	$58.54
16	First Security	Spencer F. Eccles	$2.63	$44.84	$47.47
17	Central Bancshares of the South	Harry B. Brock, Jr.*	$4.89	$38.25	$43.15
18	Fruehauf	T. Neal Combs	$16.20	$21.14	$37.34
19	Holiday	Michael D. Rose	$14.01	$20.94	$34.94
20	Cullen/Frost Bankers	Thomas C. Frost*	$8.90	$25.95	$34.85
21	Beneficial Corp.	Finn M.W. Caspersen	$3.37	$29.87	$33.23
22	Yellow Freight System	George E. Powell, Jr.	$0.86	$30.90	$31.76
23	Data General	Edson D. deCastro*	$1.89	$29.79	$31.68
24	Equitable Bancorporation	H. Grant Hathaway	$11.01	$17.23	$28.24
25	Imperial Corp. of America	Kenneth J. Thygerson	$24.98	$2.52	$27.51

Note: Sample consists of CEOs in companies ranked 251 to 430 by 1988 sales. *Denotes founder or founding-family CEO.

Buffett of Berkshire Hathaway leads this list with $446 per $1,000, followed by William Swindells, Jr. of Williamette Industries, Joe Allbritton of Riggs National, and Barron Hilton of Hilton Hotels. Again, the importance of large stockholdings is clear.

Indeed, one problem with current compensation practices is that boards often reward CEOs with substantial equity through stock options but then stand by to watch CEOs undo the incentives by unloading their stockholdings. Boards seldom provide contractual constraints or moral suasion that discourage the CEO from selling such shares to invest in a diversified portfolio of assets. One of the ironies of the situation is that the corporation itself often funds executive financial counseling by consultants whose common mantra is "sell and diversify, sell and diversify." While this can be personally advantageous to executives, it is not optimal for shareholders or society because it significantly reduces CEOs' incentives to run their companies efficiently.

Pay-related incentives are under the direct control of the compensation committee and the board. The table "Best Paid CEOs of Large Companies" lists the 25 companies that reward their CEOs in a way that provides the best incentives from pay-related wealth alone–changes in salary and bonus, long-term incentive plans, dismissal likelihood, and stock options. Each of these estimates is given in the table, along with the sum of the effects in the last column. The table makes clear that the major contributors to pay-related incentives are stock options and the present value of the change in salary and bonus.

Authors' note: The accompanying tables present estimates of pay-for-performance sensitivities for only a fraction of the CEOs in our full survey. Readers who would like a copy of the full 430-company survey, along with a detailed technical appendix fully describing our methodology, can write to Professor Kevin J. Murphy at the William E. Simon Graduate School of Business, University of Rochester, Rochester, NY 14627.

Best Paid CEOs of Large Companies

Change in Pay-Related Wealth Corresponding to Each $1,000 Change in Shareholder Wealth

Rank	Company	CEO	Change in Salary + Bonus over Two Years	Present Value of Pay Change	Change in Wealth due to Dismissal Likelihood	Change in Value of Stock Options	Change in All Pay-Related Wealth
1	Paine Webber Group	Donald B. Marron	$4.11	$46.91	$1.18	$7.51	$55.59
2	Carter Hawley Hale	Philip M. Hawley*	$0.03	$0.54	$0.98	$21.83	$23.36
3	Cummins Engine	Henry B. Schacht	$1.11	$18.29	$0.03	$0.14	$18.46
4	Walt Disney	Michael D. Eisner	$0.72	$11.35	$0.00	$4.27	$15.62
5	George A. Hormel	Richard L. Knowlton	$0.76	$7.47	$0.19	$4.70	$12.36
6	UAL	Stephen M. Wolf	$0.01	$0.45	$0.02	$11.57	$12.05
7	Fleet/Norstar	J. Terrence Murray	$0.72	$10.93	$0.03	$1.02	$11.98
8	Continental Bank	Thomas C. Theobald	$0.26	$2.01	$0.04	$9.40	$11.46
9	Chrysler Corp.	Lee A. Iacocca	$0.43	$5.38	$0.02	$4.74	$10.14
10	Zenith Electronics	Jerry K. Pearlman	$0.77	$7.44	$0.05	$2.27	$9.76
11	NCNB	Hugh L. McColl, Jr.	$0.76	$8.43	$0.01	$0.63	$9.07
12	Masco	Richard A. Manoogian	$0.01	$2.38	$0.16	$6.24	$8.78
13	FMC	Robert H. Malott	$0.01	$0.13	$0.47	$7.82	$8.43
14	Turner	Alfred T. McNeill	$2.01	$4.27	$0.27	$3.52	$8.06
15	B.F. Goodrich	John D. Ong	$0.51	$4.73	$0.14	$2.85	$7.72
16	Alco Standard	Ray B. Mundt	$0.88	$5.46	$0.88	$1.28	$7.61
17	Black & Decker	Nolan D. Archibald	$0.25	$3.89	$0.34	$3.30	$7.53
18	Castle & Cooke	David H. Murdock	$0.77	$3.70	$0.04	$3.54	$7.29
19	Brunswick Corp.	Jack F. Reichert	$0.40	$6.59	$0.26	$0.00	$6.85
20	Mellon Bank	Frank V. Cahouet	$0.42	$3.69	$0.65	$2.38	$6.72
21	Enron	Kenneth L. Lay	$0.46	$3.99	$0.05	$2.58	$6.62
22	Pan Am	Thomas G. Plaskett	$0.25	$0.77	$0.13	$5.55	$6.46
23	Toys "R" Us	Charles Lazarus*	–$0.13	$1.06	$0.11	$5.27	$6.45
24	Norwest	Lloyd P. Johnson	$0.22	$1.30	$0.10	$4.98	$6.37
25	First Union	Edward E. Crutchfield, Jr.	$0.48	$5.59	$0.03	$0.08	$5.71

Note: Sample consists of CEOs in the 250 largest companies, ranked by 1988 sales. *Denotes founder or founding-family CEO.

The beauty of most compensation plans is that they always reward performance — however dismal it is.

Four Ways to Overpay Yourself Enough

by KENNETH MASON

The figures are out. Amid the blossoming of the spring's proxy statements came news of the annual salaries of the country's top executives. True, many people have found the numbers unconscionably high. Are they too high? Think of the pressure the CEO must withstand and the talent he or she must possess.

Maybe they're too low. But some companies have lost money under such well-paid helmsmanship.

How fortunate that we live in a scientific age. We don't have to ponder whether top executives are being compensated fairly. We can simply choose one of four approaches that have dominated executive remuneration planning for most of this century. Each school of thought, of course, has airtight logic and guarantees that shareholder value will be protected.

The Iron Law School. This school's central tenet is the Iron Law of Wages, according to which executives' compensation should be exactly equal to the amount that they require to subsist and reproduce, so as to perpetuate the executive population. Because of the remarkable biological diversity of executives, descended as they are from vastly different genetic pools, proponents of this theory have had to develop an enormous data base in its support. According to

---

Kenneth Mason is a former president of the Quaker Oats Company and a former director of Rohm and Haas and Harper & Row. He retired from Quaker Oats in 1979 and from all other business commitments in 1987. He now resides on the coast of Maine and is writing a novel about the inner workings of a large multinational food company.

the 1987 figures, in manufacturing concerns with $1 billion to $5 billion annual sales, entry-level accountants joining the controller's department require $24,000 per year to subsist. Beginning-level MBAs joining the marketing department require $37,500 to subsist.

Managers of Midwestern food plants employing approximately 1,000 workers can subsist on $80,000 per year plus a modest bonus, but New York advertising agency account executives supervising three peo-

> **Too many executives get entrepreneurs' rewards for bureaucrats' jobs.**

ple cannot. Just a few years ago, most *Fortune* "500" CEOs could feed and clothe themselves and their families on less than $1 million per year. Today, perhaps as a result of ozone depletion and acid rain, a rapidly increasing number need more.

The School of Supply and Demand. Followers of this school hold that executives' salaries are determined by the relationship between how many executives there are and how many are wanted. Lee Iacocca was happy to go to work for Chrysler at a salary of only $1 a year because he knew that while there was a vast supply of automobile executives clamoring for the job, there was demand for only one.

The forces of supply and demand also account for the enormous incomes earned by stockbrokers and

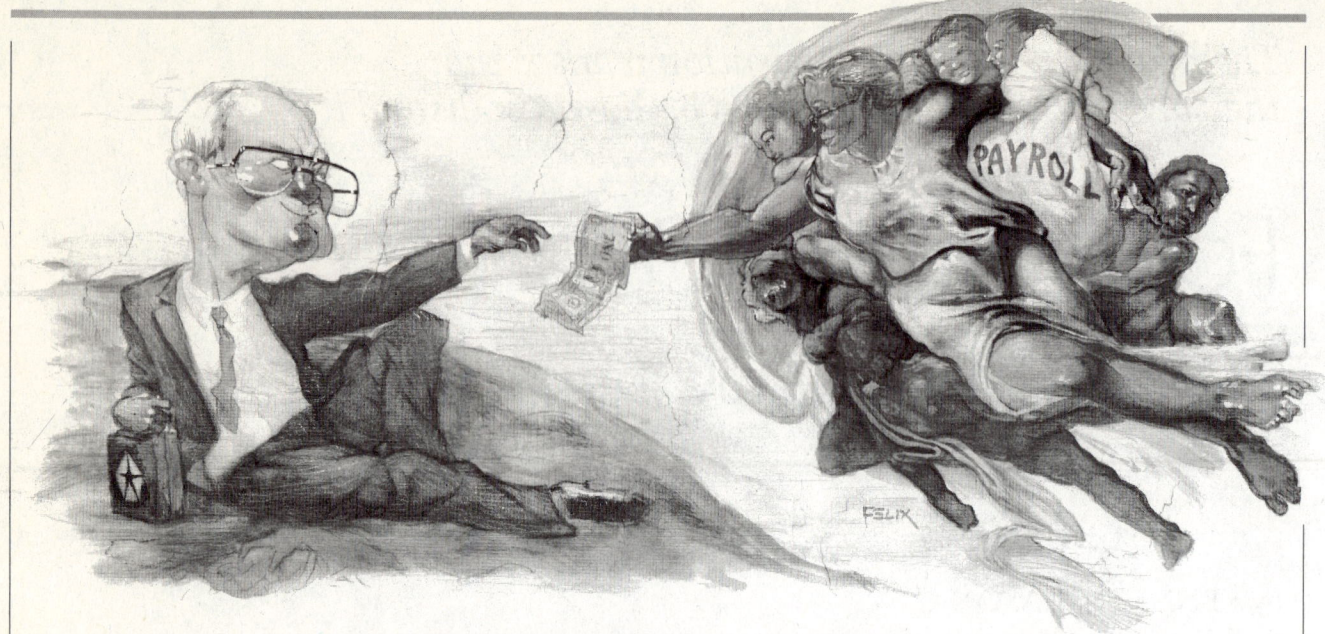

With so many executives clamoring for the job, Iacocca gladly accepted an annual salary of one dollar.

investment bankers. Most Wall Street firms will not even interview a candidate who does not have a postgraduate degree in moral philosophy, and it is a Street rule that all new employees serve a five-year apprenticeship before being permitted to contact clients directly. In view of these rigorous educational and training requirements, it is hardly surprising that few young people are attracted to a career on Wall Street these days, and that those who are can command exceptionally high salaries.

The Hay Entitlement School. It was at Camp Maxey, Texas in 1941 that an obscure master sergeant solved the problem of getting 60,000 southern draftees to salute the one black officer on the post. He simply announced that in the military you salute the uniform, not the person.

This theory's most important postwar extrapolation is the Hay Entitlement System, which posits that there is a salary range for every job title, and you pay the job title, not the job holder. One attractive feature of the Hay system is that the salary ranges allow wide discretion in determining the wages actually to be paid the executive. If performance is clearly unsatisfactory, for instance, the incumbent's pay can be held within the high-middle and low-high part of the range.

The flexibility of the Hay system also has great appeal to management: the Hay team stands ready at all times to add points to any job title whose salary maximum is preventing an increase for an incumbent who doesn't merit promotion to a higher-rated position but who is the kind of decent chap one hates to disappoint.

The Pay for Performance School. This school's highly controversial compensation theory originated in the world of professional sports. It first attracted general attention when Babe Ruth, on being asked how he could justify making more money than President Hoover, replied, "I had a better year than he did." Compensation theorists immediately recognized that the concept of linking compensation to such clear criteria as runs batted in or goals scored or sales quotas met or profit plans achieved had some real advantages over the compensation systems generally in use at that time.

The greatest advantage of the Pay for Performance approach is that, unlike the Iron Law theory, the Supply-Demand method, and the Hay Entitlement system, it enables the compensatee to play a role in the compensation process. It also allows participants to relate compensation not just to the past or present but also to the future—not just to the kind of job the executive used to do, not just to the kind of job the executive is doing now, but also to the kind of job you wish the executive would do.

This novel and powerful idea of compensation as incentive caused the emergence of a faction group, whose leaders have dominated Pay for Performance thinking throughout the post-Ruthian era. Their contributions to the discipline include such incentive devices as phantom stock, Stock Appreciation Rights, the Golden Handcuff, the Golden Parachute,

DRAWINGS BY PAUL FELIX

and, most recently, the Golden Walking Stick and the Golden Rocking Chair.

The test of any managerial tool, compensation policy included, is its effectiveness in helping achieve management's operating goals. The goal most frequently proclaimed number one by America's 1,000 largest corporations in 1987 was to increase shareholder value. Do any of the four schools of compensation support that goal?

Does the Iron Law, a school whose central thesis derives from the discredited ideas of Malthus and whose followers ignore important contemporary shibboleths like quarterly earnings and P-E ratios? Obviously not. Which is not to say the Iron Law is totally without merit in regard to shareholder value. By ensuring that each executive is paid no more than what is needed to subsist and send one child through business school, the Iron Law curbs the lavish salaries, bonuses, pensions, and postretirement consulting contracts that have reduced the earnings and, by extension, the shareholder value of more than a few American corporations in recent years. Unfortunately, restraining executives' compensation, as opposed to controlling the conditions under which it is paid, has never been shown to improve shareholder value over the long term.

According to the School of Supply and Demand, strong demand for executives committed to increasing shareholder value will create a supply of those executives, and as these executives are hired, shareholder value will creep up. While this is a highly plausible theory, in real life things are different. The demand for executives committed to shareholder value does not create a supply of executives committed to shareholder value; it creates a supply of candidates committed to being interviewed for a high-paying job. While some of these candidates may indeed have the capability of increasing shareholder value, a correlation between use of the Law of Supply and Demand for compensation and a rise in shareholder value has never been established.

It is surprising, but unfortunately true, that the Hay Entitlement system, despite its modern genesis, also has proved unhelpful to corporations whose goal is to increase shareholder value. By rating jobs instead of executives, the Hay system produces a corporate environment in which managers compete with each other for the best jobs instead of the best results. With rare exceptions, shareholder value is an objective in name only when the Hay team has been at work. Although more than 90% of companies using the Hay system increased shareholder value significantly during the 1980s, they did so by virtue of policies and conditions unrelated to compensation.

Of all the approaches to executive compensation, one would expect Pay for Performance to be the best for boosting shareholder value. A plan that ties compensation to results surely must produce those results, at least over the long term. Yet in practice, Pay for Performance works no better than the other compensation theories. The problem is that management tends to introduce a new incentive plan the moment it appears that disappointing operating results are going to produce disappointing executive bonuses. When profits are rising, compensation is tied to profits. When they begin to sink, the plan switches. Suddenly compensation is tied to achieving a corporate ROI equal to industry ROI. If results fall short of industry ROI, the compensation plan is again revised to link pay to improving ROE by a point or two.

In the 1975-1983 period, the compensation incentive plans of the 200 largest industrial companies in the United States had an average life span of less than 18 months. The Pay for Performance school seems to have evolved into the KCR school, whose theory is Keep Compensation Rising no matter what.

A familiar example of KCR at work is the underwater stock option. What better executive incentive than the stock option for a corporation whose objective is to augment shareholder value? The executive doesn't benefit unless the shareholder does. No tickee, no washee, right? Wrong, says KCR. No tickee, we give you new tickee. Within days after 1987's Black Monday stock market crash, the business press was reporting that several major corporations planned to replace their executives' newly drowned options.

When companies pay CEOs in stock, they should buy it at market rates.

This is exactly what many corporations did after the market decline of 1973. The experience of one high-level executive in the food industry is typical of that era. In 1973, he was granted an option for 2,500 shares of his corporation's stock at $40. Just after that, profits slumped. Two years later, the company replaced his stock option award with one for 7,000 shares at $15. He was not penalized by the company's decline in shareholder value; indeed, his financial future was actually enhanced as a result of it.

It's questionable whether stock options are effective incentives even in normal times because they seldom constitute a meaningful percentage of an executive's anticipated long-term compensation. True, options often turn out to be worth a lot, but for most executives they are just extra icing on an already well-frosted cake. A refreshing exception was Lee Iacocca's $1-a-year salary buttressed by a huge stock option award. His eventual payoff was enormous, but so was the risk of Chrysler going under, in which case he would have received very little.

It is a sad commentary on the intellectual vigor and financial discipline of the U.S. business community that so many corporate executives are receiving entrepreneurs' rewards for doing bureaucrats' jobs. The important decision-making jobs in American corporations today hardly ever entail financial risk to anyone except the shareholders. If my compensation package awards me $1.5 million when I meet the corporate profit plan and $1 million when I don't, where's my risk? Succeed or fail, the 20 top executives in most large corporations are almost certain to become wealthy.

Even getting fired is generally no financial blow to these executives. Personnel experts delight in figuring out a generous severance package for an executive who has been sacked after running a profitable division into the ground or making a fantastically dumb acquisition or launching five consecutive new product failures. They may not condone the executive's disastrous business decisions, but they will defend with their lives his or her right to be paid almost as much as if those decisions had been good ones. A typical severance package for an executive who has done a really bad job consists of a couple years' salary, a consulting contract, and a pension supplement giving the executive the same pension payments in early retirement that he would have gotten had he been sufficiently competent to stay the course. One executive's early retirement package included the merit increase he would have received at his annual review a few months hence had he not been fired for poor performance!

Executives' financial rewards must be linked more clearly and more emphatically to shareholders' if increasing shareholder value continues to be the first priority of U.S. corporations, and if compensation strategies are expected to play a role in achieving that objective. The Shareholder-Executive Linkage Formula (SHELF), a new incentive compensation strategy, tightens that link by introducing three long-overdue financial and ethical constraints into the corporate compensation process:

1. The annual cash compensation paid to executives of publicly held companies is limited to either 250% of the salary of the president of the United States or 25% of the compensation of the prior year's most valuable player in the National Basketball Association, whichever a corporation feels better fits its image. Are your executives more like President Reagan or Larry Bird? Strict observance of the limit by all publicly held corporations is enforced by the SEC.

2. Compensation in excess of the cash limit may be paid only in the publicly traded stock of the company. This stock must be purchased by the company on the open market and must be held by the executive for a minimum of five years. The company provides an annual interest-free loan to cover the annual income taxes due on this compensation. The executives repay the loans when they sell the shares or when they leave the company, whichever comes first.

3. The executive stock option is declared illegal and replaced by the Simultaneous Call and Put. A SCAP gives an executive a three-year call on one share of stock at a strike price of 130% of market

Why not limit executive pay to 25% of Larry Bird's salary?

price on the day of grant less dividends paid during the three-year period. At the same time, the executive commits to a three-year put on identical terms.

While some critics have dismissed SHELF as overly complicated, too risky, even radical, the plan is in no way at odds with the conventional compensation theories American industry is now following. The proposed presidential or Birdian limit on cash compensation, for instance, is entirely consistent with the Iron Law's subsistence requirement. Since the president of the United States pays no rent, it is not surprising that a CEO should require two-and-a-half times the president's wage to subsist and reproduce. Conversely, the sports star's shortened career span justifies his 4 to 1 advantage over CEOs, who often persuade their boards to let them keep playing into their dotage.

Nor does an upper limit on cash compensation violate the Law of Supply and Demand. There never has been a demand for high-salaried executives, only a large supply. The demand is for high-*performance* executives. Here there is also a large supply, but current compensation is not always a reliable clue to their identity. Many corporate executives now brazenly pay themselves annual salaries and bonuses that bear no correlation whatsoever to what any manager or company can accomplish in a single year. A corporation's paying $1 million a year for a run-of-the-mill CEO is not unlike the Pentagon's paying $150 for an ashtray: in both cases you know one just as good can be had for much less. The SEC has scores of regulations on its books designed to protect investors' interests in publicly held companies, yet under present regulations there is nothing to prevent a corporation from paying its CEO $1 million a week if it so decides. Shouldn't the shareholder be protected from such a move?

The requirement that all compensation over the cash limit be in the form of company stock and that this stock be purchased by the company on the open market serves a two-fold purpose. One is to make executives more appreciative of shareholder concerns by replacing no-risk stock options with normal-risk shares purchased at the price everyone else pays. The second is to provide a trickle-down benefit to the shareholders: the more executives are paid, the more stock the company must buy on the open market. This puts upward pressure on the stock price, boosting shareholder value.

Replacing stock options with SCAPs would put an end to a form of insider self-dealing that is extremely unfair to shareholders. Why should insiders be allowed to purchase shares at what is often a fraction of the price the public must pay? How is it fair to shareholders to dilute their ownership positions by issuing new shares for this purpose?

A call makes much more sense for executives and shareholders alike. Basing its strike price on a 10% annual growth premium makes it fair to the shareholder, while the automatic expiration date eliminates executive risk in timing the exercising of an option as well as any concern about trading on insider information. And pairing a company put with an executive call corrects a serious weakness of stock options as incentive compensation: options are a pleasant incentive when the stock is going up, but managers tend to lose interest when it isn't. With the call-put combination, managers never lose interest, no matter which direction the stock is going in.

How might a typical well-paid corporate executive expect to fare under SHELF? Consider the pretax compensation of a top executive in a large information systems company over a six-year period in the 1980s. Under a conventional compensation plan, her salary and bonus were $550,000 in year one, $600,000 in year two, $750,000 when profits surged in year three, and $700,000 for each of years four, five, and six, when profits fell and then flattened. She also received an annual stock option grant equivalent to one-fifth of compensation. The option prices and quantities for years one through six are as follows:

3,667 shares at $30   2,000 shares at $70
1,600 shares at $75   2,154 shares at $65
1,500 shares at $100 2,333 shares at $60

How many U.S. presidents is one executive worth?

Annual dividend payout during the period was $1.80, $2.00, $2.25, and, for each of the last three years, $2.50. For the whole six-year period, this executive received $4 million in cash compensation and had a paper profit of $110,000 in options for 3,667 shares of stock.

Now look at the pretax compensation history of the same executive under SHELF. Assuming the company had chosen the presidential cash cap, her cash compensation would have been $500,000 for each of the six years. Her compensation in excess of the cap would have been paid over the six years in the form of 14,766 shares of the company's stock with a current value of $885,960. In addition, the 3,667 call options received the first year would have to be exercised in year four. The strike price is calculated like this:

($30 stock price × 130%) −
($1.80 + $2.00 + $2.25) = $32.95

Since the market price of the stock in year four is $70, the executive makes a profit of:

($70 − $32.95) × 3,667 shares = $135,862

In year five, however, she has to pay the company $41,200 for the shareholders' year-two put and in year six, $93,750 for the year-three put. At $912, her call-put net for the period almost breaks even, making her total compensation for the period $3,886,872, 5% less than she would have received under the conventional method.

Now consider the future. The company's objective is to increase shareholder value. It did well at the beginning of the period, but shareholder value has declined for three straight years. Which executive has the stronger incentive to turn the company around? The executive under the conventional plan, who currently has a paper profit of $110,000 in her options and stands to make an additional paper profit of $268,710 if the stock gets back to $100 before the options expire? Or the executive under SHELF, who owns 14,766 shares of the company's stock, the value of which will increase by $590,640 if the price goes back up to $100, who stands to make $151,366 on her current calls if the stock gets back to $100 next year, and who could lose $108,115 if the stock stays where it is for another three years?

Radical though it appears to some, the Shareholder-Executive Linkage Formula proposes only two quite modest refinements to present methods of executive compensation. The first requires compensation at the highest levels to be in the form of company stock. It affects only the handful of corporate executives who make the kinds of decisions the original owners of the business made before they took the company public. As owner surrogates, shouldn't these managers share some of the risks of ownership as well as the rewards? And mightn't this dramatically improve their decision making?

The second refinement replaces stock options with simultaneous calls and puts. The call portion of SCAPs corrects the basic unfairness to shareholders of selling stock to corporate insiders at lower than market prices. The put portion does something even more important: it prevents top corporate executives from walking away from a losing game for shareholders without losing something themselves.

Too radical? Too tough? Or high time.

Reprint 88408

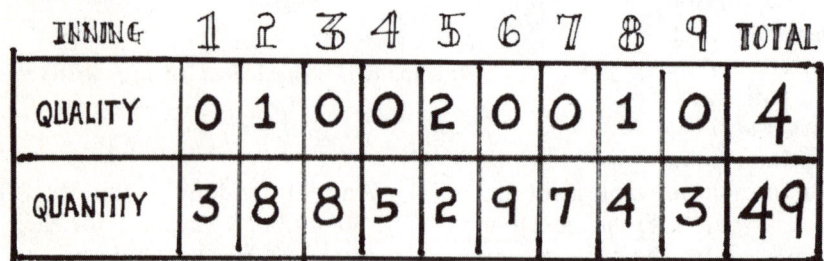

Kevin J. Murphy

Top executives are worth every nickel they get

Each spring, critics, journalists, and special-interest groups devour hundreds of corporate proxy statements in a race to determine which executive gets the most for allegedly doing the least. They're running the wrong race.

> "On average, compensation policies encourage executives to act on behalf of their shareholders and to put in the best managerial performance they can."

The "excessive" compensation paid these greedy types, we are told, gouges the nation's 30 million shareholders. Their salaries are arbitrarily set at outrageous levels without regard to either profitability or performance. Moreover, the six- and seven-digit base salaries are just the tip of the compensation iceberg—executives fatten their already sizable paychecks severalfold through bonuses, stock options, and other short- and long-term incentive plans. As a result, the public view prevails that executives are paid too much for what they do and that compensation policies are irrational and ignore the needs of shareholders.

Mr. Murphy is an assistant professor at the Graduate School of Management of the University of Rochester, where he teaches economics. A recognized expert in the field of executive compensation, he consults with a wide range of corporations on their practices and has published in the Journal of Accounting and Economics *and, with Michael Jensen, in the* New York Times.

Simply put, the public view is wrong and based on fundamental misconceptions about the managerial labor market. One reason for these misconceptions is that executive compensation is an emotional issue. And because critics become wound up in their emotions, they rely on a blend of opinion, intuition, and carefully selected anecdotes to prove their points.[1] Of course, such anecdotal evidence is not useless and may even be valuable in identifying abuses in the compensation system when carefully interpreted. Critics cannot use such evidence, however, to show compensation trends or to support across-the-board condemnations of compensation policies.

I have devised a better way to test the validity of the complaints about executive pay by subjecting each proposition to a series of logical and statistical tests. My data are drawn, in part, from an examination of the compensation policies of almost 1,200 large U.S. corporations over ten years and are supplemented by the findings of a 1984 University of Rochester symposium, "Managerial Compensation and the Managerial Labor Market."[2] My results paint a very different picture of executive compensation by showing that:

☐ The pay and performance of top executives are strongly and positively related. Even without a direct link between pay and performance, executives' incomes are tied to their companies' performance through stock options, long-term performance plans, and, most important, stock ownership.

☐ Compensation proposals like short- and long-term incentive plans and golden parachutes actually benefit rather than harm shareholders.

☐ Changes in SEC reporting requirements and a shift toward compensation based on long-term performance explain most of the apparent compensation "explosion." This shift links compensation closely to shareholder wealth and motivates managers to look beyond next quarter's results.

| Exhibit I | **Relationship between rate of return on common stock and percentage changes in executive salary and bonus** 1975-1984 |

	1975-1984		1975-1979		1980-1984	
Annual rate of return on common stock	Number of executive-years in sample	Average annual change in salary and bonus	Number of executive-years in sample	Average annual change in salary and bonus	Number of executive-years in sample	Average annual change in salary and bonus
Entire sample	6,523	7.8%	3,314	6.9%	3,209	8.8%
Less than −20%	639	0.4%	257	0.5%	382	0.4%
−20% to 0%	1,734	5.3%	1,002	5.5%	732	4.9%
0% to 20%	1,917	8.3%	989	7.5%	928	9.2%
20% to 40%	1,212	9.6%	538	7.1%	674	11.6%
More than 40%	1,021	13.8%	528	11.1%	493	16.6%

Note: Rates of return and percentage pay increases have been adjusted for inflation. As an example of how the rate of return is calculated, suppose that a share of stock worth $10 at the beginning of the year had increased in price to $12 by the end of the year and that the company paid cash dividends of $1 per share during the year. The holder of a share of the company's common stock would have realized a return of $3, or 30% for the year. Salary and bonus data were constructed from *Forbes* annual compensation surveys from 1975 to 1984. The sample consists of 1,948 executives in 1,191 corporations.

Of course, some executives are overpaid or underpaid or paid in a way unrelated to performance. But, on average, I have found that compensation policies encourage executives to act on behalf of their shareholders and to put in the best managerial performance they can.

Pay & performance

Because shareholders are the owners of the corporation, it makes sense to analyze the executive compensation controversy from their perspective. One way to motivate managers is to structure compensation policies that reward them for taking actions that benefit their shareholders and punish them for taking actions that harm their shareholders. Shareholders measure corporations in terms of stock price and dividend performance. Thus a sensible compensation policy would push an executive's pay up with good price performance and down with poor performance.

A common criticism of compensation policies is that they encourage executives to focus on short-term profits rather than on long-term performance. Assuming efficient capital markets, current stock price reflects all available information about a company, thus making its stock market performance the appropriate measure of its long-term potential. My analysis (shown in *Exhibits I* and *II*) indicates that compensation gives executives the incentive to focus on the long term since it is implicitly or explicitly linked to their companies' stock market performance.

The statistics in *Exhibit I* compare the rate of return on common stock (including price appreciation and dividends) with percentage changes in top executives' salaries and bonuses over ten years. I have grouped the data, which represent sample averages, by the companies' stock price performance, but experiments with alternative measures like sales growth and return on equity yield similar qualitative results.

Throughout the ten-year period, executives received inflation-adjusted average annual increases in salary and bonus of 7.8%; more important is the positive relationship shown between the rate of return on common stock and average percentage changes in salary and bonus. When returns were less than −20%, executives received pay increases of only .4%; when performance exceeded 40%, pay increases averaged 13.8%.

As *Exhibit I* shows, the relationship between pay and performance has remained positive over time and has actually become stronger in recent years. Chief executives in companies with returns greater

---

Author's note: I am indebted to Michael Jensen and Jerold Zimmerman for their help. I gratefully acknowledge financial support from the Managerial Economics Research Center.

than 40% received inflation-adjusted average annual increases in salary and bonus of 11.1% from 1975 to 1979 and 16.6% from 1980 to 1984.

You can also use statistical regression techniques to estimate changes in executives' salaries and bonuses corresponding to each additional 10% of shareholder return. A company realizing a 10% return on its common stock will boost executive pay by some percentage, and you can use an estimate of the average pay increase to measure the magnitude of the relationship between pay and performance. By dividing the sample into subperiods, you can see if the relationship between pay and performance strengthens or weakens over time.

Exhibit II shows the results of the regression analysis. For every 10% rise in a company's stock price over the ten-year sample, the top executive's salary and bonus rose an average of 1.1%. Moreover, the relationship was stronger in the last half of the decade than in the first half. For each 10% shareholder return, annual salaries and bonuses increased by .8% from 1975 to 1979 and by 1.5% from 1980 to 1984.

As measured by the rate of return on common stock, a strong, positive statistical relationship exists between executive pay and company performance. These results are sharply at odds with recent studies that compare pay levels with measures of profitability and conclude that compensation is independent of performance.[3] The problem with such studies is that they look at the level of executive compensation across companies at a particular time instead of considering the extent to which compensation varies with companies' performance *over time*. This is an important distinction. Whether a company has well-paid — or low-paid — executives tells us nothing about the sensitivity of pay to performance.

To illustrate, consider two well-documented relationships — the positive relationship between company size and executive compensation and the negative one between company size and the average rate of return realized by shareholders.[4] From these it follows that a large company would have low rates of return and well-paid executives, while a small company would have high rates of return and low-paid executives. You'd conclude that pay and performance didn't correlate, and you'd be right if you took this kind of snapshot of the relationships. But if you took a moving picture — that is, looked at the results over time — you'd see that the pay of individual executives and the performance of their companies are strongly and positively related.

It is better to study how executive pay varies from year to year in a given company. *Exhibit I* and *Exhibit II* show that changes in executive pay mirror changes in shareholders' wealth. Two studies presented at the Rochester symposium corroborate this result. The first was based on a sample of 461 executives in 72 manufacturing companies over 18 years; in it I examined salary, bonus, stock options, deferred compensation, total compensation, and stock ownership. It shows that executive compensation parallels corporate performance as measured by the rate of return on common stock.[5]

Another study of 249 executives from as many companies from 1978 to 1980 reaches the same conclusion. It found a strong, positive correlation between changes in executive compensation and stock-price performance (adjusted for marketwide price changes). Ranking companies on the basis of their stock-price performance, it suggests that those in the top 10% will raise their executives' compensation by an inflation-adjusted 5.5% and those in the bottom 10% will lower pay by 4%. In addition, the study finds that chief executives in the bottom 10% of the performance ranking are almost three times more likely to leave their companies than executives in the top 10%.[6]

The expanded compensation package

Suppose that I had not found a positive relationship between cash compensation and performance. Could I then conclude that executives do not act on behalf of their shareholders? The point is not moot; although I've shown a positive relationship between cash compensation and performance, I could easily find some companies where the relationship does not exist. So it is important to determine whether *total* compensation policies are doing the best job possible.

To do so requires that you look at more than just salary and bonus. Most studies in the financial press consider *only* salary and bonus and ignore potentially crucial variables like restricted stock, stock options, and long-term performance plans. In fact, these plans have become increasingly important. By their very nature, these plans tie executives' ultimate compensation directly to their companies' performance.

Executives' holdings of their companies' common stock constitute a large part of their wealth. The value of these stock holdings obviously goes up in good years and down in bad ones, quite independently of any relationship between performance and base pay. Suppose an executive with $4 million of stock sees the share price drop 25%. Because of his company's poor performance in the securities market, he has lost a million dollars — a loss that trivializes anything a board of directors might do to his base pay.

To assess the importance of inside stock ownership, I collected a 20-year time series of

Exhibit II **Average increase in executive salary and bonus corresponding to each additional 10 % rate of return on common stock 1975-1984**

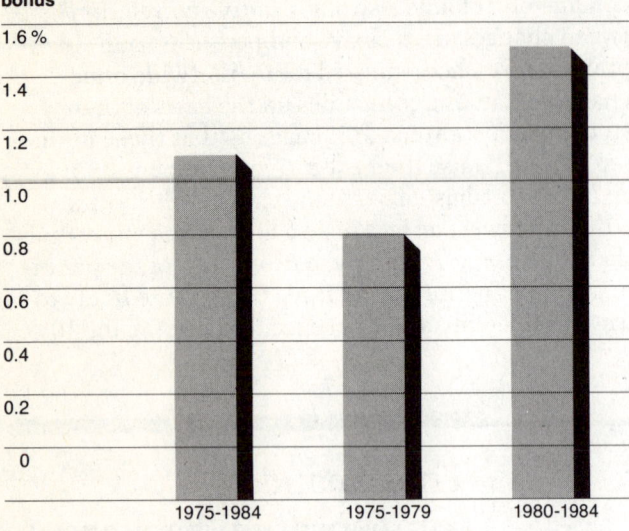

Note:
The percentage changes are estimated coefficients from regressions of percentage changes in salary and bonus on shareholder return. All estimates are statistically significant at confidence levels exceeding 99.99 %.

chief executive officer data from the proxy statements of 73 *Fortune* "500" manufacturing companies. Executives in this sample, which covered fiscal years 1964 through 1983, held an average (in 1984 constant dollars) of almost $7 million in their companies' common stock. Although this sample does not include shares held by family members and outside trusts, it does include a few executives with extraordinary stock holdings; the median stock holding for executives in this 20-year period is $1.5 million. That is, 50% of the chief executives in the 73 sample companies held more than $1.5 million in their companies' common stock.

Exhibit III depicts the relationships among company performance, salary and bonus, and changes in the value of executives' stock holdings for all chief executives in the 73 companies from 1964 to 1983. The point is clear; year-to-year changes in the value of executives' individual stock holdings often exceed their cash compensation. In companies with returns of less than −20%, executives lost an average of $2.9 million each on their stock holdings (compared with an average salary and bonus of $506,700); the median executive lost $643,800. In companies with returns greater than 40%, executives saw their stock holdings go up by an average of $3.6 million each (the median figure was $635,600) compared with an average salary and bonus of $494,300.[7]

Does generosity backfire?

Executive employment contracts are determined by the board of directors, which in turn is elected by shareholders. A cooperative relationship between executives and their directors is usually required for corporate success, and some have incorrectly interpreted this fact as evidence that executives can set their own salaries by pushing their compensation plans past "captive" directors. A friendly relationship between executives and their boards does not mean that the executives are free of constraints; rather, constraints usually operate in subtle yet powerful ways.

For example, some corporations have adopted short- and long-term compensation plans that pay off only if the executives meet a certain performance standard. Golden parachutes, which compensate executives if they leave their company after a takeover, have also grown in popularity. If, as some critics contend, these plans benefit executives and harm shareholders, you would expect stock prices to fall at the announcement of the plan. Likewise, if these plans benefit shareholders, you would expect prices to rise.

Three symposium studies examined market reaction. One found that average stock prices rise by about 11% when companies make the first public announcement of bonus and other plans that reward short-term performance.[8] Another concluded that shareholders realize a 2% return when companies adopt long-term compensation plans.[9] A third study found that, on average, stock prices increase by 3% when companies announce the adoption of a golden parachute provision.[10] This favorable reaction supports the contention that golden parachutes benefit shareholders by removing managers' incentives to block economically efficient takeovers. The price increase may also indicate that takeovers are more likely when golden parachutes are adopted but does not indicate that these provisions harm shareholders.

In each study, stock values not only increase when companies announce compensation plans but also continue to trade at the new, higher levels. The studies thus support the idea that such plans help align the interests of executives and shareholders and signal "good times ahead" to the market. They refute the view that executives "overreach" when they adopt lucrative compensation schemes.

On average, executives do not harm shareholders when they alter employment-contract

Exhibit III **Relationships among rate of return on common stock, executive salary and bonus, and change in value of inside stock holdings**
1964-1983

Annual rate of return on common stock	Number of executive-years in sample	Average annual salary and bonus	Average annual change in value of inside stock holdings	Median annual change in value of inside stock holdings
Entire sample	1,394	$541,700	$270,900	$27,600
Less than −20%	243	$506,700	−$2,914,200	−$643,800
−20% to 0%	361	$559,900	−$883,200	−$93,000
0% to 20%	360	$574,400	$560,600	$125,500
20% to 40%	223	$541,700	$2,260,700	$464,300
More than 40%	207	$494,300	$3,594,500	$635,600

Note: All variables have been adjusted for inflation (1984 constant dollars). Rate of return on common stock includes price appreciation and dividends. Inside stock holdings include only shares held directly and do not include shares held by family members or trusts. The change in the value of inside stock holdings is calculated by multiplying the value of each executive's share holdings (at the beginning of the fiscal year) by the rate of return on common stock. Data were constructed from proxy statements for 213 chief executives in 73 Fortune "500" manufacturing corporations from 1964 to 1983. Data were unavailable for 66 of the 1,460 possible executive-years.

provisions nor do they arbitrarily set their own salaries. If executives were truly able to set their salaries, why wouldn't they make them comparable with those of rock stars like Michael Jackson, whose income is many times that of even the highest paid executive? The only way the "set-their-own-salaries" argument works is if you assume that these salaries are somehow within some reasonable range of the competition—what other executives in similar industries are paid.

What's out of hand?

"Top management pay increases have gotten out of hand," warns Arch Patton, citing an apparent "explosion in top management compensation."[11] Indeed, a casual (but careless) look at compensation totals published in the business press seems to justify such concern. *Exhibit IV* shows the total compensation received by the nation's best paid executives from 1974 to 1984 using *Forbes* data (unadjusted for inflation). Before 1977, the fattest paycheck hovered around $1 million but then jumped to $3.4 million in 1978, $5.2 million in 1979, and $7.9 million in 1980. Warner Communications' Steven Ross shattered the eight-digit barrier with a total compensation of $22.6 million in 1981; in 1982, Frederick Smith of Federal Express received a total package of $51.5 million. The figure "plummeted" in 1983 to the mere $13.2 million received by NCR's retiring William Anderson but rebounded in 1984 to the $23 million received by Mesa's T. Boone Pickens, Jr.

A closer look at the data reveals that the apparent increase stems, in part, from a shift in the structure of compensation and has been exaggerated by changes in SEC reporting requirements. Moreover, the increase does not indicate that the conflict of interest between executives and their shareholders has worsened. Rather, the trend reflects a growing reliance on stock options and other long-term performance plans designed to link compensation more closely with shareholder wealth. The often spectacular payoffs are a once-in-a-lifetime experience.

For example, Frederick Smith's 1982 salary and bonus of $413,600 accounted for less than 1% of his $51.5 million total compensation; if the ranking had been based on salary and bonus alone, he wouldn't have made the top 300. NCR's William Anderson received only 8% of his 1983 compensation in the form of salary and bonus; his salary and bonus of $1,075,000 was only the nation's thirty-seventh highest. (Mr. Pickens's 1984 salary and bonus of $4.2 million was indeed the nation's highest but included $3 million for services provided in 1982 and 1983 when bonuses were not awarded.) In any given year, only a small percentage of executives enjoy big gains from stock options or other performance plans. The overwhelming majority get most of their compensation in the form of salaries and cash bonuses.

30 Compensation

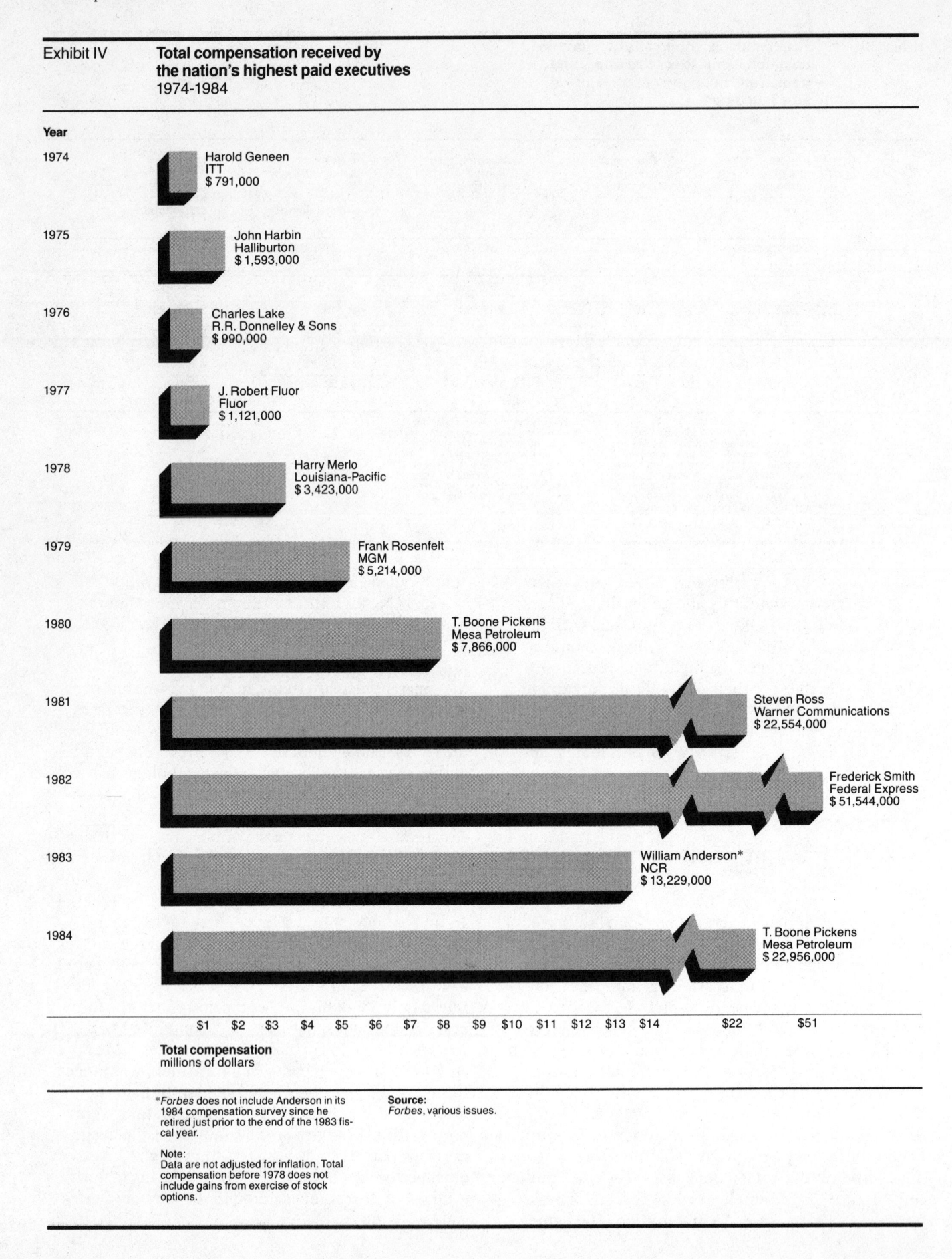

Exhibit IV	**Total compensation received by the nation's highest paid executives** 1974-1984

Year

1974 — Harold Geneen, ITT, $791,000

1975 — John Harbin, Halliburton, $1,593,000

1976 — Charles Lake, R.R. Donnelley & Sons, $990,000

1977 — J. Robert Fluor, Fluor, $1,121,000

1978 — Harry Merlo, Louisiana-Pacific, $3,423,000

1979 — Frank Rosenfelt, MGM, $5,214,000

1980 — T. Boone Pickens, Mesa Petroleum, $7,866,000

1981 — Steven Ross, Warner Communications, $22,554,000

1982 — Frederick Smith, Federal Express, $51,544,000

1983 — William Anderson*, NCR, $13,229,000

1984 — T. Boone Pickens, Mesa Petroleum, $22,956,000

$1 $2 $3 $4 $5 $6 $7 $8 $9 $10 $11 $12 $13 $14 $22 $51

Total compensation millions of dollars

*Forbes does not include Anderson in its 1984 compensation survey since he retired just prior to the end of the 1983 fiscal year.

Note: Data are not adjusted for inflation. Total compensation before 1978 does not include gains from exercise of stock options.

Source: Forbes, various issues.

Even so, the great popularity of stock options and other long-term performance plans has several implications. First, an executive's pay in any given year reflects amounts actually accrued or earned over several years and tends to increase the maximum compensation observed, just as a switch from weekly to monthly pay periods will increase the maximum compensation observed in any given week (for example, the last week of the month).

Second, long-term performance plans give high rewards for excellent performance but are neutral toward poor or mediocre performance. It's the same as designing a state lottery with one grand prize of $1 million rather than a hundred prizes of $10,000 each; you increase the amount paid to the winner but not the total amount awarded. If the chief executives of ten different companies were each awarded stock options at the beginning of the year, their value at the date of grant might be similar. By the end of the option period, however, only a few would be worth a great deal of money; the others would be worthless.

Third, most long-term performance plans are based on stock prices. The stock market boom produced high payoffs from 1981 to 1983, while the market decline in the 1970s produced low or zero payoffs. Thus an executive awarded an equal number of stock options or performance plan units each year would have realized zero gains during the stock market decline and large gains during the boom; cyclical movements produced increases in the dollar amounts realized even though the amounts granted under these plans remained relatively constant.

Finally, before 1978, the payoffs from stock options and other long-term plans were reported in a somewhat incomprehensible table at the back of corporate proxy statements. Changes in SEC reporting rules have moved these payoffs to the front of the statement, where they are much more accessible to the media. Compensation totals published in *Forbes* (see *Exhibit IV*) and other business periodicals before 1978 exclude option realizations; data published after 1978 include them. The editors of these compensation surveys warn against making year-to-year comparisons when the definitions have changed. Unfortunately, critics have often ignored these warnings.

Why such controversy?

The recent attacks on executive compensation come mainly from a few individuals and special-interest groups who use the controversy to further their own agendas. In 1984, for example, former U.S. Trade Representative William Brock assailed "excessive" auto executive bonuses to argue against Japanese import quotas. Labor unions have used the executive pay issue to bolster demands for higher wages for their members. Mark Green's condemnation of "overreaching" executives continues the general Nader-Green attack on the corporation. In each case, the executive compensation question is virtually unrelated to the ultimate objectives of the attackers.

Such highly publicized assaults cause confusion about executive compensation, a confusion exacerbated by the second-rate research conducted and reported by most media commentators. How compensation is determined is complex; current performance is only one of the many factors that affect executive pay. Thus performance cannot explain all or even most of an individual's compensation even though the relationship between pay and performance is strong, positive, and statistically significant. In any case, estimating the relationship between pay and performance is tricky and cannot be done by making simple cross-sectional comparisons.

Another source of confusion is the use of isolated examples and anecdotal evidence. The quoted numbers are usually taken out of context and fail to tell the whole story. Single examples purporting to show no relationship between pay and performance mislead since they often include big long-term payoffs but never changes in the value of the executive's stock holdings.

Some executives are undoubtedly abusing the compensation system, and anecdotal evidence may help identify and eliminate these excesses. I believe, however, that the true excesses are not made by the million-dollar executives, who are, by and large, rewarded for a history of superior performance in behalf of shareholders. Real abuses are more likely found among lower paid executives whose pay is both unrelated to performance and out of line with the pay of their peers in similar companies. Even if the critics were to identify real excesses, it is unfortunate that their isolated examples would help justify a blanket condemnation.

The nation's shareholders need not fear that they are being swindled by greedy executives. Compensation policies normally make a great deal of sense. Companies are, moreover, adopting compensation plans that benefit shareholders by creating better managerial incentives.

My evidence cannot prove that all or even most boards of directors are doing the best possible job of tying executive pay to company performance. Some executives are undoubtedly being overpaid, while others are being underpaid or paid in a way unrelated to performance. But even so, the evidence does indicate that executive compensation in U.S. corporations is characterized not by madness but by basic corporate common sense.

References

1 See, for example, Joseph E. Muckley,
"'Dear Fellow Shareowner',"
HBR March-April 1984, p. 46;
Mark Green and Bonnie Tenneriello,
"From Pay to Perks to Parachutes:
The Trouble with
Executive Compensation,"
Democracy Project Report No. 8,
March 1984.

2 Papers presented at the symposium
are published in the
Journal of Accounting and Economics,
April 1985.

3 See, for example, Carol Loomis,
"The Madness of Executive Compensation,"
Fortune, July 1982, p. 42.

4 The relationship between compensation
and sales is reported by
Harland Fox,
Top Executive Compensation,
Report No. 854
(New York: Conference Board, 1985).
Evidence relating company size and
shareholder return appears in
the Symposium on
Size and Stock Returns,
published in the
Journal of Financial Economics,
June 1983.

5 Kevin J. Murphy,
"Corporate Performance and
Managerial Remuneration:
An Empirical Analysis,"
Journal of Accounting and Economics,
April 1985, p. 11.

6 Anne T. Coughlan and Ronald M. Schmidt,
"Executive Compensation, Management
Turnover, and Firm Performance:
An Empirical Investigation,"
Journal of Accounting and Economics,
April 1985, p. 43.

7 For more evidence on the importance
of executive stock holdings, see
George J. Benston,
"The Self-Serving Management
Hypothesis: Some Evidence,"
Journal of Accounting and Economics,
April 1985, p. 67.

8 Hassan Tehranian and James Waegelein,
"Market Reaction to Short-Term
Executive Compensation Plan Adoption,"
Journal of Accounting and Economics,
April 1985, p. 131.

9 James Brickley, Sanjai Bhagat,
and Ronald C. Lease,
"The Impact of Long-Range Managerial
Compensation Plans on
Shareholder Wealth,"
Journal of Accounting and Economics,
April 1985, p. 113.

10 Richard A. Lambert and David F. Larcker,
"Golden Parachutes,
Executive Decision Making, and
Shareholder Wealth,"
Journal of Accounting and Economics,
April 1985, p. 179.

11 Arch Patton,
"Those Million-Dollar-A-Year Executives,"
HBR January-February 1985, p. 56.

The money-making citizen

By one class of journals, wealth, the science of wealth, and the classes that acquire wealth, are favorite topics of railing. The money-getting spirit is continually anathematized by all the believers in medieval virtue and patriarchal simplicity. They use the utmost license of vituperation, too, against the plodding industry of the mercantile and manufacturing classes; though no persons are more anxious than the literary hangers-on of the aristocracy, to rival or to share the wealth and the splendor of successful men of business. Our sentimental feudalists are never tired of writing against the grasping, hardhearted money makers, and sowing dissension between them and the laborers. On this specific account, as well as illustrating a general principle of society, it is important to connect the peace of society with the progress of wealth.

In fact, every man who acquires anything by his industry gives by that a hostage to order. He becomes interested in possessing tranquillity in proportion to his acquisition. His savings are generally put out to interest. He relies therefore on the future. He depends on production hereafter. He is a creditor of society, and his advances can only be repaid by peace and success. Theoretically, the matter is perfectly plain. Those who are destitute must be ready for every change. Those who are industrious, provident, and wealthy are desirous of peace and enjoyment. But what is true of individuals seems, by writers against wealth, to be considered as not true of society, and the men who are assiduous in their respective callings, who look closely after their ledgers, and endeavor to win much and waste nothing, are satirized and vilified as publicly injurious. It is supposed, according to the old antitrade, antisocial theory, and according to some practices, too much honored by these writers, that all which the plodding classes gain, produce, or possess, is taken from somebody else. They have no faith in honest exertions, and seem to believe that they are not naturally rewarded. The bookseller who employs his capital in printing a work, which, but for his aid, would never be published at all, is accused of growing rich at the expense of authors. The manufacturer who erects a mill, and finds employment for a thousand persons, is too often described as injuring and oppressing those, who but for his inventions and schemes might have wanted food. It seems of some consequence to rescue the money-getting, wealth-making classes from this kind of undeserved opprobrium, by pointing out the connection between order and tranquillity...

From
"The Progress of Wealth and
the Preservation of Order,"
The Economist,
July 14, 1849.

From the Boardroom

Peter G. Scotese

Fold up those golden parachutes

Boards must take responsibility for curbing this abuse of executive privilege

Amid the merger and acquisition furor of the past several years, boards have written golden parachute agreements into their top managers' contracts with increasing frequency. Nor do these multimillion dollar settlements look unreasonable, given the array of cash and noncash benefits that have become standard options in sophisticated executive compensation packages.

But familiarity has lulled chief executives and their boards into an inappropriate sense of complacency, this author argues. In fact, the golden parachute phenomenon may have done more to discredit CEOs among the general public than such widely publicized instances of white-collar crime as fraud and embezzlement—and rightly so.

Golden parachutes invert traditional employment contracts, which recruit and reward executives for their work within a company. And they fly in the face of the work ethic on which our business system rests. Thus it is not surprising that they have aroused widespread public protest and sparked preliminary action by the government.

Clearly the time has come for responsible board members to address this problem. Self-monitoring and remedial measures are essential to eliminate this abuse of executive privilege, regain public confidence, and avert government regulation.

Mr. Scotese is chairman of the executive committee of the board of Springs Industries, Inc., which has no golden parachutes. He is, or has been, a director of nine other companies including Bell & Howell and National Distillers & Chemical Corporation. He has a lively interest in directors' responsibilities and has contributed a chapter to the Handbook for Corporate Directors, *to be published by McGraw-Hill in 1985.*

In an era of accelerating deregulation, it is noteworthy that the government has decided that certain business practices are underregulated. And the fact that these practices relate to executive compensation—a keystone of the free enterprise system—sends a message that is disturbingly loud and clear: namely, that a groundswell of complaint is obliging the government to take corrective action.

Publicity is focused on golden parachutes, the common term for agreements whereby top executives of publicly owned companies leave their jobs, usually under the duress of a takeover, with compensation packages worth many times their annual salaries. The question raised is a simple one: Why reward an executive so generously at the moment his or her contribution to the company ceases? The approach flies in the face of the American work ethic, which is based on raises or increments related to the buildup of seniority and merit. When an employee departs, seniority and merit come to an abrupt end.

Consider the SEC's recent actions with regard to golden parachutes. In revising Item 402 of Regulation S-K, which governs public disclosure of top management's compensation, the SEC ruled that as of January 1, 1984, registrants' statements had to include any parachute agreements valued at more than $60,000 with executives who might be forced out or relegated to lesser managerial roles as a result of a takeover or merger.

At the same time the SEC held over for further consideration the July 8, 1983 recommendation of its Advisory Committee on Tender Offers that shareholders' opinions be given greater weight in determining whether executives receive golden parachutes. The committee proposed that companies disclose the terms and parties of executive compensation agreements in more detailed proxy statements. It also recommended that shareholders should vote, on a nonbinding advisory basis, on golden parachute policies. And it urged that the government put an end to the practice of companies making executive compensation deals after a takeover attempt had commenced.

Critics' charges that multimillion dollar parachute packages drain corporate coffers to provide windfalls for top executives have also gotten a receptive hearing in Congress. Remedial measures, such as penalty excise taxes and disallowing business deductions for excessive payments, were included in the Tax Reform Act of 1984. Moreover, even though the consequences of this legislation are unknown until it is applied, the direction it marks out could not be more plain. Unless the business community begins to regulate itself, the government will be quite prepared to do the job.

Resentment directed against those who garner huge rewards is probably inevitable at a time when many hourly workers find it hard to make ends meet. The feeling is also prevalent among members of America's middle class—and middle management levels—who readily cite cases in which corporate leaders appear to grab much larger pieces of the pie than their efforts warrant.

The situation is exacerbated, of course, when the media spotlight individual recipients and describe their compensation packages chapter and verse. The responsiveness of the audience, however, only reflects the widespread sense that it is the man in the street or the small investor who, one way or another, winds up paying for huge golden parachute settlements like David J. Mahoney's $35 million package from Norton Simon.

William M. Agee's $4.1 million award from Bendix was one of the more sensational parachutes of the early 1980s. But there have been many others. Nick A. Caporella received a similar sum from Burnup & Sims, and GK Technologies awarded Robert Jensen $7.8 million. Ralph Bailey received approximately $4 million from Conoco and Robert Davis deposited checks from Thiokol for a like amount. Dorman L. Commons and Kenneth G. Reed were given a total of $6.6 million from Diamond Shamrock and Natomas.

Golden parachutes first appeared during the early 1970s when takeovers were prevalent, but they were rare until the 1980s brought renewed interest in acquisitions. Then they began to multiply. In 1982, some 1,500 companies introduced golden parachutes into their bylaws and charters. And a 1983 survey of 560 Fortune "1000" companies by Ward Howell International identified more than 25% with top-echelon golden parachutes, compared with 15% in the previous year.

Is the trend abating? Probably not, although there are indications that companies are beginning to rethink the wisdom of such arrangements, especially in light of growing government scrutiny. Allied, for example, scrapped agreements for 21 executives, citing adverse public reaction. But since Allied was alone among the nation's leading corporations in taking this step, it appears unlikely that a countermovement is in the making. Revlon Chairman and CEO Michel Bergerac, for instance, recently received a new parachute valued at roughly $11.7 million as part of an estimated $30 million compensation package should Revlon be acquired.

Why the indignation?

Golden parachutes differ markedly in content and intent from other forms of executive compensation. Traditional employment contracts are highly effective in attracting, retaining, and rewarding capable top executives. Such agreements are designed to ensure that new top executives do not risk too much in leaving posts where they may have accrued considerable tenure and financial investment and that they will not be whisked away by other attractive offers. In sum, they are retention oriented. Golden parachutes, in contrast, are departure oriented—a whole different ball game.

Technically, what distinguishes a golden parachute from the usual employment contract or severance agreement is its "change in corporate control" provision. The standard for an effective change in control varies. Some companies use a percentage of outside stock ownership (usually 20% to 40%). Others focus on the composition of the board, with particular reference to the inclusion of hostile directors. Still others refer to an executive's status change—in job location, in duties, or the inability to carry out duties (presumably because the new management is restricting decision-making powers).

Many arrangements allow beleaguered executives to pull their own rip cords following the redistribution of stock ownership or the realignment of executive responsibilities. Others are set up so that once the company becomes an acquisition candidate, a tender offer or the accumulation of stock by outsiders through other means (friendly or otherwise) can trigger the chute.

The current shareholder uprising against golden parachutes is atypical. Apart from a few well-known corporate gadflies, who play an interesting role in the checks and balances of corporate governance, American shareholders generally are a docile group. As absentee owners, on the whole they are permissive, especially when things appear to be going well. And even when things are not quite right, they are disposed to believe corporate managers are professionals who understand what needs to be done and do it.

In fact, most shareholders want to believe that corporate management is qualified and conscientious because they are too busy with their own affairs to question, criticize, or interfere. Thus they are willing to tolerate the rich rewards companies bestow on CEOs and others for running the business, and they are reassured by the belief that CEOs are stars with special capabilities.

Trouble arises, however, when executives seek to multiply their just rewards and ensure that they keep coming at a time when they no longer contribute to the running of the business because they have lost their jobs. This tactic is outrageous, and shareholders justifiably feel they have a right to question it—as they are doing.

What's the rationale?

At some companies golden parachute coverage is extensive. AMF, for example, has devised a protective exit plan for 28 officers, Celanese has insulated 130 of its top executives, and Beneficial has extended takeover contracts to no fewer than 250 executives, from assistant vice presidents upward. Usually, however, parachutes apply only to a few key officers: the chairman, the CEO and/or president, and the chief financial officer.

The CEOs of successful public companies are tremendous assets. These executives usually have extraordinary business acumen; they work hard and they put in long hours and many years before they rise to the top. They are continually measured in terms of the bottom line, EPS, ROI, and other financial yardsticks; and their performance must be consistently outstanding throughout their careers.

Corporate leaders who meet these tests are richly rewarded. Well-publicized studies show that a record 46 executives of public companies earned more than $1 million in salary and bonuses in 1983. Nor should we dismiss the $655,000 median salary-plus-bonus (excluding stock options) paid to the CEOs of the 100 largest industrials.

But figures tell only part of the story. Most executives believe that their high salaries are not largesse but rather earnings that rightfully reflect the value of their experience, achievements, capabilities, and contributions. And their commitment to the success of their companies should not be underestimated. They analyze, review, restructure, and worry over corporate strategy conscientiously, with diligence and savvy. When their decisions succeed, the corporation, the economy, and large numbers of employees also succeed. When they fail, they must answer.

Increasingly, therefore, companies expect CEOs not only to explain poor results but also to accept adjusted remuneration that reflects those results. Thus in 1982, Cabot's President and CEO Robert A. Charpie's total compensation dropped to $178,696 from a high of $1.6 million the previous year, due in large part to a decline in profits. And William Agee took a 49% pay cut in 1982, reflecting Bendix's nonrave fiscal performance, before leaving the company in 1983 with his parachute prize. When Firestone Tire & Rubber had a dismal year in 1982, with earnings off by 96%, the compensation of John J. Nevin, chairman and CEO, also dropped, by 24%. David Mahoney's take-home pay was likewise shaved in the shadow of lackluster results at Norton Simon and a shareholders' suit.

Sometimes CEOs make these trade-offs deliberately. Astute executives will often sacrifice or delay short-term gains, which will make them look good, in favor of achieving longer term strength for the company and its shareholders.

But sometimes CEOs act to delay poor results until they have left the scene, to the detriment of the company. As Lester B. Korn, Korn-Ferry International, has noted:

"We have all seen too many instances of chief executive officers retiring after fifteen straight quarters of record earnings. We cover these executives with glory for their stupendous achievements. Then, two years later, the companies they left behind are on the rocks. Only then do we learn that they achieved their gains by slashing R&D budgets or, for example, by closing down operations—decisions that were expedient at the time but disastrous for the long run."[1]

In either case, as the pivotal decision maker and corporate figurehead, the CEO is often in a precarious position. Whereas a CEO's average tenure was ten years around 1950, it is now about five as a result of burnout, mergers, executive competition, and mobility. Thus CEOs perceive that their rich rewards can be tempered, that judicious long-term decisions may go unappreciated, and that their jobs are increasingly insecure. Devoted and capable executives may find themselves plagued by circumstances beyond their control and attacked by shareholders and media who do not acknowledge their dedication or their operating rationale. Right or wrong, they feel under the gun with every major move.

When a takeover or merger is imminent these feelings intensify—and with good cause. Gilbert E. Dwyer of Ward Howell International has pointed out that only one CEO in ten in acquired companies ends up with the new parent's top post. Most are relegated to lesser positions, phased out, or just fade away. Incumbent CEOs faced with an impending merger are, therefore, inevitably concerned.

It is against this backdrop that apologists for golden parachutes make their case. CEOs and directors claim that parachutes, with their provision of long-term personal protection, are necessary to dissipate executives' apprehensions and ensure objectivity during merger negotiations. CEOs will not take the shareholders' point of view in evaluating offers, the argument goes, if they believe that their livelihoods and careers are at stake.

Others involved in corporate acquisitions also defend the practice by pointing out that parachute costs are negligible compared to the megabucks involved in major mergers. Takeover attorneys Joseph Flom and Martin Lipton, for instance, insist that an executive's freedom to negotiate is well worth the price. They also argue that the costs do not deter bona fide acquisition offers.

Many shareholders dispute these views, and they often have both

---

1 Lester B. Korn, "Window of Danger in Executive Leadership," *Financier,* March 1982, p. 41.

voting rights and the right to initiate antiparachute class actions. Companies, too, sometimes voice their opposition strongly—occasionally to the point of action. Recently, for example, one large corporation objected strenuously to an acquisition candidate's golden parachutes and succeeded in having them eliminated before acquiring the company.

Personally, I think that those who defend golden parachutes are giving America's CEOs a bad rap. Most CEOs are ethical, objective, and take their obligations to shareholders seriously. Arguments on behalf of golden parachutes attempt to legitimize giving million-dollar bribes to executives for doing what they were paid to do anyway. The parachute protagonists, moreover, presuppose a readiness—if not an outright alacrity—on the part of CEOs to place their own interests ahead of the shareholders'. While this may be a keen observation about human nature in general, I believe that it maligns most American chief executives.

Directors' responsibility

As the guardians of corporate progress for the shareholders, board members are directly concerned with the caliber, continuity, and compensation of top management. Thus the responsibility for perpetuating or checking golden parachutes lies squarely in their court.

Boards attest to the value of top management's contribution to company well-being when they designate the leading officers as key employees. Moreover, they back up their valuation with special considerations, including a fine array of perks and compensation packages, that others in the organization do not receive. But boards give these rewards to top executives to induce them to join, work for, and remain with the company, and to do demanding and critical jobs in the shareholders' interest while in the company's employ. When these conditions no longer hold, corporate rewards should come to an end.

After all, the CEO and other top executives in publicly owned companies are employees, and the shareholders-owners are entitled to view their compensation in terms of work rendered.

Along with business acumen, objectivity is a primary qualification of a board member. Recognizing that inside directors may lack objectivity to some degree, most public companies have tried in recent decades to balance their boards by including outside directors. More than anything else in current corporate governance, these efforts have shored up lopsided corporate organizations and brought new respectability to publicly owned companies. At the same time, they place a heavy onus on outside directors to offset any biases that inside directors may unwittingly bring to board meetings and operational decisions.

Let us assume, therefore, that outside directors are hardheaded and clearheaded enough to act in the interests of the shareholders. And let us also assume that their objectivity can withstand the softening that sometimes accompanies exposure to top management in board meetings and elsewhere. For when it comes to the sensitive area of a CEO's claim to a golden parachute, it is hard for directors to avoid being swayed—for or against—by their personal relations with the CEO.

To preserve their objectivity and fulfill their responsibilities to the shareholders, directors must always be concerned with long-term planning and goals as opposed to crisis management. While inevitable from time to time, crisis management may have the effect of diluting objectivity if there is no established overriding long-term policy, or if such a policy is weak to begin with. Furthermore, top executives tend to define and present crises to the board. And though management-defined crises may indeed be serious problems for high-level executives, they need not be matters of life and death for the company. A CEO, for example, can view a takeover attempt as a crisis because it challenges his or her job and career. But the takeover may represent opportunity to the shareholders.

Rigorous corporate self-monitoring of golden parachutes is the only effective way to blunt further shareholder resentment and restrictive government regulations. Accordingly, I propose the following:

☐ All existing golden parachutes should be eliminated if their value exceeds two and one-half times the recipient's current annual compensation including deferred payments and bonuses.

☐ No board should give golden parachutes to its CEO or key executives if the company has performed below the industry average over the previous five years as measured by return on investment.

☐ CEOs and other directors—both inside and outside—should disqualify themselves from active negotiation on tender or takeover offers if their equity and other interests would be materially improved by the transaction, i.e., if they would receive more than the equivalent of three years cash compensation or 1% of the transaction's cash value.

☐ In the event of a takeover in which an executive's job is forfeited, new management should honor all benefits under existing employment contracts through their current termination period or for three years, whichever is greater.

Finally, remember that integrity cannot be bought. The best defense against excesses such as golden parachutes is a company's culture and the quality of the people it employs. In a recent *New York Times* article, America's corporate chiefs were charged with losing sight of moral standards in their frenzy to become rich. If we are to do away with this impression, these proposals are realistic. If we do little or nothing, we will have legislation and regulations that are harmful, restrictive, and punitive—and they will be richly deserved. ▽

GROWING CONCERNS

How to conserve cash and still attract the best executives

Compensation and Benefits for Startup Companies

by Joseph S. Tibbetts, Jr. and Edmund T. Donovan

You've decided to start a company. Your business plan is based on sound strategy and thorough market research. Your background and training have prepared you for the challenge. Now you must assemble the quality management team that venture investors demand. So you begin the search for a topflight engineer to head product development and a seasoned manager to handle marketing, sales, and distribution.

Attracting these executives is easier said than done. You've networked your way to just the marketing candidate you need: a vice president with the right industry experience and an aggressive business outlook. But she makes $100,000 a year in a secure job at a large company. You can't possibly commit that much cash, even if you do raise outside capital. How do you structure a compensation package that will lure her away? How much cash is reasonable? How much and what type of stock should the package include? Is there any way to match the array of benefits—retirement plans, child-care assistance, savings programs—her current employer provides? In short, what kind of compensation and benefits program will attract, motivate, and retain this marketing vice president and other

> **Be realistic about your limitations. But don't ignore the advantages of being small.**

key executives while not jeopardizing the fragile finances of your startup business?

Selecting appropriate compensation and benefits policies is a critical challenge for companies of all sizes. But never are the challenges more difficult—or the stakes higher—than when a company first takes shape. Startups must strike a delicate balance. Unrealistically low levels of cash compensation weaken their ability to attract quality managers. Unrealistically high levels of cash compensation can turn off potential investors and, in extreme cases, threaten the solvency of the business. How to proceed?

First, be realistic about the limitations. There is simply no way that a company just developing a prototype or shipping product for less than a year or generating its first black ink after several money-losing years of building the business can match the current salaries and benefits offered by established competitors. At the same time, there are real advantages to being small. Without an entrenched personnel bureaucracy and long-standing compensation policies, it is easier to tailor salaries and benefits to individual needs. Creativity and flexibility are at a premium.

Second, be thorough and systematic about analyzing the options. Compensation and benefits plans can be expensive to design, install, administer, and terminate. A program that is inappropriate or badly conceived can be a very costly mistake. Startups should evaluate compensation and benefits alternatives from four distinct perspectives.

How do they affect cash flow? Survival is the first order of business for a new company. Even if you have raised an initial round of equity financing, there is seldom enough working capital to go around. Research and development, facilities and equipment, and marketing costs all make priority claims on resources. Cash compensation must be a lower priority. Despite this awkward tension (the desperate need to attract first-rate talent without having the cash to pay them market rates), marshaling resources for pressing business needs must remain paramount.

What are the tax implications? Compensation and benefits choices

---

Joseph S. Tibbetts, Jr. is managing partner of the Price Waterhouse Entrepreneurial Services Center in Cambridge, Massachusetts. Edmund T. Donovan, a tax attorney, is manager of employee benefits services at Price Waterhouse in Boston.

have major tax consequences for a startup company and its executives; startups can use the tax code to maximum advantage in compensation decisions. Certain approaches, like setting aside assets to secure deferred compensation liabilities, require that executives declare the income immediately and the company deduct it as a current expense. Other

> No startup is an island. Factor regional and industry trends into your salary calculations.

approaches, like leaving deferred compensation liabilities unsecured, allow executives to declare the income later while the company takes a future deduction. Many executives value the option of deferring taxable income more than the security of immediate cash. And since most startups have few, if any, profits to shield from taxes, deferring deductions may appeal to them as well.

What is the accounting impact? Most companies on their way to an initial public offering or a sellout to a larger company must register particular earning patterns. Different compensation programs affect the income statement in very different ways. One service company in the startup stage adopted an insurance-backed salary plan for its key executives. The plan bolstered the company's short-term cash flow by deferring salary payments (it also deferred taxable income for those executives). But it would have meant heavy charges to book earnings over the deferral period— charges that might have interfered with the company's plans to go public. So management backed out of the program at the eleventh hour.

What is the competition doing? No startup is an island, especially when vying for talented executives. Companies must factor regional and industry trends into their compensation and benefits calculations. One newly established law firm decided not to offer new associates a 401(k) plan. (This program allows employees to contribute pretax dollars into a savings fund that also grows tax-free. Many employers match a portion of their employees' contributions.) The firm quickly discovered that it could not attract top candidates without the plan; it had become a staple of the profession in that geographic market. So it established a 401(k) and assumed the administrative costs, but it saved money by not including a matching provision right away.

Events at a Boston software company illustrate the potential for flexibility in startup compensation. The company's three founders had worked together at a previous employer. They had sufficient personal resources to contribute assets and cash to the new company in exchange for founders' stock. They decided to forgo cash compensation altogether for the first year.

Critical to the company's success were five software engineers who would write code for the first product. It did not make sense for the company to raise venture capital to pay the engineers their market-value salaries. Yet their talents were essential if the company were to deliver the software on time.

The obvious solution: supplement cash compensation with stock. But two problems arose. The five prospects had unreasonably high expectations about how much stock they should receive. Each demanded 5% to 10% of the company, which, if granted, would have meant transferring excessive ownership to them. Moreover, while they were equal in experience and ability and therefore worth equal salaries, each had different cash requirements to meet their obligations and maintain a reasonable life-style. One of the engineers was single and had few debts; he was happy to go cash-poor and bank on the company's growth. One of his colleagues, however, had a wife and young child at home and needed the security of a sizable paycheck.

The founders devised a solution to meet the needs of the company and its prospective employees. They consulted other software startups and documented that second-tier employees typically received 1% to 3% ownership stakes. After some negotiation, they settled on a maximum of 2% for each of the five engineers. Then they agreed on a formula by which these employees could trade cash for stock during their first three years. For every $1,000 in cash an engineer received over a base figure, he or she forfeited a fixed number of shares. The result: all five engineers signed on, the company stayed within its cash constraints, and the founders gave up a more appropriate 7% of the company's equity.

Cash vs. stock

Equity is the great compensation equalizer in startup companies—the bridge between an executive's market value and the company's cash constraints. And there are endless variations on the equity theme: restricted shares, incentive stock options, nonqualified options, stock appreciation rights (SARs), phantom stock, and the list goes on. This dizzying array of choices notwithstanding, startup companies face three basic questions. Does it make sense to grant key executives an equity interest? If so, should the company use restricted stock, options, or some combination of both? If not, does it make sense to reward executives based on the company's appreciating share value or to devise formulas based on different criteria?

Let's consider these questions one at a time. Some company founders are unwilling to part with much ownership at inception. And with good reason. Venture capitalists or other outside investors will demand a healthy share of equity in return for a capital infusion. Founders rightly worry about diluting their control before obtaining venture funds.

Alternatives in this situation include SARs and phantom shares— programs that allow key employees to benefit from the company's increasing value without transferring voting power to them. No shares actually trade hands; the company compensates its executives to reflect the appreciation of its stock. Many

"Peterson, run down and tell my wife that I'll come out and play as soon as I've wrapped up these contracts and not a minute before."

executives prefer these programs to outright equity ownership because they don't have to invest their own money. They receive the financial benefits of owning stock without the risk of buying shares. In return, of course, they forfeit the rights and privileges of ownership. These programs can get complicated, however, and they require thorough accounting reviews. Reporting rules for artificial stock plans are very restrictive and sometimes create substantial charges against earnings.

Some founders take the other extreme. In the interest of saving cash, they award bits of equity at every turn. This can create real problems. When it comes to issuing stock, startups should always be careful not to sell the store before they fill the shelves. That is, they should award shares to key executives and second-tier employees in a way that protects the long-term company interest. And these awards should take place only after the company has fully distributed stock to the founders.

The choice of whether to issue actual or phantom shares should also be consistent with the company's strategy. If the goal is to realize the "big payoff" within three to five years through an initial public offering or outright sale of the company, then stock may be the best route. You can motivate employees to work hard and build the company's value since they can readily envision big personal rewards down the road.

The founder of a temporary employment agency used this approach to attract and motivate key executives. He planned from the start to sell the business once it reached critical mass, and let his key executives know his game plan. He also allowed them to buy shares at a discount. When he sold the business a few years later for $10 million, certain executives, each of whom had been allowed to buy up to 4% of the company, received as much as $400,000. The lure of cashing out quickly was a great motivator for this company's top executives.

For companies that plan to grow more slowly over the first three to five years, resist acquisition offers, and maintain private ownership, the stock alternative may not be optimal. Granting shares in a company that may never be sold or publicly traded is a bit like giving away play money. Worthless paper can actually be a demotivator for employees.

In such cases, it may make sense to create an artificial market for stock. Companies can choose among various book-value plans, under which they offer to buy back shares issued to employees according to a pricing formula. Such plans establish a measurement mechanism based on company performance—like book value, earnings, return on assets or equity—that determines the company's per-share value. As with phantom shares and SARs, book-value plans require a thorough accounting review.

If a company does decide to issue shares, the next question is how to do it. Restricted stock is one alternative. Restricted shares most often require that an executive remain with the company for a specified time period or forfeit the equity, thus creating "golden handcuffs" to promote long-term service. The executive otherwise enjoys all the rights of other shareholders, except for the

> **Shares in a company that will never go public can actually demotivate your people.**

right to sell any stock still subject to restriction.

Stock options are another choice, and they generally come in two forms: incentive stock options (ISOs) and nonqualified stock options (NSOs). As with restricted shares, stock options can create golden handcuffs. Most options, whether ISOs or NSOs, involve a vesting schedule. Executives may receive options on 1,000 shares of stock, but only 25% of the options vest (i.e., executives can exercise them) in any one year. If an executive leaves the company, he or she loses the unexercised options. Startups often prefer ISOs since they give executives a timing advantage with respect to taxes. Executives pay no taxes on any capital gains until they sell or exchange the stock, and then only if they realize a profit over the exercise price. ISOs, however, give the company no tax deductions—which is not a major drawback for startups that don't expect to earn big profits for several years. Of course, if companies generate taxable income before their executives exercise their options, lack of a deduction is a definite negative.

ISOs have other drawbacks. Tax laws impose stiff technical requirements on how much stock can be subject to options, the maximum exercise period, who can receive options, and how long stock must be held before it can be sold. Moreover, the exercise price of an ISO cannot be lower than the fair market value of the stock on the date the option is granted. (Shares need not be publicly traded for them to have a fair market value. Private companies estimate the market value of their stock.)

For these and other reasons, companies usually issue NSOs as well as ISOs. NSOs can be issued at a discount to current market value. They can be issued to directors and consultants (who cannot receive ISOs) as well as to company employees. And they have different tax consequences for the issuing company, which can deduct the spread between the exercise price and the market price of the shares when the options are exercised.

NSOs can also play a role in deferred compensation programs. More and more startups are following the lead of larger companies by allowing executives to defer cash compensation with stock options. They grant NSOs at a below-market exercise price that reflects the amount of salary deferred. Unlike standard deferral plans, where cash is paid out on some unalterable future date (thus triggering automatic tax liabilities), the option approach gives executives control over when and how they will be taxed on their deferred salary. The company, meanwhile, can deduct the spread when its executives exercise their options.

One small but growing high-tech company used a combination of stock techniques to achieve several compensation goals simultaneously. It issued NSOs with an exercise price equal to fair market value (most NSOs are issued at a discount). All the options were exercisable immediately (most options have a vesting schedule). Finally, the company placed restrictions on the resale of stock purchased with options.

This program allowed for maximum flexibility. Executives with excess cash could exercise all their options right away; executives with less cash, or who wanted to wait for signs of the company's progress, could wait months or years to exercise. The plan provided the company with tax deductions on any options exercised in the future (assuming the fair market value at exercise exceeded the stock's fair market value when the company granted the options) and avoided any charges to book earnings in the process. And the resale restrictions created golden handcuffs without forcing executives to wait to buy their shares.

The benefits challenge

No startup can match the cradle-to-grave benefits offered by employers like IBM or General Motors, although young companies may have to attract executives from these giant companies. It is also true, however, that the executives most attracted to startup opportunities may be people for whom standard benefit packages are relatively unimportant. Startup companies have special opportunities for creativity and customization with employee benefits. The goal should not be to come as close to what IBM offers without going broke, but to devise low-cost, innovative programs that meet the needs of a small employee corps.

Of course, certain basic needs must be met. Group life insurance is important, although coverage levels should start small and increase as the company gets stronger. Group medical is also essential, although there are many ways to limit its cost. Setting higher-than-average deductibles lowers employer premiums (the deductibles can be adjusted downward as financial stability improves). Self-insuring smaller claims also conserves cash. One young com-

> **You'll never match IBM's benefits. So you have to be creative.**

pany saved 25% on its health-insurance premiums by self-insuring the first $500 of each claim and paying a third party to administer the coverage.

The list of traditional employee benefits doesn't have to stop here—but it probably should. Most companies should not adopt long-term disability coverage, dental plans, child-care assistance, even retirement plans, until they are well beyond the startup phase. This is a difficult reality for many founders to accept, especially those who have broken from larger companies with generous benefit programs. But any program has costs—and costs of any kind are a critical worry for a new company trying to move from the red into the black. Indeed, one startup in the business of developing and operating progressive child-care centers wisely decided to wait for greater financial stability before offering its own employees child-care benefits.

Many young companies underestimate the money and time it takes just to administer benefit programs, let alone fund them. Employee benefits do not run on automatic pilot. While the vice president of marketing watches marketing, the CFO keeps tabs on finances, and the CEO snuffs out the fires that always threaten to engulf a young company, who is left to mind the personnel store? If a substantial benefits program is in place, someone has to handle the day-to-day administrative details and update the program as the accounting and tax rules change. The best strategy is to keep benefits modest at first and make them more comprehensive as the company moves toward profitability.

Which is not to suggest that the only answer to benefits is setting strict limits. Other creative policies may not only cost less but they also may better suit the interests and needs of executive recruits. Take company-supplied lunches. One startup computer company thought it was important to create a "think-tank" atmosphere. So it set up writing boards in the cafeteria, provided all employees with daily lunches from various ethnic restaurants, and encouraged spirited noontime discussions.

Certainly, Thai food is no substitute for a generous pension. But benefits that promote a creative and energetic office environment may matter more to employees than savings plans whose impact may not be felt for decades. One startup learned this lesson after it polled its employees. It was prepared to offer an attractive – and costly – 401(k) program until a survey disclosed that employees preferred a much different benefit: employer-paid membership at a local health club. The company gladly obliged.

Deciding on compensation policies for startup companies means making tough choices. There is an inevitable temptation, as a company shows its first signs of growth and financial stability, to enlarge salaries and benefits toward market levels. You should resist these temptations. As your company heads toward maturity, so can your compensation and benefits programs. But the wisest approach is to go slowly, to make enhancements incrementally, and to be aware at all times of the cash flow, taxation, and accounting implications of the choices you face.

Reprint 89111

Employee
Compensation

The attack on pay

Rosabeth Moss Kanter

Status, not contribution, has traditionally been the basis for the numbers on employees' paychecks. Pay has reflected where jobs rank in the corporate hierarchy—not what comes out of them.

Today this system is under attack. More and more senior executives are trying to turn their employees into entrepreneurs—people who earn a direct return on the value they help create, often in exchange for putting their pay at risk. In the process, changes are coming into play that will have revolutionary consequences for companies and their employees. To see what I have in mind, consider these actual examples:

☐ To control costs and stimulate improvements, a leading financial services company converts its information systems department into a venture that sells its services both inside and outside the corporation. In its first year, the department runs at a big profit and employees begin to wonder why they can't get a chunk of the profits they have generated instead of just a fixed salary defined by rank.

☐ In exchange for wage concessions, a manufacturer offers employees an ownership stake. Employee representatives begin to think about total company profitability and start asking why so many managers are on the payroll and why they are paid so much.

☐ To encourage initiative in reaching performance targets, a city government offers large salary increases to managers who can show major departmental improvements. After a few years, the amount in managers' paychecks bears little relationship to their levels in the organization.

In traditional compensation plans, each job comes with a pay level that stays about the same

Ms. Kanter is the Class of 1960 Professor of Business Administration at the Harvard Business School. She has written numerous books, including Men and Women of the Corporation *(Basic Books, 1979) and* The Change Masters: Innovation and Entrepreneurship in the American Corporation *(Simon & Schuster, 1983). Her HBR article "Power Failure in Management Circuits" (July-August 1979) won that year's McKinsey Award.*

regardless of how well the job is performed or what the real organizational value of that performance is. Pay scales reflect such estimated characteristics as decision-making responsibility, importance to the organization, and number of subordinates. If there is a merit component, it is usually very small. The surest way—often the only way—to increase one's pay is to change employers or get promoted. A mountain of tradition and industrial relations practice has built up to support this way of calculating pay.

> *Reward performance you want to encourage.*

Proponents of this system customarily assert that the market ultimately determines pay, just as it determines the price of everything else that buyers wish to acquire. Compensation systems cannot be unfair or inappropriate, therefore, because they are incapable of causing anything. Actually, however, because it is so difficult to link people's compensation directly to their contributions, all the market really does is allow us to assume that people occupying equal positions tend to be paid equally and that people with similar experience and education tend to be worth about the same. So while the market works in macroeconomic terms, the process at a microeconomic level is circular: we know what people are worth because that's what they cost in the job market; but we also know that what people cost in the market is just what they're worth.

Given logic like this, it's not hard to see why such strange bedfellows as feminist activists and entrepreneurially minded managers both attack this traditional system as a manifestation of the paternalistic benefits offered across the board by Father Corporation. "We've got corporate socialism, not corporate capitalism," charged the manager of new ventures for a large industrial company. "We're so focused on consistent treatment internally that we destroy enterprise in the process."

These old arrangements are no longer supportable. For economic, social, and organizational reasons, the fundamental bases for determining pay are under attack. And while popular attention has focused on comparable worth—equalizing pay for those doing comparable work—the most important trend has been the loosening relationship between job assignment and pay level.

Four separate but closely related concerns are driving employers to rethink the meaning of worth and look beyond job assignments in determining pay—equity, cost, productivity, and the rewards of entrepreneurship.

It's not fair!

Every year, routine company surveys show fewer employees willing to say that traditional pay practices are fair. In particular, top management compensation has been assailed as unjustifiably high, especially when executives get large bonuses while their companies suffer financial losses or are just recovering from them.

Despite economic data showing an association between executive compensation and company performance, many professionals still argue that the amounts are excessive and reflect high status rather than good performance. Likewise, the existence of layers on layers of highly paid managers no longer seems entirely fair. Employees question why executives should be able to capture returns others actually produce. And they are beginning to resent compensation plans like the one in a leading well-run bank that gives managers bonuses of up to 30% of their pay for excellent branch performance, while branch employees get only a 6% to an 8% annual increase.

If executives get bonuses for raising profits, many urge, so should the workers who contribute to those profits. Indeed, this is the theory behind profit sharing in general. Such programs, and there are several widely used variants, have in common the very appealing and well-accepted notion that all employees —not just management—should share in the gains from enhanced performance.

Profit sharing is ordinarily a straightforward arrangement in which a fraction of the net profits from some period of operation are distributed to employees. The distribution may be either immediate or deferred, and the plan may not include all employees.

The plan at Lincoln Electric, the world's largest manufacturer of arc-welding products, is particularly generous. Every year, Lincoln pays out 6% of net income in common stock dividends—the "wages of capital." The board determines another sum to be set aside as seed money for investment in the future. The balance, paid to all employees, ranges from 20% of wages and salary, already competitive, to more than 120%. The company has remained profitable even in the face of sales declines in the 1981-1983 recession, to the benefit of employees as well as stockholders.

Overall, probably about a half million companies have some form of profit sharing, if both deferred and cash payouts are included. In private enterprises other than those categorized as small businesses, government statistics show that by 1983 19% of all production employees, 27% of all technical and clerical employees, and 23% of all professional and administrative employees were covered by profit-sharing agreements.

The variant known as gain sharing takes profit sharing one giant step further by attempting, usually with some elaborate formula, to calculate the contributions of specific groups of employees whose contingent pay depends on those varying results. Although the basis for calculation varies from one gain-sharing plan to another, the plans have two principles in common: first, the payout reflects the contribution of groups rather than individuals (on the theory that teams and collective effort are what count), and second, the rewards to be shared and the plan for their distribution are based on objective, measurable characteristics (so that everyone can see what is owed and when).

According to experts, several thousand companies have gain-sharing programs of some sort. These programs already involve millions of workers and seem to be growing in popularity. The Scanlon Plan, probably the oldest, best-known, and most elaborate gain-sharing system, usually distributes 75% of gains to employees and 25% to the company. In addition, this plan is organized around complex mechanisms and procedures that spell out how employees at various levels are to participate, not only in control of the process but also in opportunities to help improve performance and thereby their own shares. At Herman Miller, Inc., gain sharing is described not simply as a compensation system but rather as a way of life for the company.

Group or all-employee bonuses, especially when linked to fairly specific indicators, provide another way to share some of the benefits of good performance more equitably. But evidence shows that their potential far exceeds their use. Although group performance bonuses are continuing to grow, top exec-

---

Author's note: I thank Barry Stein, Cynthia Ingols, Paul Loranger, Carolyn Russell, Wendy Brown, and D. Quinn Mills for their valuable contributions.

utives are much more likely to capture a portion of the benefits of increased profitability than employees are. In a recent Conference Board study of 491 companies, 58% had top executive bonus plans but only 11% had profit-sharing plans, 8% all-employee bonuses, 3% group productivity incentives, and fewer than 1% group cost-control incentives.

Performance-related compensation plans generally ignore employees other than top management and, to a lesser extent, some middle managers. And even in incentive-conscious high-technology companies, gain sharing is rare. While more than half the high-tech companies included in a recent Hay Associates compensation survey had cash or stock awards for individuals, only 6% had gain-sharing or group profit-sharing programs. Concerns about equity—including those framed in terms of comparable worth—are not altogether misplaced therefore.

Companies have long been concerned with one fundamental fairness issue—the relative compensation of employees in general. Now, however, they face two new issues that are complex, hard to resolve, and rapidly getting worse. The first, evident in the debate over gain sharing and profit sharing, sets up what employees get against what the organization gets from their efforts. The second, evident in the debate over comparable worth, is how groups in an organization fare in relation to each other. At the very least, these issues call for better measurement systems or new principles on which various constituencies can agree.

Let them eat dividends

Facing challenges from competitors, companies in every field are seeking ways to reduce fixed labor costs. One sure way is to peg pay to performance—the company's as well as the individual's. Merit awards, bonuses, and profit-sharing plans hold out the promise of extra earnings for those who truly contribute. But it is their cost-reduction potential that really makes executives' eyes sparkle with dollar signs.

Making pay float to reflect company performance is the cornerstone of MIT economist Martin L. Weitzman's proposal for a "share economy." If many companies can be induced to share profits or revenues with their employees, Weitzman argues, then the cure for stagflation would be at hand. Among other things, companies would have an incentive to create jobs because more workers would be paid only in proportion to what they have brought in.[1]

For organizations struggling to compete, these macroeconomic implications are a lot less tantalizing than the more immediate benefits to be gained by asking workers to take their lumps from business cycles—or, employees would add, poor management decisions—along with their companies. Moreover, a similar logic clearly accounts for some of the appeal of employee ownership, especially to companies in industries where deregulation has created enormous cost competitiveness.

According to one recent book about employee ownership, *Taking Stock: Employee Ownership at Work*, at least 6 major airlines and 15 trucking companies have adopted employee ownership plans in response to deregulation.[2] Overall, the authors estimate that some 11 million employees in 8,000-plus businesses now own at least 15% of the companies employing them.

While many companies have found employee ownership attractive primarily as a financing scheme, there is little doubt that, properly designed and managed, it can positively affect corporate success. Take Western Air Lines as an illustration. After losing $200 million over four years, this company created the Western Partnership by trading a 32.4% ownership stake, a meaningful profit-sharing plan, and four seats on the board of directors for wage cuts and productivity improvements of 22.5% to 30%. In 1985 Western distributed more than $10 million to its 10,000 employees—$100 each in cash and the rest in employees' accounts. Now employees are making about $75 million on Western's sale to Delta.

Such schemes have obvious advantages over another highly visible alternative for fixed-labor-cost reduction—two-tier wage systems, which bring in new hires at a lower scale than current employees. Most of us can see the obvious inequity in paying two groups differently for doing exactly the same job. But pay pegged to actual performance? Earnings tied to company profits? What could be more fair?

The clear problems—that lower paid employees cannot afford income swings as readily as the more highly paid and that employee efforts are not always directly related to company profitability—do not seem to deter the advocates. The fixed part of the paycheck is already shrinking in many American companies. Even the bonus is being used to supplement these efforts, especially among manufacturing companies. A recent study by the Bureau of National Affairs reveals that one-shot bonus payments, replacing general pay increases, were called for in almost 20% of all 1985 union contract settlements outside the construction industry, up from a mere 6% in 1984. Similarly, 20% of the 564 companies in Hewitt Associates' 1986

---

1 Martin L. Weitzman,
*The Share Economy:
Conquering Stagflation*
(Cambridge:
Harvard University Press, 1984).

2 Michael Quarrey, Joseph Blasi,
and Corey Rosen,
*Taking Stock:
Employee Ownership at Work*
(Cambridge, Mass.: Ballinger, 1986).

"Used to be sort of a Yuppy myself, but we called it 'up-and-comer.'"

compensation survey gave one-time bonuses to white-collar workers, up from 7% in 1985.

These one-time payments do not raise base pay, nor do they affect overtime calculations. In fact, just the opposite occurs: they reduce the cost of labor. More than two-thirds of the bonus provisions the BNA studied were accompanied by wage freezes or decreases.

Bucks for behavior

The cost attack is one straightforward way for companies to become more competitive, at least in the short run. In the long run, however, pay variations or rewards, contingent on specific and measurable achievements of individuals at every level, are likely to be even more effective in stimulating employee enterprise and channeling behavior. What better way could there be, proponents argue, to help employees recognize what is most useful and to guide their efforts appropriately?

Merrill Lynch's compensation system for its 10,400 brokers, introduced in February 1986, is a good example. To encourage brokers to spend more time with larger, more active customers, the firm has cut commissions for most small trades and discounts and rewards the accumulation of assets under its management. The pay system was developed in direct response to new products like the firm's Cash Management Account because the old system wasn't adequate to reward performance in new and growing areas management wanted to stress.

Commissions and bonuses for sales personnel are standard practice in most industries, of course. What seem to be changing are the amounts people can earn (for example, more than double one's salary at General Electric Medical Systems' Sales and Service Division), the number of people who can earn them, and the variety of productivity bonuses, especially in highly competitive new industries.

PSICOR is a small Michigan company supplying equipment and professionals (called perfusionists) for open-heart surgery. Perfusionists are in great demand and frequently change employers, so founder Michael Dunaway searched for a way to give them immediate rewards because the standard 10% increase at the end of the year was too remote.

First he tried random bonuses of $100 to $500 for superior performance, but tracking proved difficult. Then in 1982 he hit on the idea of continuous raises—increases in every paycheck—calculated to add up to at least a 5% annual raise over base salary, with up to 8% more in a lump sum at year-end based on overall performance. Employee response was positive, but the accounting department was soon drowning in paperwork.

PSICOR's latest system combines quarterly raises of up to 5% a year, based solely on performance, with a series of additional bonuses to reward specific activities: higher caseloads, out-of-town assignments, professional certification, and the like. Turnover is less than 2% and drops to less than $1/2$% for those employed two years or more.

Of course, some companies are going in exactly the opposite direction—for seemingly good reason. As an ex-director of sales compensation for IBM confessed, "We used to give bonuses and awards for every imaginable action by the sales force. But the more complex it got, the more difficult it was to administer, and the results were not convincing. When we began to ask ourselves why Digital Equipment had salespeople, who are tough competitors, on straight salary, we decided perhaps we'd gone overboard a bit."

Even in commercial real estate leasing, long a highly performance-oriented business, one major and very effective Boston company—Leggat, McCall & Werner, Inc.—has for years had its brokers on salary.

Nevertheless, the tide is moving in the other direction—toward more varied individual compensation based on people's own efforts. This trend reaches its fullest expression, however, not in pay-for-performance systems like those just described but in the scramble to devise ways to reward people in organizations for acting as if they were running their own businesses.

A piece of the action

The prospect of running a part of a large corporation as though it were an independent business is one of the hottest old-ideas-refurbished in American industry. Many companies are encouraging potential entrepreneurs to remain within the corporate fold by paying them like owners when they develop new businesses. And even very traditional organizations are looking carefully at the possibility of setting up new ventures with a piece of the action for the entrepreneurs. "If one of our employees came along with a proposition, I'm not sure how anxious we'd be to do it," one bank executive said. "But ten years ago, we wouldn't have listened at all. We'd have said, 'You've got rocks in your head.'"

Most of the new entrepreneurial schemes pay people base salaries, generally equivalent to those of their former job levels, and ask them to put part of their compensation at risk, with their ownership percentage determined by their willingness to invest. This investment then substitutes for any other bonuses, perks, profit sharing, or special incentives they might have been able to earn in their former jobs. Sometimes the returns are based solely on percentages of the profits from their ventures; sometimes the returns come in the form of phantom stock pegged to the companies' public stock prices. Potential entrepreneurs cannot get as rich under this system as they could if they were full owners of independent businesses who shared ownership with other venture capitalists. But they are also taking much less risk.

AT&T's new venture development process, begun just before divestiture, illustrates how large corporations are trying to capture entrepreneurship. Currently seven venture units are in operation, each sponsored by one of AT&T's lines of business. One started in 1983, three in 1984, and three more in 1985. The largest is now up to 90 employees.

William P. Stritzler, the AT&T executive responsible for overseeing this process, offers venture participants three compensation alternatives corresponding to three levels of risk.

Option one allows venture participants to stick with the standard corporate compensation and benefits plan and to keep the salaries associated with their previous jobs. Not surprisingly, none of the seven has chosen this option.

Under option two, participants agree to freeze their salaries at the levels of their last jobs and to forgo other contingent compensation until the venture begins to generate a positive cash flow and the AT&T investment is paid back (or, with the concurrence of the venture board, until the business passes certain milestones). At that point, venture participants can get one-time bonuses equal to a maximum of 150% of their salaries. Five of the seven venture teams have selected this option.

The third option, chosen by two self-confident bands of risk takers, comes closest to simulating the independent entrepreneur's situation. Participants can contribute to the venture's capitalization through paycheck deductions until the venture begins to make money and generate a positive cash flow. Investments are limited only by the requirement that salaries remain above the minimum wage—to avoid legal problems and prevent people from using personal funds. In exchange, participants can gain up to eight times their total investment.

To date, participants have put in from 12% to 25% of their salaries, and one of the two ventures has already paid several bonuses at a rate just below the maximum. The other, a computer-graphics-board venture housed outside Indianapolis, could return $890,000 to its 11 employee-investors in the near future.

The numbers show just how attractive AT&T employees find this program: ideas for new ventures began coming in before the program was announced, and in the planning year alone, 300 potential entrepreneurs developed proposals. Perhaps 2,000 ideas have been offered since, netting a venture formation rate of about 1 from every 250 ideas. People from every management level have been funded, including a first-line supervisor and a fifth-level manager (at AT&T, roughly equivalent to those just below officer rank), and in principle, management is even willing to offer this option to nonmanagers.

Entrepreneurial incentives are especially prevalent at high-technology companies—not surprising given the importance and mobility of innovators. For example, a 1983 random sample of 105 Boston-area companies employing scientists and engineers compared the high-tech enterprises, dependent on R&D for product development, with their more traditional, established counterparts. The high-tech companies paid lower base salaries on average but offered more financial incentives, such as cash bonuses, stock options, and profit-sharing plans.[3]

The entrepreneurial paycheck is on the rise wherever management thinks that people could do as well or better if they were in business for themselves—in high tech and no-tech alike. Au Bon Pain, a Boston-based chain of bakeries and restaurants, with $30 million in revenue from 40 stores nationwide, is launching

---

3 Jay R. Schuster,
Management Compensation in High Technology Companies: Assuring Corporate Excellence
(Lexington, Mass.: Lexington Books, 1984).

a partnership program that will turn over a big piece of the action to store managers. Under the plan, annual revenues exceeding $170,000 per store will be shared fifty-fifty with the partners.

If business developers and revenue growers are getting a chance to share in the returns, will inventors in the same companies be far behind? Probably not. The inventors' rights challenge is another nudge in the direction of entrepreneurial rewards.

Traditional practice has rewarded salaried inventors with small bonuses (often $500 to $1,000) for each patent received and some nonmonetary incentives to encourage their next inventions. Recognition ranges from special awards and promotion to master status entailing the use of special laboratories, freedom of project choice, sabbaticals, and the like. Cash awards are often given, but they are generally not tied to product returns. For outstanding innovation, IBM, for example, offers awards (which can be $10,000 or more) and invention achievement ($2,400 and up).

Increasingly, however, we are seeing strong competitive and legal pressures to reward employed inventors as if they were entrepreneurs by tying their compensation to the market value of their output. They too want a piece of the action and a direct return on their contributions.

The challenge to hierarchy

If pay practices continue to move toward contribution as the basis for earnings, as I believe they will, the change will unleash a set of forces that could transform work relationships as we know them now. To illustrate, let's look at what happens when organizations take modest steps to make pay more entrepreneurial.

In 1981, the city of Long Beach, California established a pay-for-performance system for its management as part of a new budgeting process designed to upgrade the city government's performance against quantifiable fiscal and service delivery targets. Under the new system, managers can gain or lose up to 20% of their base salaries, so the pay of two managers at the same level can vary by up to $40,000. Job category and position in the hierarchy are far weaker determinants of earnings. In fact, at least two people are now paid more than the city manager.

While the impact of a system like this on productivity and entrepreneurship is noticeable, its effect on work relationships is more subtle. People don't wear their paychecks over their name badges in the office, after all. But word does get around, and some organizations are having to face the problem of envy head-on. In two different companies with new-venture units that offer equity participation, the units are being attacked as unfair and poorly conceived. The attackers are aggrieved that venture participants can earn so much money for seemingly modest or even trivial contributions to the corporation overall, while those who keep the mainstream businesses going must accept salary ceilings and insignificant bonuses.

> *The iron cage of bureaucracy is being rattled.*

In companies that establish new-enterprise units, this clash between two different systems is self-inflicted. But sometimes the conflict comes as an unwelcome by-product of a company's efforts to expand into new businesses via acquisition. On buying a brokerage firm, a leading bank found that it had also acquired a very different compensation system: a generous commission arrangement means that employees often earn twice their salary in bonuses and, once in a while, five times. In 1985, six people made as much in salary and commissions as the chairman did in his base salary, or roughly $500,000 each. These people all made much more than their managers and their managers' managers and virtually everyone else in the corporation except the top three or four officers, a situation that would have been impossible a few years ago.

Now such discrepancies cannot be prevented or kept quiet. "People in the trade know perfectly well what's happening," the bank's senior administration executive told me. "They know the formula, they see the proxy statements, and they are busy checking out the systems by which we and everybody else compensate these people."

To avoid the equivalent of an employee run on the bank—with everyone trying to transfer to the brokerage operation—the corporation has felt forced to establish performance bonuses for branch managers and some piece-rate systems for clerical workers, though these are not nearly as generous as the managers' extra earning opportunities.

This system, though it solves some problems, creates others. The executive responsible recognizes that although these new income-earning opportunities are pegged to individual performance, people do not work in isolation. Branch managers' results really depend on how well their employees perform, and so do the results of nearly everyone else except those in sales (and even there a team effort can make a difference). Yet instead of teamwork, the bank's practices may encourage competition, the hoarding of good leads, and the withholding of good ideas until one person can claim the credit. "We talk about teamwork at training sessions," this executive said, "and then we destroy it in the compensation system."

Team-based pay raises its own questions, however, and generates its own set of prickly issues. There is the "free rider" problem, in which a few nonperforming members of the group benefit from the actions of the productive members. And problems can arise when people resent being dependent on team members, especially those with very different organizational status.

> *The new bottom line is what you contribute.*

There are also pressure problems. Gainsharing plans, in particular, can create very high peer pressure to do well, since the pay of all depends on everyone's efforts. Theodore Cohn, a compensation expert, likes to talk about the Dutch company, Philips, in which twice-yearly bonuses can run up to 40% of base pay. "Managers say that a paper clip never hits the floor—a hand will be there to catch it," Cohn recounts. "If a husband dies, the wake is at night so that no one misses work. If someone goes on vacation, somebody else is shown how to do the job. There is practically no turnover."

Similarly, Cohn claims that at Lincoln Electric, where performance-related pay is twice the average factory wage, peer pressure can be so high that the first two years of employment are called purgatory.[4]

Another kind of pressure also emerges from equity-ownership and profit-sharing systems—the pressure to open the books, to disclose managerial salaries, and to justify pay differentials. Concerns like these bubble up when employees who may never have thought much about other people's pay suddenly realize that "their" money is at stake.

These concerns and questions of distributional equity are all part of making the system more fair as well as more effective. Perhaps the biggest issue, and the one most disturbing to traditionalists, is what happens to the chain of command when it does not match the progression of pay. If subordinates can outearn their bosses, hierarchy begins to crumble.

Social psychologists have shown that authority relationships depend on a degree of inequality. If the distance between boss and subordinate declines, so does automatic deference and respect. The key word here is *automatic*. Superiors can still gain respect through their competence and fair treatment of subordinates. But power shifts as relationships become more equal.

Once the measures of good performance are both clearly established and clearly achieved, a subordinate no longer needs the goodwill of the boss quite so much. Proven achievement reflected in earnings higher than the boss's produces security, which produces risk taking, which produces speaking up and pushing back. As a result, the relationship between boss and subordinate changes from one based on authority to one based on mutual respect.

This change has positive implications for superiors as well as subordinates. For example, if a subordinate can earn more than the boss and still stay in place, then one of the incentives to compete for the boss's job is removed. Gone, too, is the tension that can build when an ambitious subordinate covets the boss's job and will do anything to get it. In short, if some of the *authority* of hierarchy is eliminated, so is some of the *hostility*.

In most traditional organizations, however, the idea of earning more than the boss seems insupportable and, to some people, clearly inequitable. There are, of course, organizational precedents for situations in which people in lower ranked jobs are paid more than those above. Field sales personnel paid on commission can often earn more than their managers; star scientists in R&D laboratories may earn more than the administrators nominally placed over them; and hourly workers can make more than their supervisors through overtime pay or union-negotiated wage settlements. But these situations are usually uncommon, or they're accepted because they're part of a dual-career ladder or the price of moving up in rank into management.

To get a feeling for the kinds of difficulties pay imbalances can create in hierarchical organizations, let's look at a less extreme case in which the gap between adjacent pay levels diminishes but does not disappear. This is called pay compression, and it bothers executives who believe in maintaining hierarchy.

In response to an American Management Association survey of 613 organizations, of which 134 were corporations with more than $1 billion in sales, 76% reported problems with compression.[5] Yet only a few percentage points divide the organizations expressing concern from those that do not. For example, the average earnings difference between first-line production supervisors and the highest paid production workers was 15.5% for organizations reporting com-

---

4 Theodore H. Cohn, "Incentive Compensation in Smaller Companies," *Proceedings of the Annual Conference of the American Compensation Association* (Scottsdale, Ariz.: ACA, 1984), pp. 1-7.

5 James W. Steele, *Paying for Performance and Position* (New York: AMA Membership Publishing Division, 1982).

pression problems, and only a little higher, 20%, for those not reporting such problems. In the maintenance area, the difference was even less—a 15.1% average earnings difference for those who said they had a problem versus 18.2% for those who said they did not. Furthermore, for a large number of companies claiming a compression problem, the difference between levels is actually greater than their official guidelines stipulate.

What is most striking to me, however, is how great the gap between adjacent levels still is—at least 15% difference in pay. Indeed, it is hard to avoid the conclusion that the executives concerned about compression are responding not to actual problems but to a perceived threat and the fear that hierarchy will crumble because of new pay practices.

What organizations say they will and won't do to solve compression problems supports this interpretation. While 67.4% of those concerned agree that an instant-bonus program would help, 70.1% say their companies would never institute one. And while 47.9% say that profit sharing for all salaried supervisors would help, 64.7% say that their companies would never do that either. In fact, the solutions least likely to be acceptable were precisely those that would change the hierarchy most—for example, reducing the number of job classifications, establishing fewer wage levels, and granting overtime compensation for supervisors (in effect, equalizing their status with that of hourly workers). On the other hand, the most favored solutions involved aids to upward mobility like training and rapid advancement that would keep the *structure* of the hierarchy intact while helping individuals move within it.

Innovative thoughts

The attacks on pay I've identified all push in the same direction. Indeed, they overlap and reinforce each other as, for example, a decision to reward individual contributors makes otherwise latent concerns about equity much more visible and live. Without options, private concerns can look like utopian dreams. Once those dreams begin to appear plausible, however, what was "the way things have to be" becomes instead a deliberate withholding of fair treatment.

By creating new forms for identifying, recognizing, and ultimately permitting contributions, the attack on pay goes beyond pay to color relationships throughout an organization. In the process, the iron cage of bureaucracy is being rattled in ways that will eventually change the nature, and the meaning, of hierarchy in ways we cannot yet imagine.

Wise executives, however, can prepare themselves and their companies for the revolutionary changes ahead. The shift toward contribution-based pay makes sense on grounds of equity, cost, productivity, and enterprise. And there are ways to manage that shift effectively. Here are some options to consider:

☐ Think strategically and systematically about the organizational implications of every change in compensation practices. If a venture unit offers an equity stake to participants, should a performance-based bonus with similar earning potential be offered to managers of mainstream businesses? If gain sharing is implemented on the shop floor, should it be extended to white-collar groups?

☐ Move toward reducing the fixed portion of pay and increasing the variable portion. Give business unit managers more discretion in distributing the variable pool, and make it a larger, more meaningful amount. Or allow more people to invest a portion of their salary in return for a greater share of the proceeds attributed to their own efforts later on.

☐ Manage the jealousy and conflict inherent in the more widely variable pay of nominal peers by making standards clear, giving everyone similar opportunities for growth in earnings, and reserving a portion of the earnings of stars or star sectors for distribution to others who have played a role in the success. Balance individual and group incentives in ways appropriate to the work unit and its tasks.

☐ Analyze—and, if necessary, rethink—the relationship between pay and value to the organization. Keep in mind that organizational levels defined for purposes of coordination do not necessarily reflect contributions to performance goals, and decouple pay from status or rank. And finally, be prepared to justify pay decisions in terms of clear contributions—and to offer these justifications more often, to more stakeholder groups. ⏚

Management, labor, and the golden goose

How exit barriers and high labor costs squeeze and then strangle mature businesses once the economic fairy tale ends

William E. Fruhan, Jr.

What is the source of the problems of mature industries in the United States? Some say foreign competition, which is subsidized by governments and supported by new plants and by low costs for production and capital. Others say U.S. managers' obsession with short-term earnings and lack of attention to product quality. Missing from this analysis is a realistic appraisal of the financial economics of today's competing industries.

To put it in the simplest terms, management and labor have bargained their way into an economic corner. They have set wages and fringe benefits at levels far beyond the ability of many companies to pay. Had the escalation not occurred, many mature industries would not suffer as they now do and they would have access to the capital necessary to modernize. Through case studies of the employee buyout of Weirton Steel, the upheaval in the meatpacking industry, and the competition between railways and trucking companies, the author shows where management and labor made their mistakes and suggests how to avoid these mistakes in the future.

Mr. Fruhan is professor of business administration at the Harvard Business School, where he teaches corporate finance. He has written three other HBR articles. During the past five years, his primary research has centered on the financial dilemmas facing executives of mature industries. He is the author of Revitalizing Businesses: Shareholder Work Force Conflicts *(Division of Research, Harvard Business School, 1985) and of* Financial Strategy *(Richard D. Irwin, 1979) and co-editor of* Case Problems in Finance *(Richard D. Irwin, 1981).*

Across mature industries, a "revolution," we are told, has occurred:

☐ The employees of the Weirton division of National Steel have bought the ownership of their plant in the largest employee buyout in history.

☐ Eastern Air Lines has given its employees 25% of its common stock, agreed to lucrative profit sharing when net earnings exceed $90 million, and said it will give back wage increases when productivity rebounds.

☐ United Air Lines has set up a two-tiered wage structure under which it will hire new pilots on a scale 40% lower than that of those already employed.

Recognizing that current operating costs are too high, the managers of mature and deregulated businesses have used concessionary bargaining to restructure industrywide wage agreements. Wage reductions are as common today as double-digit annual wage increases were only a few years ago. A good thing? A bad thing? A good thing too late?

After five years of study of basic industries, I believe that bargaining decisions that have resulted in a rising standard of living and economic health for employees—and that have satisfied the short-term concerns of managers—have also destroyed the economic structures of numerous mature industries. In labor contracts, managers have bargained away their competitiveness on the assumption that if every domestic company faced the same wage structure, none would suffer a competitive disadvantage. The consumer would pay for the consequences—not labor, management, or the shareholders. But the consumer has not paid.

In negotiation after negotiation, companies have not carefully considered the long-run implications of their decisions. In the fairy tale atmosphere of the 1950s and 1960s, both management and labor

Exhibit I

Pro forma financial projections for Weirton division of National Steel Corporation under various operating assumptions
1984 – 1989
in millions of dollars

		1984	1985	1986	1987	1988	1989	Six-year total	Assumption
Pro forma income statement									
1	Net sales	$1,019	$1,150	$1,250	$1,342	$1,395	$1,402	$7,558	Before modernization expenditures
2	Cost of goods sold	976	1,071	1,154	1,230	1,285	1,303	7,019	
3	Gross profit	43	79	96	112	110	99	539	
4	Other operating expenses	104	111	117	122	128	133	715	
5	Operating profits	−61	−32	−21	−10	−18	−34	−176	
6	Depreciation of existing equipment	21	21	21	21	21	21	125	
7	Other noninterest expense	6	11	6	6	7	7	43	
8	Pretax profit before financing charges	−88	−64	−48	−37	−46	−62	−344	
9	Savings from cost improvements	26	28	29	30	32	34	179	After modernization expenditures
10	Savings from capital investment expenditures	3	3	8	8	53	50	125	
11	Depreciation of new equipment	5	11	18	24	31	37	126	
12	Pretax profit before financing charges	−64	−44	−29	−23	8	−15	−166	
13	Savings from labor cost reductions	120	130	135	139	141	141	806	After 32% labor cost reduction and modernization expenditures
14	Pretax profit before financing charges	56	86	106	116	149	126	640	
Uses of funds statement									
15	Uses of funds as capital expenditures	72	84	83	83	81	81	484	After modernization expenditures
16	Uses of funds as an increase in working capital	−4	3	1	0	−1	1	0	
17	Total uses of funds	68	87	84	83	80	82	484	

thought that their companies were like golden geese that would lay golden eggs whenever needed.

The cases of the steel, meat-packing, rail, and trucking industries prove otherwise. The lessons to be learned are varied and apply to a wide range of industries. They show that management should:

1   Fully analyze the economic consequences of the "contingent obligations" they incur in bargaining with labor, including shutdown benefits, early retirement provisions, and health care obligations for retirees. At a seminar for senior financial officers, for example, I asked how many were involved in negotiating major investment decisions; essentially all said they were. When asked whether they evaluated, negotiated, or even participated in major wage and benefit contracts, almost none said they did. While such a sampling is unscientific, it indicates a problem. The one big investment decision in a mature business has been completely escaping the scrutiny of the CFO.

2   Avoid getting trapped in uneconomic businesses. Managers must guard the exit door at least as carefully as they guard current operating costs, and they must understand that diversification helps preserve the exit. While much current management philosophy (in both financial and strategic circles) stresses the idea of "doing what you know best," management will lose bargaining power with labor if it has to contemplate getting out of one business before it becomes firmly established in another.

The experience of these mature industries indicates that management has failed to adequately consider the ramifications of its actions at the bargaining table for the financial health of the business. In the end, a significant segment of mature industry has become owned, de facto, by the work force. In some cases, employees have even become the legal owners.

Steel: a hapless goose?

In the past 25 years the steel industry has experienced an unprecedented redistribution of corporate wealth. Collective bargaining has yielded impressive improvements in pension and health care benefits during the same time that the industry has come under pressure from stagnant demand and increased foreign competition.

The terms under which steelworkers can retire have become more and more generous as incremental enhancements have erected barriers to corporate exit from the industry. If a steel company wants to close a plant, it becomes obligated to pay unreserved and unfunded pension and health care costs that generally far exceed the liquidation value of the plant and related working capital. In financial terms, an uneconomic but operating steel plant has a large negative net present value for its shareholder owners.

This general industry problem achieved public recognition when National Steel turned over the assets of the Weirton division in January 1984 to its employees and made it the largest employee-owned enterprise in America. The purchase culminated 22 months of joint owner and employee effort to save the facility from liquidation; the final decision turned on management's analysis that the company could not economically operate or modernize the facility.

On a business-as-usual basis (without modernization expenditures), National estimated pretax losses for 1984-1989 would total $334 million before financing charges. Even if National were to reduce costs as aggressively as possible and increase capital spending to almost $500 million, it would still lose $166 million.

The financial forecasts shown in *Exhibit I* were clearly unattractive to National Steel executives. The financial consequences flowing from past investments in projects with inadequate returns are all too clearly reflected in *Exhibit II*. From 1972 to 1981, National achieved a return on equity of more than 10% in only one year; shareholders increased their equity investment by nearly $500 million, while the market value of that equity fell more than $300 million. The destruction of the shareholder wealth produced by capital investment in projects that had inadequate returns continued over a long period of time.

Too many golden eggs at once

The details of the Weirton buyout have been well publicized. But the most important aspect of the story—the lesson for management—has not. It is the story of compounding contingent liabilities and failing to anticipate the cost of these contingent liabilities. It is the story of how a management—always believing that it could walk away from Weirton if necessary yet systematically cutting off its option to walk away—negotiated itself into a position of negative net present value. It is the story of the expropriation of a business once the option to exit became too expensive to exercise.

What started it all was a collective bargaining process that began with the watershed year of 1959—notable because of the invocation of the Taft-Hartley Act and a subtle shift in bargaining emphasis. Management in the steel industry first began to trade away its economic options; although it realized it had

Exhibit II **National Steel Corporation common stock market value – book value ratio and corporate profitability**
1972-1981

	1972	1973	1974	1975	1976	1977	1978	1979	1980	1981
Market value / Book value	.74	.52	.52	.59	.69	.49	.42	.36	.33	.29
Return on equity	.070	.092	.147	.048	.068	.047	.084	.089	.058	.058

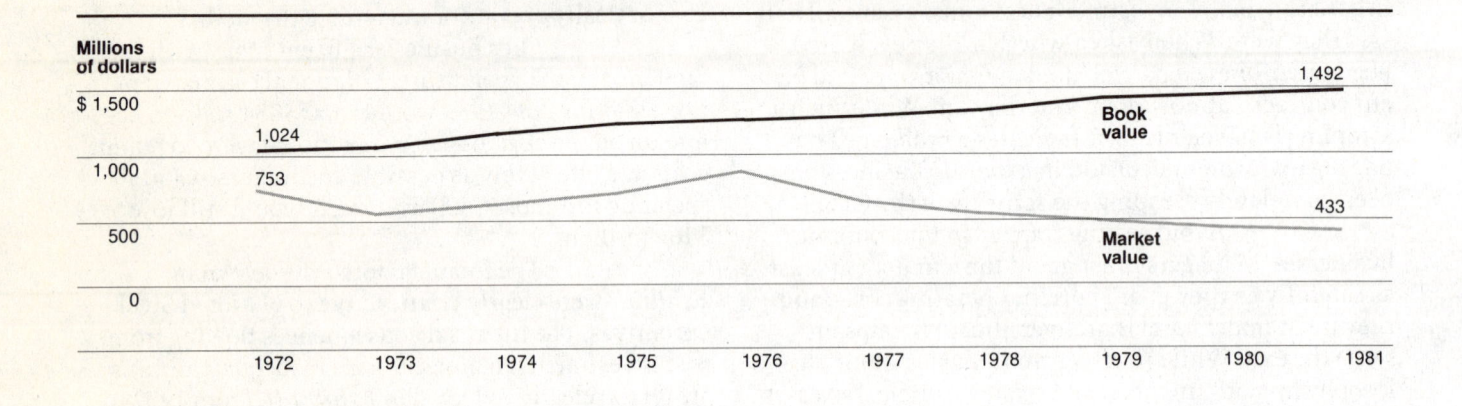

Millions of dollars — Book value: 1,024 (1973) rising to 1,492 (1981); Market value: 753 (1972) declining to 433 (1981).

short-term difficulties, it believed the long run would bring relief. Instead, the situation worsened.

In the 1959 negotiation, for example, the union rank and file were angling for improved fringe benefits, including expanded hospitalization, company-paid insurance, a lower retirement age, and more generous pensions, while their union leaders wanted higher wages. But the steel industry, fearing an onslaught of foreign steel imports and seeking more production efficiency, wanted to be free of the contractual necessity to keep on a certain number of workers in each plant. The battle cry was "management rights"; if labor would agree to allow automation and production efficiencies, management would agree to meet the unions halfway.

But management went more than halfway. The next year brought a rosier outlook for steel than 1959. A Republican administration under electoral heat persuaded steel executives that changes in union work rules to allow production efficiencies were unnecessary – that management could achieve its objectives within existing rules. Not only did management respond to these political and economic pressures by granting "normal" wage increases, but it improved employee fringe benefits as well. One new benefit (a "contingent" liability) was potentially devastating: the so-called 70/80 provision, which permits workers who begin continuous employment at age 18 to retire early on an unreduced pension if the plant closes after they reach 49 (see the early retirement provision of the 1969 agreement in *Exhibit III*). Management began to close off its options. The contingent liability was acceptable to management because it was inconceivable that it would become economically significant.

In 1966, collective bargaining produced a "30 and out" option, whereby a worker completing 30 years of service could retire early for any reason. A plant shutdown or layoff was not a precondition. But because of the pension supplement offered under the 70/80 provision, employees with 30 years of service facing a plant shutdown would probably choose to retire under this provision – not the 30 and out alternative – and the cost of a shutdown to producers would rise.

In the same way, a "rule of 65" became effective in 1978 and permitted a worker who began continuous employment in a steel plant somewhat later in life to enjoy benefits similar to, but somewhat less than, those available under the 70/80 provision.

Despite what these provisions meant should management want to close a plant, nowhere did Weirton's accounting system reflect their potential impact.

The goose gets too expensive

While workers' fringe benefits improved dramatically in the 1960s, steel wages increased but did not rise any faster than wage levels in other manufacturing industries. Steel wages remained at about the same ratio (31%) above the average of wages in other manufacturing industries. It is important to grasp the fact that as long as steel wages increased in the same magnitude as those in other manufacturing industries – and thus maintained their historic relationship – steel companies stayed in reasonably good health.

After 1973, the economics of the steel industry changed; compensation concessions then proved fatal. The reason for such corporate largesse was the seemingly rosier economic climate. Imports had stabilized at around 12% of the market (they now account for more than 25%), demand had pressured capacity, and management had sought labor peace. Unions agreed to the Experimental Negotiating Agreement; it gave management relative freedom from the threat of strikes (and the resulting pressure from the hedge-buying of imported steel) in return for general cost-of-living adjustments to labor's pay.

From 1973 through 1982, steel led all major U.S. industries in wage progress. For example, it was up 146% during the period in comparison with 133% for motor vehicles and car bodies, 130% for aircraft, 123% for tires and inner tubes, and 108% for electric and electronic equipment. All manufacturing wages together rose 108% in 1973-1982. The result: wages climbed from a level 31% above the wages in all manufacturing to one 64% higher than those paid to other manufacturing workers. (See *Exhibit IV.*)

The change in the relationship of total compensation (including fringe benefits) was even more dramatic. From 1964 to 1973, the total compensation of steelworkers was roughly 31% higher than the total compensation of workers engaged in all manufacturing (see *Exhibit V*). By 1982, total compensation of steelworkers had jumped to a 92% premium above that in all manufacturing.

When the wage ratio premium rises, either the work has become more difficult – or the employees have gotten a better deal. The consequences of the latter are telling. For example, if the ratio between the total hourly compensation of steelworkers and that of workers in all manufacturing remained stable after 1973, by 1982 steelworkers' compensation

Exhibit III	Evolution of the early retirement pension benefits in the basic steel pattern plan 1960-1982		
Year applicable	Early retirement provision	Basic pension benefit	Supplement to basic benefit if plant shuts down
1960	Applicable at age 60 with 15 years' service under an actuarially reduced pension. Following plant shutdown, two-year layoff or, with consent of company, early retirement with 15 years' service if age plus years of service equal 80 (or 75 if employee is over 55).	1% of average compensation over the last 10 years of service times years of service, offset by a portion of Social Security.	None.
1966	Applicable after 30 years.	Social Security offset reduced.	None.
1969	Following plant shutdown, early retirement possible if age plus service equal 80 (or 70 – not 75 – if employee is over 55).	Social Security offset eliminated.	Supplement of $900 a year until start of Social Security.
1972	No change.	Slightly increased.	Supplement increased to $1,260 per year.
1975	If employee retires after age 62 with 15 years' service, pension is no longer actuarially reduced.	Basic pension calculation based on highest 5 of the last 10 consecutive years.	Supplement increased to $2,760 per year, payable until Social Security starts at age 62.
1978	Following plant shutdown, layoff, or consent of company, early retirement with 20 years' service if age plus service equal 65 and company makes no offer of suitable substitute employment.	Calculation changed to 1.155% of average compensation (highest 5 of last 10 consecutive years) multiplied by years of service for up to 30 years. Multiple is 1.26% if years of service are more than 30.	Supplement increased to $3,600 until age 62. Supplement reduced by 50% of earnings after retirement for payments exceeding $4,500 a year.
1981	No change.	No change.	Supplement raised to $4,800 a year.

would have averaged $16.81 per hour, 30% below the actual figure. The change in this ratio added $60,000 in compensation cost for the average steelworker employed throughout the 1974-1982 period (see column 8 of *Exhibit V*). Theoretically, if this extra $60,000 per person had not been paid to the 8,000 members of the Weirton work force, it would almost have totaled the $484 million National needed to modernize the Weirton facility in 1984 (see line 15, *Exhibit I*). Simply stated, the modernization budget went into the pay packet of the Weirton work force.

Exhibit IV Hourly earnings trends of production workers in selected major industries

	Average hourly earnings 1973	1982*	Percent of increase 1973-1982
Selected manufacturing industries			
Blast furnaces and steel mills	$5.61	$13.80	146%
Motor vehicles and car bodies	5.70	13.30	133
Aircraft	5.09	11.72	130
Tires and inner tubes	5.23	11.68	123
Electric and electronic equipment	3.91	8.14	108
Major industrial groups			
Mining	4.75	10.78	127
Manufacturing	4.09	8.50	108
Services	3.47	6.84	97
Construction	6.41	11.47	79

*Data for the month of June 1982.

Sources:
Audrey Freedman and William E. Fulmer, "Last Rites for Pattern Bargaining," HBR March-April 1982, p. 30;
U.S. Department of Labor, *Employment and Earnings*, 1909-1978;
U.S. Department of Labor, *Employment and Earnings*, July 1983.

Of course, National's management tried but could not pass on the added costs to steel consumers in the form of higher prices. The combination of a strong U.S. dollar, foreign subsidies, stagnant worldwide demand, domestic competition from nonunion minimills, increasing production capacity in the developing world, and aggressive foreign price competition prohibited such a strategy. As I said earlier, productivity gains could not cover the gap either. Only the providers of capital remained to shoulder the cost of the compensation gains for labor.

As we have seen in *Exhibit II*, steel shareholders bore the brunt of labor's gain, so at National Steel (as well as at the other integrated U.S. steel producers) equity capital providers went on strike. National Steel's management got the message and stopped new investments at Weirton, its least efficient major facility. (In 1984, National tried to throw in the towel on the balance of its steel production business by agreeing to sell this business to U.S. Steel, but opposition by the U.S. Justice Department helped cancel the agreement. National then sold a 50% interest in what remained of its steel operations to Nippon Kokan K.K. for $292 million, and it reached – but then recently terminated – an agreement to merge with Bergen Brunswig in a stock-for-stock transaction valued at $580 million.)

Hoping for a new goose

Under normal business economics, once a company rules out new investment at a big facility like Weirton, the idea of closing the plant almost inevitably follows. But collective bargaining destroyed the normal economics in this case.

The three early retirement options described before were bargained into the fabric of the basic steel pattern agreement over an 18-year period (see *Exhibit III*). In the event of a shutdown at Weirton, for example, 4,100 of the 8,000 employees would have been entitled to retire under one of these options. Almost 3,200 workers would be entitled to a basic pension supplement under the early retirement options of *Exhibit III*. An employee joining National at age 18 in 1951 would have 31 years of service, be 49 years old in 1982, and be entitled to a pension equal to about 36% of his or her average annual wages for the past five years plus an annual supplement of $4,800, under the 70/80 provision.

Taken together, the present value of the future cost of the added pension obligation – a "contingent liability" that would be converted into an "actual liability" by a Weirton closing – was estimated at $318 million, of which almost $125 million came from pension supplements. Not included were the costs of health care benefits, life insurance protection, and termination pay. Like most companies, National Steel bore these costs and carried them as items of current expense only as they were incurred. In 1983 the cost of health care coverage was about $2,500 per family for retirees under age 65 and about $1,000 per family for retirees over age 65 whose primary insurer was Medicare. The present value of the future health care costs of early retirement could easily reach $25,000 per retiree.

The growing size of these obligations for retirees has caught the attention of the Financial Accounting Standards Board. The FASB has stated that companies should not treat such obligations on a pay-as-you-go basis but should accrue them over the periods in which employees render service. According to FASB 81 (issued in November 1984), corporate annual reports for 1984 were to include some limited disclosure of the cost of health care benefits to retirees. Recommendations for more stringent reporting requirements are expected to follow.

Exhibit V **Average wage and compensation data for workers engaged in steel production and for workers in all manufacturing industries 1964-1982**

Year	1 Average hourly earnings Steel	2 All manufacturing	3 Percent premium*	4 Average hourly total compensation Steel	5 All manufacturing	6 Percent premium*	7 Average hours steelworkers work per week	8 Steelworkers' annual compensation premium†
1982	$13.96	$8.50	64%	$23.78	$12.36	92%	33.3 hours	$13,215
1981	13.11	7.99	64	20.16	11.39	77	36.4	9,985
1980	11.84	7.27	63	18.45	10.36	78	35.7	9,105
1979	10.77	6.70	61	15.92	9.28	72	37.5	7,397
1978	9.70	6.17	57	14.30	8.46	69	37.9	6,395
1977	8.67	5.68	53	13.04	7.81	67	36.7	5,405
1976	7.86	5.22	51	11.74	7.21	63	36.4	4,388
1975	7.11	4.83	47	10.59	6.67	59	35.1	3,418
1974	6.38	4.42	44	9.08	5.96	52	37.7	1,532
1973	5.56	4.09	36	7.68	5.39	43	38.5	1,275
1972	5.15	3.82	35	7.08	5.03	41	37.3	982
1971	4.57	3.57	28	6.26	4.77	31	36.1	43
1970	4.22	3.35	26	5.68	4.50	26	36.7	−381
1969	4.09	3.19	28	5.38	4.21	28	38.6	−245
1968	3.82	3.01	27	5.03	3.94	28	37.7	−225
1967	3.62	2.82	28	4.76	3.67	30	37.0	−72
1966	3.56	2.71	31	4.63	3.50	32	38.2	113
1965	3.46	2.61	33	4.48	3.34	34	37.7	218
1964	3.41	2.53	35	4.36	3.28	33	38.3	145
Average data for 1964-1972			~31			~31		

Sources:
Report to the President on Prices and Costs in the United States Steel Industry by the Council on Wage and Price Stability, October 1977; American Iron and Steel Institute, *Annual Statistical Report, 1982*; *Economic Report of the President*, February 1984; U.S. Department of Labor, *Monthly Labor Review*, December 1983.

*The percent premium is the gap between the earnings in steel and the earnings in all manufacturing divided by the earnings in all manufacturing; it shows how much more pay the steelworker gets than the typical worker in all manufacturing.

†Column 8 is the total additional compensation earned by the average steelworker in the year indicated measured against the compensation the steelworker would have earned if steelworker compensation had continued to exceed the compensation of the average worker in "all manufacturing" by only 31% (the average 1964-1973 premium).

Owning the goose

Why is it important to worry about the present value of the future costs of employee benefits? If you analyzed the net present value of the future health care costs for early retirees if Weirton closed its doors, you would probably find that the bill exceeds $100 million. The magnitude of such exposure creates major problems when a company wants to close a plant. Obviously, the plant will no longer produce any income with which to pay these unreserved and unfunded future benefits. Who will pay? Lawsuits have grown around that question.

Colt Industries recently tried to terminate the medical benefits for 4,200 retirees of its Crucible Steel division, which had been closed and sold to Jones & Laughlin Steel Corporation. Litigation initiated by the United Steelworkers of America and public pressure from Crucible's retirees produced a one-year interim solution that requires modest monthly contributions from retirees. If a settlement is not negotiated within one year, the litigation will be reinstated. Following the Colt action, Bethlehem Steel decided nonunion retirees should shoulder a large share of their health insurance costs. Legal action commenced and Bethlehem was forced on an interim basis to restore all benefits. A court-approved settlement was reached in mid-1985 that ensures future health insurance coverage at a modest cost to nonunion retirees.

In Weirton's case, the present value of the unreserved and unfunded total cash outlays precipitated by early retirements resulting from a plant shutdown would exceed $418 million. The cost of severance pay and health care continuation payments for about 4,000 other terminated employees not qualifying for early retirement (or qualifying with only a reduced pension) would easily bring the total shutdown costs to $450 million as of December 31, 1982. Spread over a base of 8,000 employees, the cost would amount to approximately $56,000 per employee.

While collective bargaining gains were improving the lot of the work force, they were devastating the value of National Steel's investment in Weirton. *Exhibit VI* shows the impact. Because the book value of National Steel's net investment was $448 million (see line 8 of this exhibit), unless National Steel could liquidate the assets of Weirton at slightly more than book value (a hopelessly optimistic assumption), National Steel would be ahead of the game if it could give away its investment rather than liquidate the assets. Indeed, under the "most likely" liquidation value assumptions as presented—albeit in a highly simplified way—in *Exhibit VI*, National Steel should have been indifferent to the two choices: (1) paying a responsible buyer $295 million in cash to take on the net assets and ongoing business responsibilities of Weirton or (2) liquidating the facility.

Management was caught in a web of contingent liabilities of staggering proportion. Of course, collective bargaining has vastly improved the economic lot of Weirton's work force. But competition has caused that success to reduce profitability and to frighten off the providers of capital. With no profits and no access to new capital, a business obviously cannot continue. Because management has guaranteed—and escalated—exit payments (early retirement, plant shutdown supplements, and retiree health care benefits), National must pay the Weirton work force far more than the value it could obtain from selling the Weirton net assets in order to be able to get out of the business.

One reason that companies aren't forced to recognize the potential economic consequences of their collective bargaining actions is that the contingent obligations associated with these agreements don't have to be disclosed. The magnitude of the exit barrier at Weirton was not evident from any financial statement. Yet once the exit barriers described in *Exhibit III* had finally locked in place, the escalating wage trap of *Exhibit IV* and *Exhibit V* was ready to be sprung. Weirton Steel was no longer owned by

Exhibit VI	Estimate of the value to National Steel of the net assets of the Weirton division assuming a liquidation of the division's assets

in millions of dollars

		Book value	Most likely liquidation value
1	Current assets	$ 314	$ 314
2	Other assets (primarily property, plant, and equipment)	326	33
3	**Total assets**	**$ 640**	**$ 347**
4	Current liabilities	$ 101	$ 101
5	Other liabilities	91	91
6	Employee-related liabilities	–	450
7	**Total liabilities**	**$ 192**	**$ 642**
8	**Value of National Steel's investment**	**$ 448**	**– $ 295**

National Steel's shareholders but by the Weirton work force long before the formal purchase negotiations took place. The ownership was de facto. The formal purchase negotiations simply made the work force's ownership de jure.

Could National Steel's management have made Weirton a viable business as of 1982? If the compensation of the Weirton work force were reduced by 32%, Weirton's employees would still enjoy a total compensation level 31% higher than the average level of workers in all U.S. manufacturing. At this rate Weirton's workers would presumably still be receiving at least a free market rate of compensation based on historical wage relationships between steel and all manufacturing.

Line 14 of *Exhibit I* suggests how Weirton's profitability might have changed between 1984 and 1989 if the union employees had accepted the 32% decrease. These profitability levels would allow Weirton two advantages:

> Access to the capital markets to fund both the acquisition of Weirton's net assets and the capital expenditures required for modernization.

> Recovery in later years of much of the value of the 32% compensation reduction via profit sharing and/or equity participation.

While the *Exhibit I* numbers suggest that Weirton could still be a viable business beyond 1982 with substantial compensation reductions, National had no leverage available to gain these concessions. Exceptionally high exit barriers made the cost of a closedown too high to pursue. The Weirton employees would only accept the reduction in return for their acquisition of the company's net assets by way of an employee stock ownership plan, which was to start in January 1984.

A total of 6,203 out of 6,977 union employees voted in favor of the pay reduction needed to complete the acquisition transaction. For Weirton's net assets the employees paid $75 million in cash (supplied by lenders) and $119 million in bargain-interest-rate, long-term subordinated notes (supplied by the seller), which National valued at $75 million. At the same time, National agreed to absorb $204 million of employment-related costs associated with the sale — essentially giving the work force the assets for nothing. National Steel got quite a bargain nonetheless since the company might have been willing to pay the work force a far greater sum to accept the net assets.

In the first year of operations (1984) Weirton earned $60 million, a figure exceeding the forecasts.

A wolf in steer's clothing?

Am I making too much of this incident? Didn't the steel industry suffer from a foreign competitor subsidized by its government? What has happened in the steel industry is not an isolated incident. While Weirton provides one of the more extreme examples (since the work force wound up with ownership of the business essentially for nothing), similar dramas are being played out — and will be played out — across many industries. But in other mature industries, where managers have retained some bargaining options, the end point need not be the same.

The meat-packing industry, for example, had an industrywide wage agreement like that in steel, but management left an exit door open.

Just as the steelworkers bargained under a master agreement, so a similar arrangement between the United Food and Commercial Workers International Union and the principal companies governed meat-packing; it included fringes and an adjustment for increases in the cost-of-living index. For many years, wage levels for meat-packers remained at about the same percentage (between 14% and 15% above the average) of all manufacturing. The fringe benefits negotiated — particularly the termination benefits paid to workers in case of plant closings — were not as high as those in the steel industry, however. The master agreement provided for six months' advance notice, eight weeks' severance pay, and early retirement for employees over age 55 with ten years of service. Total added cost: about $15,000 per employee — substantially below the $56,000 per employee figure projected at Weirton.

Like a steer in the night

Enter IBP, formerly Iowa Beef Processors, whose management understood that the economics of the industry allowed room for a competitor to cut costs, reduce prices, and earn a higher return than the industry average. It introduced new technologies, located plants near midwestern cattle suppliers, and achieved high levels of profitability by paying lower wages than those specified in the master agreement. IBP's low cost structure and fast growth rate forced the meat-packing industry to restructure.

Meat-packing executives were caught, as were those in steel, but not to the same extent. Large conglomerates like LTV Corporation, Greyhound, and Esmark had acquired the major old-line meat-packing companies in 1967-1970. Because the meat-packing divisions were only small pieces of these larger corporations, their problems did not threaten the viability of the parent companies (as they did in steel). Parent company executives had the leeway to take more drastic measures than those available to the National Steel managers.

The resulting transactions were complex. Because it could find no buyer for Swift, Esmark, for example, transferred all Swift assets not related to the fresh meat business to other parts of Esmark. Then it sold its Swift stock to a new company, Swift Independent Corporation (SIPCO), in a two-step transaction for cash and securities. The bulk of SIPCO's stock was sold to the public through an initial offering; Esmark retained 35% of the common stock, and 10% was reserved for employee ownership.

But before the public would buy SIPCO, Esmark had to make provisions for unreserved and unfunded liabilities. First, it contributed $16.7 million to fully fund the pension plan for the active employees and paid an additional $6.2 million to a newly established trust to fund *in advance* the cost of health care insurance for SIPCO's active employees once they reached retirement. (In the past Esmark, like other employers, had met retiree health care obligations on a pay-as-you-go basis.) Second, Esmark paid $25.8 million in employee termination pay and related obligations in order to close three plants ultimately con-

62 Compensation

Exhibit VII **Ratio of hourly wages in steel, railroads, trucking, and meat-packing in relation to wages in all manufacturing industries 1967-1984**

	Steel	Railroads	Trucking	Meat-packing
1984*	1.47	1.45	1.15	.89
1983	1.52	1.45	1.20	.97
1982	1.64	1.36	1.24	1.06
1981	1.64	1.33	1.27	1.12
1980	1.63	1.36	1.28	1.17
1979	1.61	1.33	1.27	1.15
1978	1.57	1.28	1.28	1.15
1977	1.53	1.30	1.27	1.16
1976	1.51	1.32	1.26	1.16
1975	1.47	1.25	1.27	1.17
1974	1.44	1.29	1.30	1.18
1973	1.36	1.32	1.32	1.16
1972	1.35	1.28	1.30	1.17
1971	1.28	1.22	1.27	1.18
1970	1.26	1.16	1.18	1.19
1969	1.28	1.15	1.16	1.15
1968	1.27	1.14	1.16	1.15
1967	1.28	1.15	1.17	1.15

Sources:
U.S. Department of Labor, Bureau of Labor Statistics, *Employment and Earnings,* 1909-1978;
U.S. Department of Labor, Bureau of Labor Statistics, *Employment and Earnings,* July-November 1983, March 1984, and November 1984.

*The figures for 1984 are estimates.

veyed to SIPCO so that they could reopen with more competitive labor costs. Third, Esmark assumed the pension and health care costs of employees who retired as a result of the closing of facilities conveyed to SIPCO.

Esmark's management substantially reduced the cost structure and created a more efficient operation. Before the restructuring, Esmark had to operate its meat-packing plants at an employment cost disadvantage of about $4 per hour in comparison with the competition not operating under the master agreement.

This amounted to a cost disadvantage of nearly $8,000 per employee per year ($4.00 per hour x 2,000 hours per year). By paying termination expenses of $15,000 per employee, Esmark could save $8,000 per employee per year. This was an investment opportunity with an extremely high return, and it would put the newly revamped SIPCO in a good competitive position.

Jumping the fence

Other meat-packing executives were not as fortunate as those of Esmark. LTV, Wilson Foods' parent, did not have the financial resources to fund the termination of Wilson's work force in order to achieve lowered wage levels. Wilson was thus forced into a corner. LTV spun off Wilson Foods as an independent company in July 1981. The new company did well at first because the United Food and Commercial Workers International Union agreed to a 44-month wage freeze and suspended cost-of-living adjustments. When the same union signed agreements with other companies permitting even greater wage reductions and other concessions, Wilson could not compete and saw its profits turn to losses.

The culprit? IBP, which had entered the pork business and forced more than 100 pork-processing plants in the Midwest to close between 1980 and 1983. Many of these plants reopened with lower wages and benefits and left Wilson paying a wage package almost 40% higher than theirs. By early 1983, the margins between the price received for fresh pork and the cost to buy and butcher hogs fell to a historic low for the whole industry. Wilson vainly tried to renegotiate the wage contract, ran up against its loan covenants, and faced insolvency.

What could Wilson's management, running out of time and money, do? Wilson could wait until the current labor agreement ran out to renegotiate the rate (at a pretax cost disadvantage of $145 million, if it could survive for 29 months). It could close the plants and terminate the work force (at a cost of $100 million, or 6,500 union workers at $15,000 in termination costs). Or it could file for bankruptcy, pay no termination expenses, and achieve cost advantages almost at once (until the work force struck back).

In April 1983, Wilson filed a voluntary bankruptcy petition and applied to have its collective bargaining agreements rejected. Wilson's reopened plants paid $9.90 an hour in wages and benefits, 37% below the 1983 rate of $15.66, and saved an estimated $5 million a month.

In the end, however, Wilson agreed to increase its total wage and benefits package to $11 an hour because of wildcat strikes. Wilson's bankruptcy cost the company about $20 million in the form of a strike and business disruptions and yet allowed it to realize savings of approximately $40 million to $50 million a year.

IBP achieved the same objective as many foreign competitors in other industries but without the advantages usually attributed to foreign competitors. No government funded its research effort or provided subsidies to allow it to undercut U.S. prices.

IBP's management understood the economics of its industry, looked at the costs of doing business, and restructured them. From 1980 through 1984, wage levels in meat-packing fell from 1.17 times that of all manufacturing to about .89 times – a fall of 24% that probably placed wage levels at close to free market rates (see *Exhibit VII*).

How did the restructuring of the meat-packing industry differ from the restructuring of the steel industry as represented by Weirton?

First, the return on an investment in termination expenses in steel is far lower than it is in meat-packing. A $15,000 investment saves $8,000 per employee in meat-packing. A $56,000 investment would save only about $14,000 in lower annual costs per employee at Weirton.

Second, the absolute size of the exit barrier is enormously higher in steel. Closing a plant such as Weirton with 8,000 employees would cost almost $500 million. Closing a large meat-packing plant with 2,000 employees would cost only $30 million.

Finally, steel manufacturers are less well diversified than the companies owning large meat-packing subsidiaries. The closure of all or a significant portion of the entire business was less credible as a negotiating threat in steel than it was in meat-packing. The tax benefits associated with losses incurred in closure would also take longer to realize in a less diversified company.

In short, the owners of meat-packing companies were in a better position to retain some value from their investments than were the owners of steel plants. Once wage levels had become a competitive disadvantage, the size of the exit barrier in the form of negotiated contractual termination obligations to the work force made the difference.

Hardly a fairy tale

In the competitive struggle between railroads and the deregulated trucking industry, the railroads are fighting a battle similar to the steel companies'. Since 1970, when the federal government stepped in to save Conrail, railroad wage levels have grown from around 1.16 times the average paid in manufacturing to 1.45 times. In contrast, the fragmented trucking industry's average wages have risen and then settled back near the 1970 ratios (see *Exhibit VII*). Truckers have used this labor cost advantage to take market share gradually away from the railroads. While railroads will always haul heavy low-value commodities, their high labor rates are giving the truckers an ever-increasing share of shipments.

Rail management and labor face the clear choices already made in steel and meat-packing. They can reach agreement on shrinking the pay gap between trucking and railroads (see *Exhibit VII*); or if this cannot be accomplished, they can continue to invest in productivity improvements but see the benefits of these improvements go to expanding the pay gap for a rapidly shrinking work force. Or they can make a strategic decision to withdraw from the core business, as National Intergroup (formerly National Steel) did, and direct future capital investment into other businesses.

Two messages for managing mature businesses clearly emerge from the examples of steel, meat-packing, trucking, and railroads.

Guard the exit

First, make certain you have a way to get out of the business. Once you've lost the exit, you will lose the business to escalating wage costs. Your potential cost exposure in a shutdown should be monitored as carefully as your overall operating cost structure. During bargaining negotiation, always project the effects of all non-wage-contingent obligations on your exit cost. You may never have to pay them, but your successor will if you fail to take them into account.

Diversify

Second, consider new business activities. Diversification provides two critical benefits. If you do have to shut down a plant or a whole line of business, any tax benefits resulting from the write-off will be less valuable if you have no significant source of taxable income to offset. And what is equally significant, the existence of a diversified source of profit may strengthen your bargaining position in wage negotiations. For a diversified company, the closure of a plant or a business can be a credible threat even if such an action on a stand-alone basis might not be economically rational. U.S. Steel's acquisition of Marathon gave that company added strength along these two dimensions.

Managements that are vulnerable and that cannot do both of the foregoing should be ready to hand over the keys to a well-informed and ably represented work force. Owners of such businesses should count their blessings if they don't have to pay to get out the door once they've handed over the keys.

GETTING THINGS DONE

Teamwork for Today's Selling

In many companies, the Willy Loman model has given way to coordination across product lines.

by Frank V. Cespedes, Stephen X. Doyle, and Robert J. Freedman

☐ Listen to this account manager, responsible for building sales and a close relationship with a key customer, describe a recent conversation with a colleague: "I called our district manager in Phoenix and explained that I was preparing an important proposal for this big account, and would he please help with the part of it having to do with an account location in his territory. He reluctantly agreed, but I haven't seen anything yet, and he hasn't returned my last two phone calls. With friends like that—"

This is how the district sales manager sees it: "I've got monthly numbers to meet with limited time and resources. And I don't get paid or recognized for helping someone else sell. So I don't."

☐ Now let's hear from the vice president of national accounts at a major telecommunications company: "We do about $3 million a year with Zembla [a large, diversified corporation] but that's peanuts compared with the potential. A big part of Zembla's strategy is their telecommunications network, which they've sunk millions into over the past decade. Last week their information systems czar called me to complain about our salespeople in two regions. They were trying to sell a discount service to a couple of Zembla divisions, and they were succeeding. He said that this subverted his company's telecom strategy, which requires high utilization of Zembla's network to make it operate efficiently. Attempts to sell some of his people off that network were causing a lot of friction in his organization. And in ours too, I might add."

☐ Then there's the sales representative of a company where the proverbial 80% of revenue comes from 20% of the customers. She sells equipment to some of those large accounts, while other salespeople in another sales force handle related supply items to the same accounts (among others). She says: "Many customers want to coordinate their purchases of equipment and supplies because of the impact they have on their production processes. But equipment sales are usually higher priced transactions than supply sales, occur much less often, and involve contact with more people from more functions in the customer's organization. So you have more sales calls and a longer selling cycle, as well as different delivery and service requirements after the sale is made. I meet a lot with my supply brethren because, while we share all of our accounts, what's often not shared or clear are our individual goals."

☐ A sales manager comments on his company's recent annual sales meeting: "Great resort, wonderful food, and the weather was terrific. Our senior VP of sales and marketing made his annual speech on teamwork. But that's not enough. Until teamwork becomes a daily part of operations, the occasional pitch for it is only lip service."

> "Until teamwork becomes a daily part of operations, the occasional pitch for it is only lip service."

For many companies in the past two decades, selling has changed dramatically. Traditionally it was the vocation of a single energetic, persistent individual—"a man way out there in the blue, riding on a smile and a shoeshine," in Arthur Miller's memorable words. Now selling is often the province of a team composed of men and women who must coordinate their efforts across product lines (the products often made by different divisions and sold from different locations) to customers that require an integrated approach. Even when there is no formal sales team,

---

Frank V. Cespedes is an assistant professor at the Harvard Business School, where he teaches marketing. Stephen X. Doyle is president of SXD Associates, a sales management consulting firm. Robert J. Freedman is a vice president at TPF&C, where he specializes in sales and executive compensation.

moreover, it's often necessary to coordinate—as the vignettes at the start of this article show.

Mergers, acquisitions, and other changes in the business environment are forcing vendors in many industries to put greater emphasis on large customers with equally large and complex purchasing requirements. Conventional supermarkets, for example, accounted for about 75% of U.S. retail food sales in 1980. They will take in an estimated 25%

> **Vendors increasingly have big customers with big, complex purchasing requirements.**

in 1990; "super stores," "combination stores," and "warehouse stores" will account for most remaining sales. These chains possess the buying power (backed by sophisticated information systems) they need to insist on better service, lower prices, and a coordinated approach from their vendors, many of whom sell them multiple products through different sales forces.

Similar trends are evident in many industrial goods categories, where just-in-time inventory systems make customers aware of any discrepancies in prices, terms and conditions, delivery, or timely attention by vendors' salespeople in many buying locations. Internationally, the emergence of more multinational, even global customers places similar demands on many sales organizations—with distance, currency variations, and cultural differences in the vendor's sales force adding complications to the administration of these important shared accounts.

In these situations, selling depends on the vendor's ability to marshal its resources effectively across a range of buying locations, buying influences, product lines, and internal organizational boundaries. Coordination in these shared-account situations affects the company's expense-to-revenue ratio, ability to retain current business or develop new business at these accounts, and sales force morale and management. Yet, as the comments by salespeople indicate, coordination is not easy.

At four sellers of industrial goods we studied, only 11% of the salespeople involved in shared accounts were located in the same building, while 43% were in different sales districts and 7% in different countries. Of course, this dispersion erects time, expense, and scheduling barriers to coordination, and the problem is likely to get worse as many customers become more multinational in scope. Further, although development work on major accounts often takes years, one-quarter of the salespeople had been in their account positions less than five years. "It takes time to develop good working relationships on an account team," one sales manager explained, but account continuity is a recurring issue at these and many other companies.

In interviews, salespeople repeatedly cited more communication as the one thing that could most improve teamwork on shared accounts. In view of the distances and compensation involved, however, improving communication—especially the preferred mode, meetings—would raise these companies' marketing expense-to-revenue ratios to unacceptable levels. There is no doubt that a coordinated sales approach can be expensive. So, like any other expensive business resource, it should be employed where it will yield the highest returns.

Because the need for sales coordination depends on the complexity of the account, moreover, both large and small vendors face these issues. Large companies may enjoy scale advantages over the smaller competition, but they often have more products to sell and more layers in their sales and marketing hierarchies, making coordination among their salespeople difficult.

Smaller companies may have less bureaucracy than the big competition, but with fewer products and fewer resources they often base their marketing strategies on superior responsiveness to customers via customized marketing programs. Hence, this important source of competitive advantage for the smaller vendor raises the threshold of coordination required. Actually, our research showed that despite significant size differences among the various companies that we studied, the number of salespeople who must work together in shared accounts remained about the same at each company.

Our data and experience indicate three areas that are most important in sales coordination: compensation systems, the goal-setting process, and staffing and training issues that arise when shared accounts are an integral part of sales strategy.

Compensation systems

In sales management, you won't get what you don't pay for. One salesperson put it this way: "Teamwork reflects many elements. However, compensation is a foundation. An individual's belief that he or she is paid fairly spurs belief in the team concept."

Many companies have three types of teamwork situations:

1. Joint efforts on behalf of certain national or international accounts, in which all team members work exclusively with these accounts.

2. Headquarters national account managers (NAMs) or account executives coordinate with field sales reps; the NAM is dedicated to one or two accounts, but these accounts are among dozens or even hundreds that field sales representatives call on.

3. District sales managers' efforts affect important accounts that cut across sales district lines, but performance evaluations are based on intradistrict results.

To encourage the kind of teamwork required, a different compensation system may be appropriate for each type of sales rep and account situation. Flexibility is the key, and this often means complexity. Yet in big-account situations, many companies design compensation plans according to "keep it simple, stupid" criteria, however complex the sales tasks are. Top management then ignores important differences tied to account assignments and often re-

About Our Research

In gathering material for this article, we concentrated on four companies with sizable sales forces selling industrial goods. We administered a comprehensive questionnaire, which 835 people completed. About two-thirds were sales representatives and one-third, sales managers. About half of the group had worked in sales for more than a decade.

The perspectives in this article also reflect many conversations with sales managers, marketing managers, field sales representatives, and senior executives at these and other companies.

wards selling activity that neglects coordination at the customer.

If there are many salespeople calling on key accounts and teamwork is important, then a bonus based on total account sales often makes more sense than traditional, individually oriented incentive arrangements. Interep is the nation's largest radio "rep" firm; its salespeople in major U.S. cities call on ad agencies and advertisers to sell time on the more than 3,000 radio stations it represents. To avoid bureaucracy and maintain an entrepreneurial spirit, Interep's chairman, Ralph Guild, has spread the company's sales efforts among six different sales forces.

Mergers among big advertisers and ad agencies, however, have made customers increasingly receptive to a rep firm that can act as a coordinated supplier across various radio markets for different product categories. In response, Interep uses a team approach to selling that cuts across each sales force. A prime element is the compensation system. Unlike the plans at most other rep firms, where incentives are staunchly "Lone Ranger" in design, Interep has salespeople with shared-account responsibilities participate in a bonus pool based on the particular account's sales volume. The approach has been effective: Interep's sales are growing faster than the industry's, and according to market surveys, ad agencies generally view Interep as more responsive than competitors.

Another important compensation issue is the time frame employed. Sales efforts at big accounts often take months, sometimes years, to pan out. But compensation plans usually tie incentives to quarterly or annual snapshots of performance. The usual result, as one salesperson acknowledged, is this: "Because our compensation plan is short-term oriented, I put my efforts where there are short-term benefits. Also, many short-term sales goals can be met with a minimum of teamwork; the longer term results require the hassle of working with lots of other people." Bonuses for multiple-year performance, or for qualitative objectives like building relationships with certain account decision makers, can encourage team effort.

Sharing of sales credit is a nettlesome issue. Surveys of major account sales programs show that only a minority use credit splitting to help coordinate NAMs and field sales reps.[1] In shared accounts, split credits are often better than mutually exclusive credit decisions.

But not always. One sales rep noted how a common attitude toward split credits can fuel resentment and block teamwork: "Most salespeople feel that when the split is 50/50, they're losing 50% instead of gaining 50% of the incentive pay. A lot of time and energy is wasted arguing over splits."

Actually, a company can give full credit to those involved and still not (as many managers fear) pay twice for the same sale. The key is having a good understanding of the sales tasks involved and an information system capable of tracking performance so that shared sales volume can be taken into account when setting objectives. Consider an example: two salespeople last year sold about $500,000 each to individual accounts and about $500,000 to shared accounts. Their combined sales amounted to about $1.5 million. Two approaches to goal setting and credits are possible:

☐ The employer sets targets and bonuses so that each person receives $25,000 for $750,000 in sales, with credit from shared account sales split 50/50. If each sells $500,000 in individual sales and $500,000 to shared accounts, each makes the $750,000 target and gets a bonus.

☐ The employer pays a $25,000 bonus for $1 million of sales with all shared-account volume double counted and fully credited to both people. Each salesperson must then rely on team effort for about 50% of target sales, but each also receives full credit for team sales.

A participant in the first plan may reason that an incremental $250,000 in individual sales (perhaps developed at the expense of time devoted to the more complicated joint sales effort) could reach the $750,000 target. Consequently, he or she might decide to concentrate on individually assigned accounts, encourage the colleague to continue to work hard on the team accounts, and hope to gather those half-credit sales with little or no effort. Coordination and major account penetration are likely to suffer. Under the second plan, there is at least no compensation barrier to expenditure of effort on the more labor-intensive team sales.

Compensation alone won't harness teamwork if other control systems are out of kilter. But ill-defined compensation plans can thwart teamwork even when other control systems support coordination.

Setting and meeting goals

Compensation means money. A less expensive way to foster teamwork is by clarifying goals – defining individual salespeople's main responsibilities and desired accomplishments (like opening new accounts, maximizing sales from existing accounts, and launching new products). When goals are unclear, selling can be frustrating because salespeople cannot know where they stand in relation to some standard. Good performance may appear then to be a random occurrence, independent of effort. This confusion can

---
1. Gary Tubridy, "How to Pay National Account Managers," *Sales & Marketing Management*, January 13, 1986, p.52.

discourage effort, especially in those tasks that require working with other people.

Disseminating information about company strategy helps to clarify sales goals and the effort top management wants. Yet few companies regularly pass on information to the sales force about the company's objectives in its various market segments. Many so-called "strategic plans" do not make meaningful reference to the sales force's role in implementing strategy. Instead, the

> **A close fit of sales goals with strategic goals, clearly understood, is essential.**

goals coming out of senior executive negotiations are usually kept secret because of fear that wide dissemination would unwittingly include competitors.

A strategy that does not imply certain behavior by the sales force, however, is often no strategy; it's merely an interesting idea. In the context of sales teamwork, moreover, competitive cost data are usually not what salespeople want; they need information about the company's goals in the marketplace, the nature of its potential competitive advantage, and their role in achieving those goals. Withholding this information is counterproductive. If salespeople are not selling in accordance with corporate goals, withholding information about strategy will not help; and if salespeople *are* selling in accordance with corporate goals, competitors will learn about them anyway.

One company we studied makes automatic testing equipment that is often bought to function as part of a total quality-control system at customer locations. Hence extensive customization for customers' production processes and information networks is necessary. These products are technologically dynamic and complex, demanding comprehensive product knowledge on sales-people's part. So the sales force is divided into product-oriented units.

The company holds semiannual sales meetings where the importance of integrated selling strategies is high on the agenda and where, in small groups, salespeople and senior executives talk about joint sales work and cross-selling activities on specific accounts. Top management considers these sessions as both an important input and output of strategic planning in a business where product development costs and an increasingly multinational customer base make account selection and incremental sales to major customers a key aspect of strategy.

In situations like this, where goal clarity and information about those goals are intertwined, managers might use the following checklist of questions to perform a quick audit of sales teamwork:

1. Do the goals spelled out to salespeople fit the company's strategic objectives? The compensation plan? One U.S. company, responding to the increasing globalization of its markets, began joint ventures with Japanese and German companies, realigned its product line and manufacturing operations at great cost, and established an ambitious "global account management" program. Quotas for the U.S. sales force, however, continued to focus on domestic accounts, and commissions were tied to domestic deliveries. Sales goals and corporate objectives were out of sync. Sometimes U.S. sales reps even tried to talk customers with foreign operations out of buying a product from one of the company's overseas operations! The frequent result: no sale at all.

2. Does the sales force understand the goals? Attention must be paid to "recommunicating" goals regularly — not least because the makeup of the sales force is always changing.

At IBM, account planning sessions spanning three to five days and often involving as many as 50 people have long been standard features of big-account management. The sales force discusses each account's business conditions and decision-making processes, and the staff concerned reviews all account applications, installations, and maintenance issues. The chief objective is an updated account plan for sales personnel.

Another goal is to acquaint people with the status of the account, including people in support roles. The impact on their morale and on the coordination of their efforts is an often overlooked, but crucial, aspect of sales teamwork. At one large medical equipment supplier, fast delivery is an important aspect of service to major hospital accounts. So account meetings include the truck drivers who regularly deliver to these accounts. "Knowing the warehouse," they can often make the difference in expediting a key customer's order.

3. Are the goals measurable? Do the sales managers reinforce them? In most busy organizations, "that which is not measured does not happen," as one sales manager sardonically noted. Some companies respond to the more protracted and more complicated nature of shared-account sales by relaxing or ignoring measures. In such cases, the field salespeople often feel "We do the work, while the major account managers play golf and get the glory." It is precisely *because* shared-account sales demand sustained attention that measures are important. Without them, the pull in most sales organizations is toward the shorter term, individually assigned accounts.

Sales volume is only one measure of shared-account performance. Profitability, cross-selling, or new product introductions are often more appropriate measures, depending on the vendor's strategy.

Qualitative as well as quantitative measures may figure in evaluation of performance. At many investment banks, for example, a common source of data for evaluating individual performance at bonus time is input from colleagues via cross-evaluation surveys of collaborators on various deals. Account executives and product specialists may evaluate each other on certain criteria, including the other's contribution in marketing and service efforts for clients. These surveys keep account people sensitive to the coordi-

"Hold it, Al...if we're going to talk marketing, I'm going to switch to my marketing hat."

nation requirements of their jobs and keep managers aware of potential problems.[2]

Staffing and training

"I've worked alone 14 years in this territory," one field sales rep said, "and I prefer an 'I'll call you, don't call me' relationship with team players." A revamped compensation plan and an effective goal-setting procedure may change her attitude, but the odds are against it.

Teamwork in sales, as in sports and many other endeavors, is the sum of individual efforts working cooperatively toward a common goal. And just as most ballplayers play better in some conditions than they do in others, some hitting right-handed pitchers better and some left-handers, so do different salespeople perform better in some circumstances than in others. This has implications for account staffing. The sales rep we quoted should not be required or even asked to work in team-selling situations. The "don't call me, I'll call you" attitude won't help and may hurt in these circumstances. As long as her performance is acceptable, she should continue where she is.

A team process for recruiting is helpful for spotting such loners. At many companies, including Digital Equipment, interviews with team members are a crucial part of the hiring procedure. A team process is also useful for acquainting a prospect with account characteristics and corporate goals.

A perennial question for many companies that have key-account sales programs is whether to fill vacancies internally or hire externally. Most of the companies we looked at preferred to promote from within on the ground that understanding of the organization is more important and useful than general sales experience or even industry familiarity picked up at another vendor. Why? One reason is that shared-account programs place salespeople in positions where they have little authority over others who affect their performance on accounts. In such a situation, things get done through persuasion (helped by an informal reckoning of personal debits and credits), a knowledge of how the organization sets budgets and allocates resources, and a network of relationships cultivated over time. Outsiders, however knowledgeable and competent, are at a disadvantage in these areas.

At one company, a vendor of medical supplies, the account executive is called the "quarterback" of the company's resources for an account, and managers use the metaphor of a lens to describe the account manager's job: to bring into focus for a key account the company's resources in areas ranging from R&D and product development to distribution and customer service. Effective performance in this role calls for account executives who know internal systems as well as they know their ac-

---

2. Robert G. Eccles and Dwight B. Crane, *Doing Deals: Investment Banks at Work* (Boston: Harvard Business School Press, 1988).

counts' buying processes and purchase criteria.

As sales tasks change, sales training should change too. In shared-account situations, product knowledge and generic selling skills (e.g., presentation expertise and time management) remain important, but the coordination requirements make other skills necessary as well. In major-account programs, salespeople usually work across product lines, often across sales forces and, increasingly, across country sales organizations that reflect different national cultures. Furthermore, line authority in these situations is often ephemeral, since coordinators, like NAMs and account executives, often have dotted-line relationships with other sales personnel. Team building is a crucial part of sales competence in these situations.

Yet, as one sales rep (echoing many others) noted to us, "All sales training I've ever seen in my company stresses development of individual skills, not teamwork. As a result, delegating responsibility and working with and through others are seen as weaknesses, not strengths, in our sales force."

Attention to team training is particularly important in companies with multiple sales forces, especially when they speak different technical or trade languages. Exposure to the other sales force's product line in training sessions can help. Mixed sales meetings encourage idea sharing across district or product lines and, equally important, build acquaintances among individuals who can later call on one another during an account crisis or opportunity.

A barrier to such training efforts is often not the money involved but the source of the money. Sales training is a significant expenditure at most companies–and, because the numbers usually do not reflect the cost of salespeople's time out of the field, a usually underestimated expenditure. But training budgets are often set according to district results or the performance of a particular sales group. The local managers who set the budgets naturally focus training on specific sales opportunities; they have little incentive to devote training to team efforts. A task for executives at many companies is to determine whether the method they use to apportion expenditures on sales training supports a goal of better sales coordination.

Situational teamwork

How a company thinks about improving sales coordination depends to a large extent on its products and the way it sells. Look at two organizations we studied, Company X, a supplier of automatic testing equipment, and Company Y, which sells business equipment and supplies.

While both handle large accounts where teamwork is essential, X sells technically complex and high unit-priced products, and Y sells technically simple products with lower unit prices. X has a small sales force and Y a large one. X's salespeople (mostly engineers) deal with long selling cycles and complex customer decision-making processes, while Y's salespeople (most without technical backgrounds) encounter shorter selling cycles and a more easily identifiable set of decision makers at their accounts. X's salespeople tend to place less emphasis on money (compensation systems, sales contests) and measurements (formal performance evaluation criteria) as control and coordination mechanisms than on "people issues" (relationships within the sales group and sales supervisors' skills). Y's salespeople tend to stress money and measurements as the key factors affecting teamwork.

These differences seem tied to the tasks facing salespeople at these companies and coincide with others' observations about the way task complexity affects the nature of the selling effort required.[3] The more complex the selling task, the more information must be exchanged between vendor and customer and the more information passed around among the vendor's salespeople working on a common account. Especially in technical sales situations, moreover, this information must be coordinated among people trained in certain core disciplines as well as in sales techniques. At the other extreme is the salesperson with the simple product whose mandate is a simple "go out and sell." Less information has to be transmitted between buyer and seller and among salespeople.

One inference to be drawn is that in complex sales tasks the initial selection of salespeople is more important. The technical skills required are expensive to obtain and keep honed through training; and the coordination skills necessary are more dependent on individual relationships. Where the sales task is less complex, however, requiring less information to be understood and communicated, "systems solutions" to coordination (mechanisms like compensation and measurement systems) are potentially more appropriate and respected by the sales force.

Organizations are often diligent in setting budgets, creating organization charts, and establishing other types of formal control systems. But they are often less attentive to the

> While most top managers support teamwork, their organizations don't focus on team effectiveness.

crucial but "softer" aspects of sales management. Sales managers in the companies we studied overwhelmingly stressed formal control systems (like compensation and quota-setting mechanisms) in their coordination efforts, while salespeople favored processes (like relationships with other salespeople and long-established company norms that aid or inhibit coordination). Sales managers are no doubt more com-

---

Authors' note: We thank Professor Benson P. Shapiro of the Harvard Business School for his helpful comments on an early draft of this article.

3. Benson P. Shapiro, "Manage the Customer, Not Just the Sales Force," HBR September-October 1974, p. 127; and Barton A. Weitz, "Effectiveness in Sales Interactions: A Contingency Framework," Journal of Marketing, Winter 1981, p. 85.

fortable with formal systems; they are easier to install and measure than initiatives aimed at nurturing process in the sales environment—and so easier to justify at budget-setting sessions. But in many situations, managers may be trying to address what salespeople perceive as interpersonal issues in teamwork with administrative "solutions."

While most top managers support teamwork, very few organizations actually focus on team effectiveness, and few managers get the process going on their own without the organization's support. As one sales executive commented, "Sales teamwork is ultimately a by-product of the organization and has to come from the top down. People in the trenches can be team players, but they need encouragement and incentives. Preaching teamwork won't work as long as senior managers' attitude toward the sales force remains at the carrot-and-stick level."

In seeking to make a sales organization more effective, however, it's important for management to keep aware of a key distinction: coordination doesn't necessarily mean consensus. That is, a team shouldn't approximate the dictionary definition of "two or more beasts of burden harnessed together." Years ago in *The Organization Man*, William Whyte skewered a certain pseudo teamwork that has a numbing and leveling effect on individual performance, creativity, and expression—qualities that are always vital in effective sales and marketing. But Whyte also missed the point: there are so many tasks in business that can only be carried on through groups. A sales manager with 20 years of experience put it this way: "You cannot legislate teamwork. It's an attitude that comes over the long term, and it's essential in a well-run sales organization. Despite this, there still needs to be plenty of room for individual success and achievement. Otherwise, teamwork becomes an amorphous concept that can lead a group to underachieve in harmony." Our suggestions can mean increased rewards for both the company and the individual salesperson.

Reprint 89205

How to pay your sales force

Choice of a plan is crucial for increasing motivation and sales

John P. Steinbrink

Using the results of a survey of 380 companies in 34 industries, this author examines three basic types of compensation plans: salary, commission, and combination (salary plus commission). Most companies in the study favored a combination plan, but such plans have some disadvantages to offset their obvious attractiveness. The author sets out the possible reasons for choosing each type of plan according to the needs of the company.

Mr. Steinbrink is editorial director of the Dartnell Corporation and is author of Dartnell's 18th and 19th Biennial Survey of Compensation of Salesmen. He is a member of the board of advisors and contributors, *Journal of Accounting, Auditing and Finance.* He was formerly director of Sales and Marketing Executives International, Chicago.

Any discussion with sales executives would bring forth a consensus that compensation is the most important element in a program for the management and motivation of a field sales force. It can also be the most complex.

Consider the job of salespeople in the field. They face direct and aggressive competition daily. Rejection by customers and prospects is a constant negative force. Success in selling demands a high degree of self-discipline, persistence, and enthusiasm. As a result, salespeople need extraordinary encouragement, incentive, and motivation in order to function effectively.

The average age of today's industrial salesman is 36 years, and about 60% have some college training or are college graduates. Today's salesman wants a challenging job with good prospects as well as payoffs now.

A properly designed and implemented compensation plan must be geared both to the needs of the company and to the products or services the company sells. At the same time, it must attract good salesmen in the first place and then keep them producing at increasing rates.

In this article, I will focus on the basic types of compensation plans, current levels of pay, and the compensation-related areas of expense practices, additional incentives, and fringe benefits. The main source of data used throughout is Dartnell's 19th Biennial Survey of Salesmen.[1] The data are based on studies of 380 companies in 34 Standard Industrial Classifications throughout the United States and Canada which employ a total of more than 15,000 salespeople.

---

1. *Compensation of Salesmen: Dartnell's 19th Biennial Survey* (Chicago: Dartnell Institute of Financial Research, Dartnell Corporation, 1978).

74 Compensation

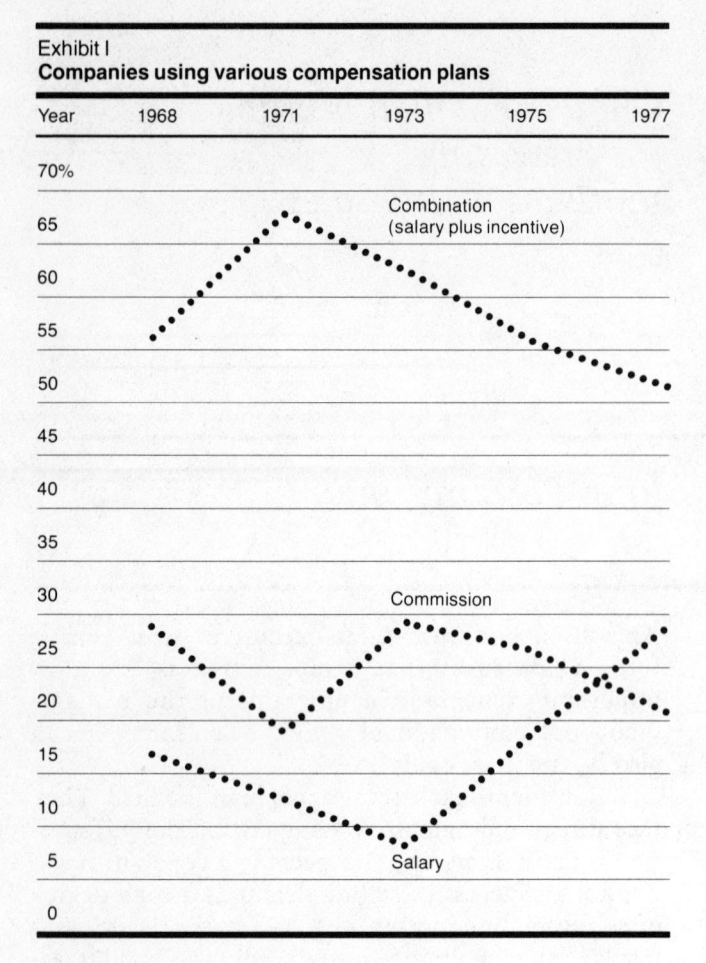

Exhibit I
Companies using various compensation plans

Year   1968   1971   1973   1975   1977

[Line graph showing three plans from 1968 to 1977: Combination (salary plus incentive) trending from ~55% in 1968, peaking around 65% in 1971, declining to ~50% by 1977; Commission line fluctuating between ~15% and ~28%; Salary line between ~5% and ~18%.]

Basic kinds of plans

Three basic compensation plans are available to sales management: salary, commission, and combination (salary plus incentive) plans.

Exhibit I shows the use of the three basic plans in recent years. While the combination plan continues to be most favored, the commission plan has been declining in recent years. For example, 1971, a recession year, was a poor commission year, while the boom year of 1973 produced commission earnings that, in many cases, were totally out of proportion to the sales effort put forth. *Exhibit II* shows selective use of the three basic plans in 34 SIC industries.

Salary plan

This kind of plan, in which salesmen are paid fixed rates of compensation, may also include occasional additional compensation in the form of discretionary bonuses, sales contest prizes, or other short-term incentives. The plan works well when the main objective is missionary work or requires a lot of time for prospecting, or if the salesman's primary function is "account servicing." Secondary objectives of increasing sales from existing accounts and opening new accounts require special incentive treatment.

The salary plan is appropriate where it is difficult to evaluate who really makes the sale, where a salesman's contribution cannot be accurately separated from the efforts of others in the company such as inside personnel and technical service persons. Sales of technical products commonly involve this form of team selling. When management finds it difficult to develop adequate measures of performance against which an equitable bonus or commission can be paid, a salary plan is desirable.

The position description for a field engineer on salary with a West Coast industrial equipment manufacturer illustrates the difficulty of measuring sales performance for incentive reward. The field engineer calls on distributors. His duties include:

□ Developing and executing sales and product training programs for distributors' sales forces.

□ Doing missionary work with selected manufacturers and major oil companies to encourage them to recommend his products to their dealers and mention them in their service and installation manuals.

□ Participating in national and local trade shows; conducting occasional training programs for trade groups and associations.

□ Suggesting ideas for new products and promotional programs; recommending changes or improvements in existing products.

Many durable goods industries experience cyclical sales patterns, which makes a salary plan more compatible with the salesman's efforts and avoids the sharp swings in income that can occur in a commission plan.

After close examination of the salary plans of many companies, I have identified the following basic advantages and disadvantages of the salary plan approach.

The salary plan has advantages for both salesmen and their companies because it:

□ Assures a regular income.
□ Develops a high degree of loyalty.
□ Makes it simple to switch territories or quotas or to reassign salesmen.
□ Ensures that nonselling activities will be performed.
□ Facilitates administration.
□ Provides relatively fixed sales costs.

However, the salary plan does have disadvantages, in that it:

Exhibit II
Type of compensation by industry, 1977

Industry	Number of companies	Salary	Commission	Combination
Aerospace	5	60%	—	40%
Appliance (household)	8	25	25%	50
Automobile parts and accessories	12	34	16	50
Automobile and truck	10	30	30	40
Beverages	6	50	—	50
Building materials	23	17	13	70
Casualty insurance	5	20	20	60
Chemicals	13	23	23	54
Cosmetics and toilet preparations	9	33	34	33
Drugs and medicines	12	25	25	50
Electrical equipment and supplies	19	26	10	64
Electronics	21	19	9	62
Fabricated metal products	26	26	19	55
Food products	14	43	14	43
General machinery	26	19	15	65
Glass and allied products	8	60	20	20
Housewares	12	25	25	50
Instruments and allied products	10	30	20	50
Iron and steel	10	20	—	80
Life insurance	5	20	20	60
Nonferrous metals	6	50	—	50
Office machinery and equipment	7	14	29	57
Paper and allied products	12	33	—	67
Petroleum and petroleum products	4	50	25	25
Printing	17	24	47	29
Publishing	14	10	30	60
Radio and television	7	—	—	100
Retailing	4	50	25	25
Rubber	8	25	—	75
Service industries	21	15	40	45
Textiles and apparel	6	33	33	34
Tobacco	4	—	100	—
Tools and hardware	11	18	36	46
Transportation equipment	5	100	—	—

☐ Fails to give balanced sales mix because salesmen would concentrate on products with greatest customer appeal.

☐ Provides little, if any, financial incentive for the salesman.

☐ Offers few reasons for putting forth extra effort.

☐ Favors salesmen or saleswomen who are the least productive.

☐ Tends to increase direct selling costs over other types of plans.

☐ Creates the possibility of salary compression where new trainees may earn almost as much as experienced salesmen.

The two lists do not necessarily cancel each other out. Every compensation plan is a compromise. Determination of marketing and sales objectives, which will in turn determine the role of the sales force, will indicate to the sales executive whether the salary plan is best for achieving his goals. *Exhibit III* shows that the average earnings of experienced salesmen on this plan have increased from $9,700 in 1964 to $20,950 in 1977.

Commission plan

In this type of plan, salesmen are paid in direct proportion to their sales. Such a plan includes straight commission and commission with draw. The plan works well at the start of a new business where the market possibilities are very broad and highly fragmented. In such situations, territory boundaries are usually rather fluid and difficult to define. Therefore, quota and customer assignments are difficult to determine, making other types of compensation plans too costly or too complex to administer.

When management desires to maximize incentive, regardless of compensation levels in other company functions, or prefers a predictable sales cost in direct relationship with sales volume, the commission plan is appropriate. However, use of the straight commission approach has declined in popularity over the past several years and is not currently preferred, as the data in *Exhibits I* and *II* show.

Following are the advantages of the straight commission plan:

□ Pay relates directly to performance and results achieved.
□ System is easy to understand and compute.
□ Salesmen have the greatest possible incentive.
□ Unit sales costs are proportional to net sales.
□ Company's selling investment is reduced.

The disadvantages of this plan are:

□ Emphasis is more likely to be on volume than on profits.
□ Little or no loyalty to the company is generated.
□ Wide variances in income between salesmen may occur.
□ Salesmen are encouraged to neglect nonselling duties.
□ Some salesmen may be tempted to "skim" their territories.
□ Service aspect of selling may be slighted.
□ Problems arise in cutting territories or shifting men or accounts.
□ Pay is often excessive in boom times and very low in recession periods.

□ Salesmen may sell themselves rather than the company and stress short-term rather than long-term relationships.
□ Highly paid salesmen may be reluctant to move into supervisory or managerial positions.
□ Excessive turnover of sales personnel occurs when business turns bad.

Commission plan salesmen have historically earned more than their counterparts in a salary or combination plan. However, this trend was reversed in 1977, with commission men earning an average of $1,650 less than combination plan salesmen, as shown in *Exhibit III*.

We note in these data that from the eight-year period of 1964 to 1971 the average yearly gain was 7.5%. However, the unusual boom year of 1973 produced a 26% increase in earnings over 1971. Several sales executives cited examples of extraordinary commission earnings for that year which they felt were undeserved and totally disproportionate with sales effort expended. The swift economic swings from 1971 to 1973 forced sales executives to seek more stable compensation arrangements, as shown in the decrease in use of commission plans and the increase in combination plans previously referred to in *Exhibit I*.

If a commission plan is desired, the disadvantages must be offset. To accomplish this, some elements of guarantee must be added to the compensation package, especially for new salesmen. These can include guaranteeing a monthly minimum income, generous draws, and starting new men on a salary-plus-commission plan until commissions reach a desired level. The effect of possible personal economic fluctuations should be balanced by strong, security-oriented fringe benefit packages including surgical and medical insurance, pensions, and educational assistance. These stabilizing elements should help in recruiting and keeping men.

Combination plan

This type of plan includes all variations of salary plus other monetary incentive plans. The variations include base salary plus commission on all sales, salary plus bonus on sales over quota, salary plus commission plus bonus, and so on.

There are many sound reasons for installing a salary-plus-incentive plan. It permits greater incentive than a salary or commission plan and provides better control of the incentive or variable income than is possible with the commission plan. Also the much greater degree of flexibility with a wide varia-

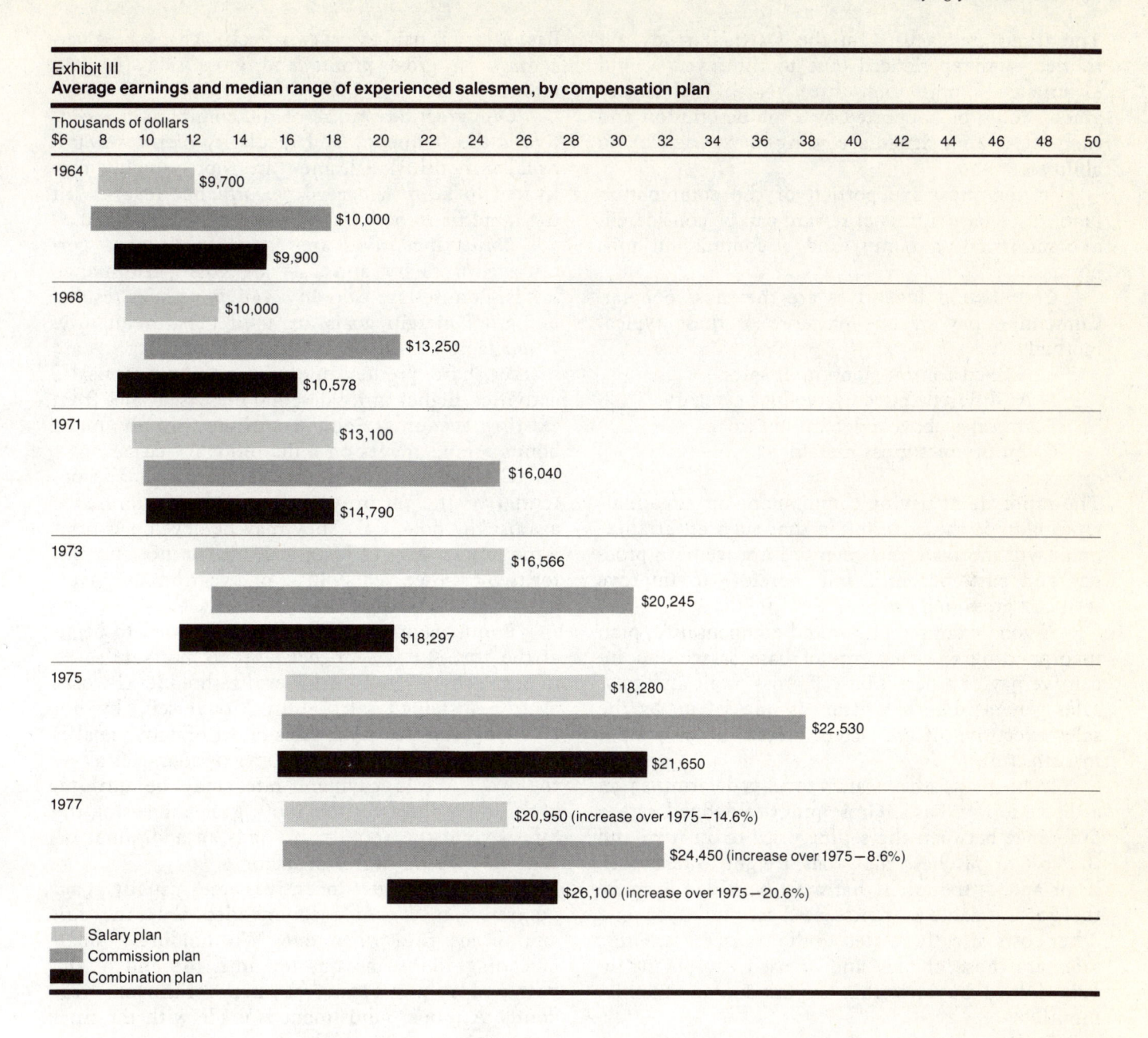

Exhibit III
Average earnings and median range of experienced salesmen, by compensation plan

Thousands of dollars

Year	Salary plan	Commission plan	Combination plan
1964	$9,700	$10,000	$9,900
1968	$10,000	$13,250	$10,578
1971	$13,100	$16,040	$14,790
1973	$16,566	$20,245	$18,297
1975	$18,280	$22,530	$21,650
1977	$20,950 (increase over 1975—14.6%)	$24,450 (increase over 1975—8.6%)	$26,100 (increase over 1975—20.6%)

Salary plan
Commission plan
Combination plan

tion in incentives to work with allows management to develop practically tailor-made plans for each salesman.

But these plans have liabilities, too. Salary-plus-incentive plans tend to be more complex than the other two methods. Thus they involve more paperwork, control, and administrative work. They need more frequent revision because of the interaction of the elements that comprise the total plan. In making individual adjustments over the years, one should be careful to avoid a gradual loss of uniformity in the plan.

The most important determination in building a sound salary-plus-incentive plan is the split between the fixed portion (salary) and the variable portion (incentive). The split is usually determined on the basis of historical sales performance and compensation records. Competitive analysis of other company programs, the base salary needed to keep good men, and an estimate of incentive potential should also be considered. Ceilings on incentive payments are usually part of combination plans.

The most frequent percentage split reported in the Dartnell study was 80% base salary and 20% incentive. A close second was a 70%/30% split, with a 60%/40% split being the third most frequently reported arrangement. As the rewards are closely tied into sales or gross margins, closer supervision and control of the plan are needed as the incentive portion of the plan increases.

Structuring the salary portion of the plan requires establishing salary grades for the sales force.

The three grades used in the Dartnell study are trainee, semiexperienced (one to three years), and experienced (more than three years). Each salary grade should be supported by a job description and each salesman assigned according to experience and ability.

In the incentive portion of the combination plan, three basic forms of reward can be considered: a commission, a bonus, and a commission plus bonus.

Commission incentives are the most popular. Companies pay by one or more of these typical methods:

1. A fixed commission on all sales.
2. At different rates by product category.
3. On sales above a determined goal.
4. On product gross margin.

The rationale of paying commissions on gross margin dollars is the assumption that such an arrangement will motivate salesmen to improve both product and customer mix and therefore to improve territory gross margin.

A good example of a sound compensation plan incorporating the elements of base salary and incentive pay of a percentage of gross profit and gross sales generated in a territory is one set up by the sales executive of an eastern electrical component manufacturer.

In his plan, a base salary level is determined on a discretionary basis. Gross profit is defined as the difference between the selling price of an item and the cost to purchase the goods, freight to transport, labor and/or materials that must be added to make the goods salable as represented to the buyer, and other costs directly related to the transaction. Gross sales are those of new and/or used equipment invoiced to a buyer within a period of a calendar month.

Each territory has a minimum requirement for gross profits and gross sales. The following three-step formula is applied:

Step 1: Sales volume up to $18,000 a month.
Base salary plus 7% of gross profits plus ½% of gross sales.

Step 2: Sales volume from $18,000 to $25,000 a month.
Base salary plus 9% of gross profits plus ½% of gross sales.

Step 3: Over $25,000 a month.
Base salary plus 10% of gross profits plus ½% of gross sales.

Base salary is paid every two weeks. The earned percentage of gross profits and gross sales is paid monthly.

One great advantage of the commission incentive is the frequency and regularity of the reward, usually monthly. Salesmen are more quickly motivated to keep or exceed performance levels with the rapid tie-in between performance and reward.

Bonus incentives are usually paid as a percentage of salary and vary by goal performance levels. Bonuses are paid on a variety of sales results, but gross margin goals are used most frequently. Other factors used as a measure for bonus goals are market share, product mix, new accounts, nonsales activities, higher unit sales, and increased sales from existing accounts. Some companies simply make bonus arrangements on a discretionary basis.

Goals may be based on an analysis of the potential of the territory and expected performance against the potential. They may be developed from a moving average of historical sales or gross margin for two or three years plus a one-year forecast averaged into the moving base.

Bonus payments should be structured to begin at the 70%- to 75%-of-goal level to motivate salesmen to achieve goals. A lower threshold level works against sustained sales effort. Conversely, by not receiving bonuses until sales effort of 100% goal is achieved, many persons become discouraged along the way. While payment rates may be uniform both under and over the 100% goal, increasing the rate beyond the 100% mark adds an additional incentive with a lower cost factor.

Because bonus incentives are usually paid quarterly, it is not recommended that the full amount be paid when due. Withholding a small percentage due each quarter until the end of the year avoids a possible overpayment for the total year bonus. A proper adjustment is made with the final quarter payment.

A bonus incentive plan is more difficult to establish and administer than a commission incentive. Also, rewards paid on a quarterly basis are not as effective motivators as weekly or monthly commission payments.

Another variation of the combination plan is one which pays *salary, commission,* and *bonus.* While this approach offers more flexibility than the other two types, it is more complex and more difficult to administer than any other plan.

Here are the elements of a good salary, commission, and bonus plan used by a midwest fabricated metal products company:

1. Base salary, company car, and all business expenses.

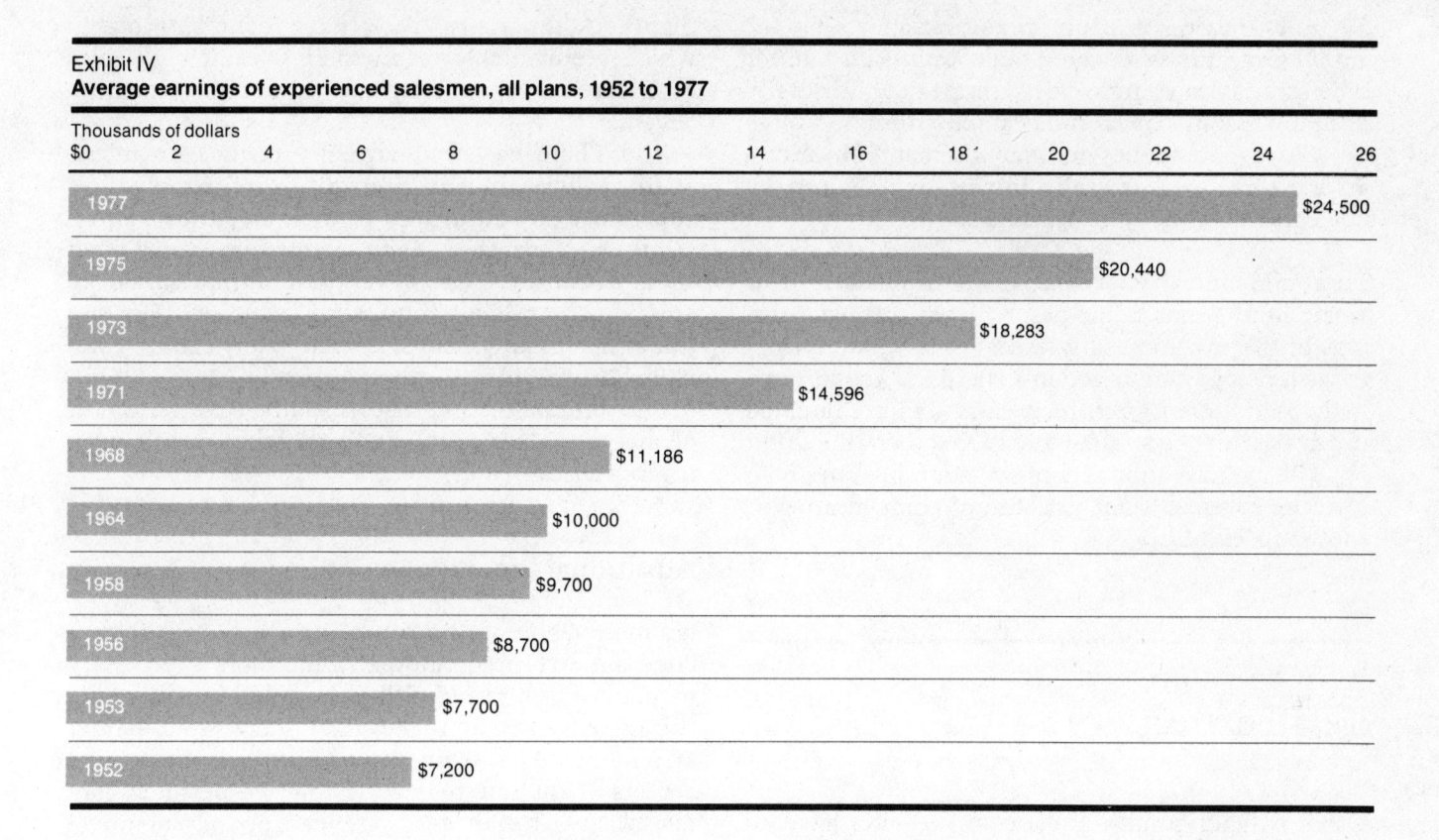

Exhibit IV
Average earnings of experienced salesmen, all plans, 1952 to 1977

Year	Earnings
1977	$24,500
1975	$20,440
1973	$18,283
1971	$14,596
1968	$11,186
1964	$10,000
1958	$9,700
1956	$8,700
1953	$7,700
1952	$7,200

2. A 5% commission, based annually and paid quarterly, on all sales volume over predetermined sales base.

3. A bonus on attainment of quota. Annual quota is divided in two parts: first six calendar months and last six calendar months. If quota is attained for the first half, bonus of 1% of all sales during that period is paid in July. This is repeated for the second half with bonus paid in January.

4. If quotas for both halves of the calendar year are attained, an additional bonus of ½% of all sales for the year is paid. Thus a total of 1½% of annual sales is paid as a bonus.

5. If quota for either of the six-month periods is not achieved but annual quota is achieved, ½% for the year is paid but not the 1% for period in which quota is not achieved.

6. "House" or "divisional manager" accounts are excluded from quota, commission, and bonus calculations.

Take another look at *Exhibit III* to see how the experienced salesperson on a combination plan has fared historically. Survey data covering the period from 1964 to 1977 are shown.

Two observations about these data are worth noting: average total earnings have increased 163% in the past 13 years; and total earnings in 1977 increased 20.6% over 1975, showing the highest increase of the three basic compensation plans for that period.

Also, average earnings of the combination plan salesperson exceeded the average earnings of the salaried person by $5,150 and the average earnings of the commission man by $1,650. This trend should continue. This fact of earnings plus relative advantages of the combination compensation plan, which follow, reinforces the continuing popularity of this plan.

Advantages are that the combination plan:
☐ Offers participants the advantages of both salary and commission.
☐ Provides greater range of earnings possibilities.
☐ Gives salesmen greater security because of steady base income.
☐ Makes possible a favorable ratio of selling expense to sales.
☐ Compensates salesmen for all activities.
☐ Allows a greater latitude of motivation possibilities so that goals and objectives can be achieved on schedule.

Disadvantages are that the plan:
☐ Is often complex and difficult to understand.
☐ Can, where low salary and high bonus or commission exist, develop a bonus that is too high a percentage of earnings; when sales fall, salary is too low to retain salesmen.

□ Is sometimes costly to administer.

□ Can, unless a decreasing commission rate for increasing sales volume exists, result in a "windfall" of new accounts and a runaway of earnings.

□ Has a tendency to offer too many objectives at one time so that really important ones can be neglected, forgotten, or overlooked.

To round out the basic compensation data, it is worth noting that in the past 25 years, average earnings of the experienced salesperson have more than tripled, rising from $7,200 in 1952 to $24,500 in 1977. Perhaps of more significance, earnings have doubled in the past 10 years. These data are shown in *Exhibit IV*. The average annual compensation broken down into the seven distinct varieties of compensation is shown in *Exhibit V*.

Related areas

Other policies besides direct compensation have an impact on both the salesperson's total pay package and the company's financial position. These are sales expenses and extra incentive plans.

Expense practices

The need for keeping a tight rein on sales-generated expenses, which have a direct effect on profits, was never more evident than in the recent turbulent economic years. With the cost of sales calls constantly rising and with increased traveling and lodging costs, companies must periodically examine their expense policies and procedures and make adjustments in order to draw that ideal fine line where expenses are kept under proper control and reimbursement to salesmen is fair and reasonable.

Respondents to the Dartnell survey indicate that 92% of the companies paid all or some of their salesmen's expenses—in addition to compensation payments.

Eight major expense categories are covered in *Exhibit VI*, which shows the percentage of companies paying all or part of salesmen's expenses by compensation plan.

A few significant observations regarding expense practices should be noted:

□ More salesmen are using air travel, with 84% of all respondent companies authorizing commercial flights. Additionally, 26% have company planes which are available to all their salesmen for sales calls based primarily on the function of territory coverage.

□ There has been virtually no change in expense policies in the past six years—80% of the companies pay all or part of their salesmen's entertainment expenses. Many companies noted that these expenses must have prior authorization or are "luncheon only" types of expenses. Expense limits are usually set. Salesmen rarely have "carte blanche" on entertainment expenses.

□ Promotion expenses usually cover the cost of meetings, local publicity, and other merchandising activities.

Additional incentives

No matter how well a compensation plan is formulated and executed, another dimension is necessary to achieve best results. What I am talking about are the incentives that make a salesman work harder all around. And again, let us consider the unique aspects of the salesman's job: limited personal contact with his manager; extended periods of travel which brings loneliness and inconvenience; decisions that require a high level of motivation (when to make the first call of the day, how many calls to make, objectives to be achieved on each call, when to quit for the day); and emotional swings between the elation of obtaining a large order and the frequent frustrations of orders lost to competitors and missed shipping dates.

Motivation calls for creating a climate in which the salesman can motivate himself with the incentives provided by management. These incentives can be financial, nonfinancial, or a combination of the two.

Financial incentives

Short-term sales contests are popular. Costs are predictable, results are usually successful, and rewards are immediate. Contests usually run for one or two months, but some as short as a week can produce results. The awards that are most favored in contests are money, trips, merchandise, and personal recognition.

A successful sales contest should include these basic elements: well-defined objectives, simple rules, short duration, goals attainable by most salesmen, inclusion of wives and families when possible, and follow-through program to sustain enthusiasm.

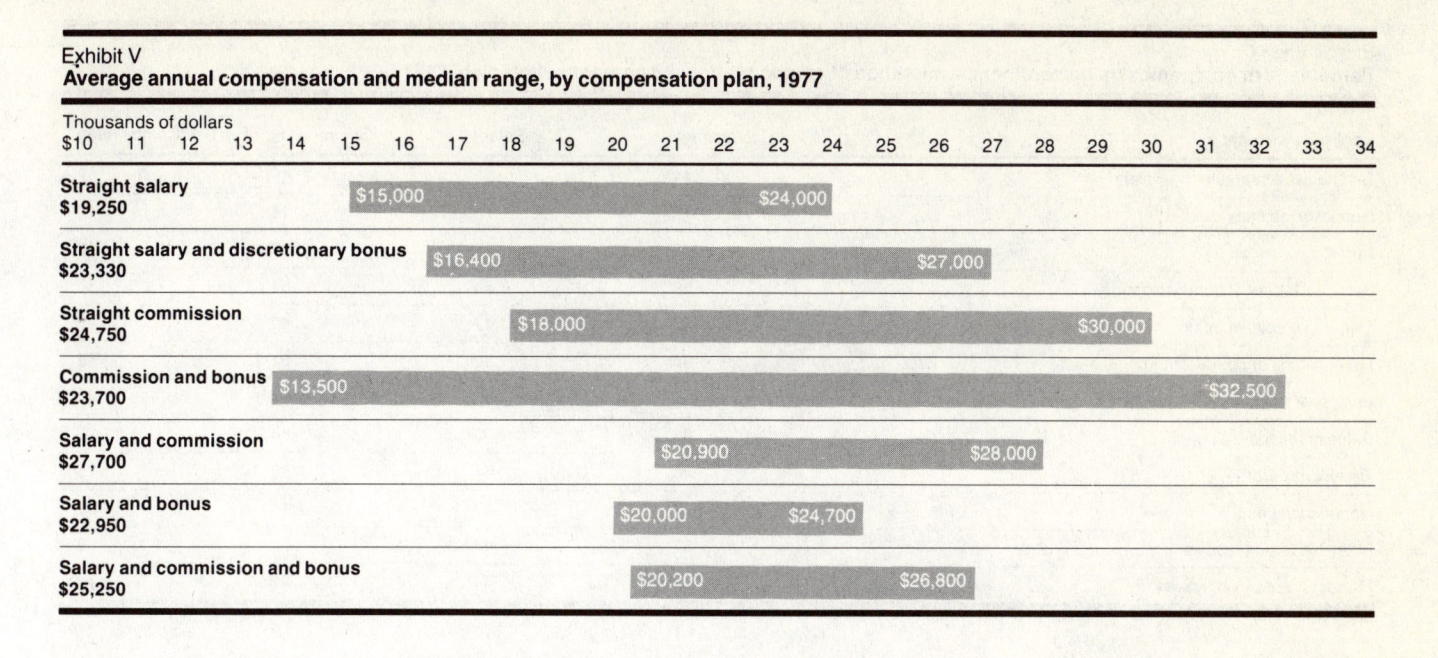

Exhibit V
Average annual compensation and median range, by compensation plan, 1977

Compensation plan	Average	Median range
Straight salary	$19,250	$15,000 – $24,000
Straight salary and discretionary bonus	$23,330	$16,400 – $27,000
Straight commission	$24,750	$18,000 – $30,000
Commission and bonus	$23,700	$13,500 – $32,500
Salary and commission	$27,700	$20,900 – $28,000
Salary and bonus	$22,950	$20,000 – $24,700
Salary and commission and bonus	$25,250	$20,200 – $26,800

Exhibit VI
Percentage of companies paying expenses, by compensation plan, 1977

Expense	All companies	Salary	Commission	Combination
Automobile (company-owned, leased, personal)	91%	97%	73%	99%
Other travel (commercial airlines, railroads, company plane)	84	88	63	88
Lodging	86	90	69	90
Telephone	87	89	75	91
Entertainment	80	86	58	86
Samples	73	75	71	75
Promotion	76	72	71	77
Office and/or clerical	73	63	73	77

Contests are like a double-bladed sword. Improperly used or used for the wrong reasons, they can create dissension and dissatisfaction within the ranks. Properly used, contests can create a competitive atmosphere that will stimulate sales and provide additional rewards.

In addition to the usual contest objectives of increased sales volume, more sales calls, new accounts, and so forth, contests can serve to build off-season business, increase the use of displays, stimulate various dealer tie-ins, revive dead accounts, and reduce costs.

Nonfinancial methods

Techniques that principally provide salesmen recognition, status, and a sense of group belonging are generally referred to as "psychic income."

This is an area in which the industrial psychologists have made positive contributions. Though many of the successful techniques have been available for a long time, it has just been within the past 10 to 15 years that sales executives have begun to realize their importance.

Over the years, as the role of the salesman has been redefined and enlarged, many companies have conferred more meaningful titles on members of their sales forces to improve their status with customers, to give them personal status symbols, and to more aptly describe their functions. Companies commonly use such titles as regional, area, or zone manager, field sales engineer, account executive, and staff associate.

Other productive ways to recognize individual good performance or encourage effectiveness are: distinguished salesman awards, honorary job titles, publicity, personal letters or telephone calls of com-

Exhibit VII
Percentage of companies using nonfinancial methods of compensation, by compensation plan, 1977

Nonfinancial method	All companies	Salary	Commission	Combination
Distinguished salesman awards	44%	31%	49%	47%
Honorary job titles	13	16	16	12
Publicity	37	39	37	36
Personal letters of commendation	59	56	54	63
Telephone calls of commendation	42	42	40	43
Face-to-face encouragement	88	90	81	88
Individual help with responsibilities	64	69	61	62
Sales meetings	91	86	88	92
Training programs	70	64	63	75
Honor societies	7	3	11	8
Published sales results	57	44	61	59
Management by objectives	43	44	32	46

mendation, face-to-face encouragement, and individual help with responsibilities.

Exhibit VII shows the percentage of companies (by compensation plan) using broad nonfinancial methods of motivation. The low percentages in most categories indicate that many companies are missing a good bet in not using these highly effective techniques. All these methods are inexpensive and convey a sense of personal communication that salesmen value highly.

Fringe benefits

The cost of maintaining medical, accident, life, and dental insurance programs on a personal basis is significant, so fringe benefits constitute an important part of the "total income" of every company employee, including the sales force.

Adding up the costs of personal use of the company or leased car, memberships, and educational expense assistance that many companies provide, the basic benefit package would cost a salesman a minimum of $1,500 a year.

Currently, many companies in most industries are paying part or all of the costs of 12 major benefits: hospitalization-surgical insurance; life, accident, and dental insurance; educational assistance; profit sharing; pension plans; stock purchase; personal use of car; club or association memberships; moving expenses; and salary continuation program. *Exhibit VIII* shows the participation by companies broken down by the three basic compensation plans and for all companies responding to the survey, regardless of compensation plan used.

The salary plan and combination plan salesmen fared about equally in all benefit provisions. As was to be expected, commission plan salesmen lagged in all categories. However, in comparison with previous studies, the commission man has made dramatic gains. As I said earlier, many companies are seeking ways of increasing company loyalty and of providing competitive advantage to attract and retain the commission salesman on the payroll.

To dramatize the significance of fringe benefits for salesmen in the total compensation package, I compared current data with that of 1958, 19 years ago. The percentage of companies providing hospital insurance increased by 16%, life insurance by 10%, educational assistance by 36%, and club or association memberships by 14%. Dental insurance, stock purchases, profit sharing, and salary continuation programs have been added to the benefit package since 1958 at an increasing rate. As general company benefits to all employees increase in scope, the salesman's benefit package will likewise increase.

Compensation plans have become more complex—the three basic methods of paying salesmen have stretched into at least seven kinds of plans, and possibly more will be designed tomorrow.

Combination plans dominate the compensation package makeup despite the complexity of administration and control. The disadvantages are far overshadowed by the flexibility in providing meaningful incentive pay tied more directly to sales per-

Exhibit VIII
Companies paying all or part of benefits, by compensation plan, 1977

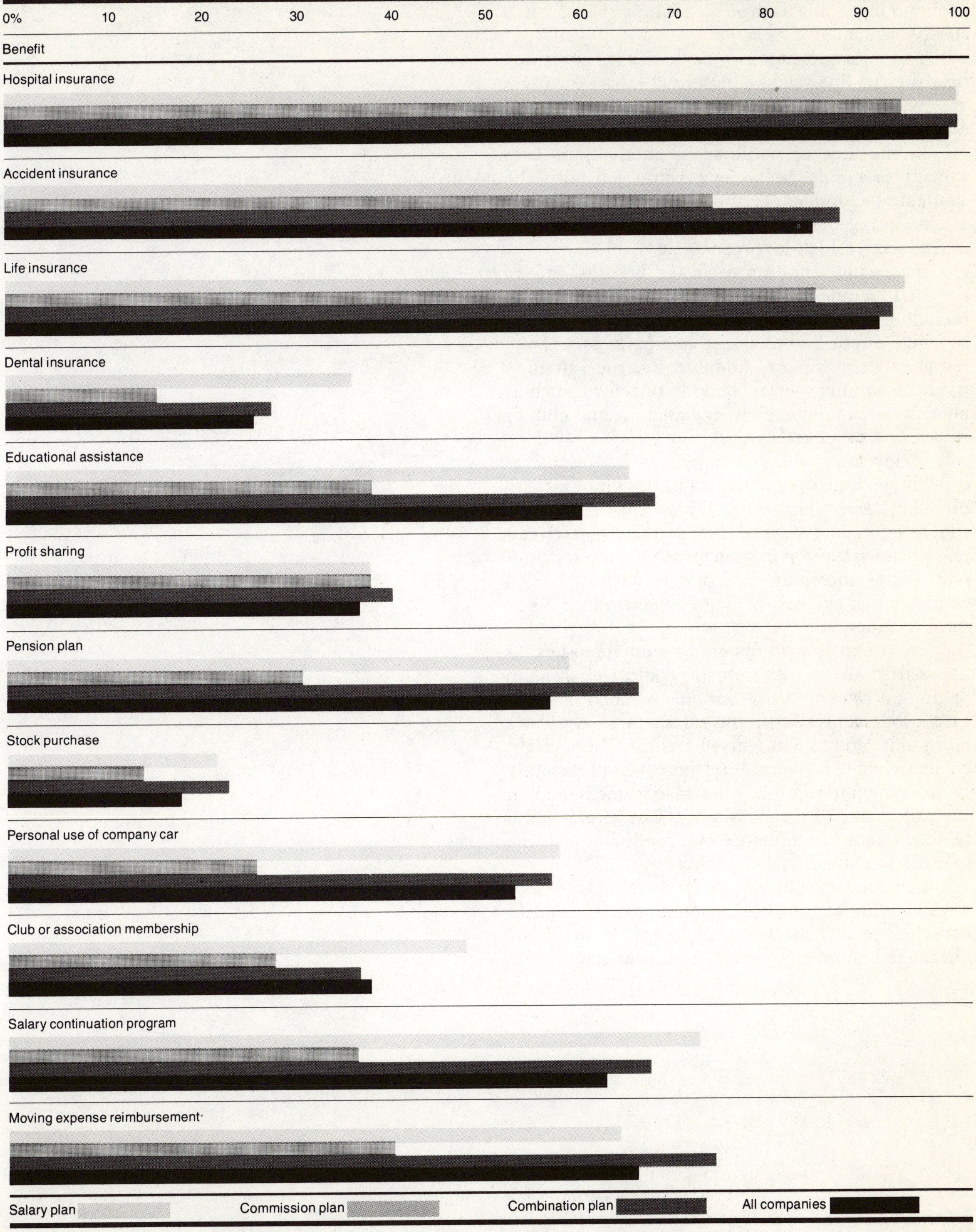

| 0% | 10 | 20 | 30 | 40 | 50 | 60 | 70 | 80 | 90 | 100 |

Benefit

Hospital insurance

Accident insurance

Life insurance

Dental insurance

Educational assistance

Profit sharing

Pension plan

Stock purchase

Personal use of company car

Club or association membership

Salary continuation program

Moving expense reimbursement

Salary plan   Commission plan   Combination plan   All companies formance—that is, applying commission and bonus to single and/or multiple sales goals. In addition, a combination plan provides the salesman with a greater range of earnings possibilities based on a steady base income.

The salesman expense policies I have examined over the last five years indicate that sales executives are exercising good judgment in controlling and administering field expenses.

In the area of nonfinancial motivation, sales executives should be doing a better job with the available techniques. Personal contact, recognition, and encouragement are needed to sustain a positive attitude and a high level of morale.

Increasing amounts of fringe benefits add to the total income package of a salesman. Employees, including salesmen, no longer regard such benefits as fringe offerings, but rather as a basic part of the terms of employment. Additionally, the salesman has been gaining special "perks" of his own, such as personal use of a company or leased car and club or association memberships.

In my many discussions with sales executives over the past two years, the subject of "profitability of sales" kept coming up. While sales executives should never lose sight of their primary objectives—to increase sales—top management pressure for profitable sales increases. It demands new rules and definitions of the cost of doing business in a given sales territory.

The trend toward obtaining profitable sales, as opposed to sheer sales volume, could well lead to defining a sales territory not only as such but also as a profit center with the salesman as the sales *and* profit producer in a given territory. This might be an awesome responsibility, but it would certainly be a new dimension in sales management and in the salesman's job responsibility. The effect would be to increase the influence of a profit factor in the salesman's compensation package.

The sales executive will have to educate and reeducate himself in this expanding sphere of profit consciousness. This is his challenge in the years ahead, and he must meet it if he is to survive.

Tie salesmen's bonuses to their forecasts

By linking sales bonuses to results, percent of quota achieved, and forecasts, managers can reward salesmen more equitably and set realistic objectives

Jacob Gonik

Compensating salespeople according to how much they sell has many advantages; it is straightforward and easy to calculate. It does not, however, account for sales territories with different potential. Compensating salespeople according to how much of their quota they achieve can also be effective, but it depends on the salesperson's forecasts which tend not to be the same as the company's objective. The incentive system described in this article accounts for unequal territories and makes good forecasting possible by rewarding a salesman according to how close his forecasts and actual results are to the company's objective. The author shows how the system is used in practice by describing a sales contest case, and provides a grid with which to calculate bonuses linked to forecasts, actual results, and objectives.

Mr. Gonik is the director of data processing marketing support at IBM Brazil. His areas of responsibility include marketing programs, education, support services, and data centers and information records. He is currently preparing a book on motivation techniques based on his experiences in Brazil.

John and Peter are two salesmen for the XYZ corporation.

John sells twice as much as Peter.

John earns twice as much as Peter, right?

Wrong. John may even earn less.

The XYZ corporation's sales compensation plan is not unique in the modern business world. In the past decade many companies have turned to sophisticated incentive plans that seem to challenge Darwin's law of survival. Throughout the years salespeople have been paid by either fixed salaries or variable incentives such as commissions and shares in profits. Other forms of payment are expense accounts and fringe benefits such as paid insurance and vacations, but these are never used alone and can be set aside when discussing the motivational aspects of compensation plans.

Most companies use a combination of straight salary and commissions. By including both a fixed monthly wage and a sales percentage bonus, managements seek to secure company control as well as provide salesmen with ample motivation. For example, at XYZ John and Peter will each earn $10,000 a year guaranteed, plus another $10,000 in bonuses which depend directly on their results. How, though, can Peter sell less and still earn more than John even though they sell the same piece of machinery for XYZ?

The dilemma is resolved if one takes into consideration how management measures John's and Peter's performance.

In this article I describe a sales compensation system which, unlike most incentive plans, rewards salespeople not only for their actual results but also for their effort and ability to forecast accurately. Before describing that system, however, let us take a look at the two basic compensation systems from which all others spring.

Basic compensation systems

Many years ago a manager's payroll slogan was quite straightforward: "Bring me more revenue and I will pay you more!" A salesperson's commissions were proportional to his or her sales. The proportion could vary from product to product, but in the end the salesperson's reward was linked to the benefit he or she brought to the company. This is a system set up to reward results.

Achievement system

Under this system, every salesman had a yearly quota, that is, a standard by which he could measure his performance on December 31, but the achievement of which brought no extra money at all. The prize and motivation to achieve that quota was often a trip to a winner's convention plus, of course, an opportunity for a promotion. But the quota had no links to earnings.

After World War II when business boomed so quickly, the flaws in the straight achievement system revealed themselves. Companies using it found that they were paying huge unexpected commissions to some salesmen for the same effort they had made before. And these sudden commissions created enormous differences in earnings between salesmen owing to inequitable territories.

In addition, as products became more and more complex, companies needed more and more investments for longer periods. Because one single product could require five years to be developed and a small mistake could turn into a big loss, planning became a fundamental business effort. Sales forecasting and quota setting became major disciplines and activities, and reaching the quota became even more important since it meant achieving the overall goal of the company.

The need to tie quota objectives to salesmen's earnings was a natural consequence of this panorama, and many different sales compensation plans sprang to life. Commissions might be paid for quota completion only, or just for sales in excess of quota. Complex payment curves were built to sharpen the importance of achieving the preset goal. The most imaginative method rewards salesmen for achieving a company's objectives.

Objective-achievement system

Ed and Charles are two factory workers and use the same type of tools for punching the same kind of holes in a television chassis. They are paid by the number of holes they punch a day. Since Ed is more experienced and quicker than Charles, he punches more holes and gets more money.

One day their manager calls Ed and tells him that since he is more experienced than Charles, it is absolutely normal that he punches more holes. From that day on, therefore, he will earn the same as Charles for doing twice as much. One can imagine the look on Ed's face.

When applied to sales effort the objective-achievement system is not as absurd as it looks in the factory case. Say a TV set manufacturing company determines each salesman's bonus according to his experience, time with the company, and merit. Frank, for instance, qualifies for a $15,000 bonus, while Steve for only $12,000. Their bonuses have no relation to their territories or objectives.

Next, let us assume that their manager has a sales quota of 700 TV units which he must split between the two of them. The manager decides that Frank has a "better" territory—i.e., one with more market potential—and should get an objective of 500 units. The remaining units he assigns to Steve. Frank and Steve each sell 200 units, but while Steve makes 100% of his quota and gets the full bonus, Frank reaches just 40% of his objective and thus only 40% of his bonus. *Exhibit I* shows how objectives and actual achievements were calculated for Frank and Steve. Although Steve did a better job because of the toughness of his territory, under the old achievement system both would have received the same amount.

Using the objective-achievement approach all managers can shuffle territories and salesmen around without the salesmen complaining. Those who must

Exhibit I
Objective-achievement system results

	Possible bonus	Objective	Achievement	Percent of objective	Actual bonus
Frank	$15,000	500	200	40%	$6,000
Steve	12,000	200	200	100	12,000

spend time on assisting customers in installing complex machinery receive a smaller sales quota. Salesmen with good sales prospects get higher objectives; thus they neither frustrate other salesmen nor eat up the company's sales budget.

The system is not only fair to salesmen but also fits into operational plans. All quotas add up to the company's total objective, or nearly. It is quite simple. Simple but tricky. The whole concept depends on a precise forecasting technique. Up to now nobody has ever invented such a precise forecasting method, particularly when dealing with the small figures of a one-man territory.

In many cases, the objective-achievement system has more holes in it than Ed and Charles will ever make in the TV sets at their plant. For instance, Mary is a young saleswoman for an air-conditioning manufacturer. She sells air conditioners to any prospective customers within a given geographic territory. She works with a list of potential buyers given to her by the headquarters staff.

In September, Mary is asked to update the prospects list, indicating how many units each customer might buy in the following year. This does not make her happy because she knows that her information will be used to set up her next year's quota which will limit her gains. Mary sees the forecasting process as an enemy.

Although every month she prepares a 90-day sales forecast pinpointing the hot prospects, near the end of the year Mary does not enhance the list with new names. The company understands that she is concentrating on the most probable buyers and does not have time to open new accounts. On December 31 the 90-day forecast is near zero. The new year rewinds everyone's production clock. Mary is back to zero sales, and ready to get a new quota, which she hopes will be low.

The board of directors, however, wants growth—a 20% increase over last year's results. The branch offices receive the same percentage increase, so do the sales managers, and so does Mary who ends up with a higher objective despite her forecast. She learns that the company had not trusted her low forecast anyway. It looks like it is a mutual cheating system.

Since Joe, another salesman, is supposed to spend his year assisting old customers, he gets half of Mary's quota. Life goes on. Mary has a tough year, barely reaching 100% of her objective, while she watches Joe get 300% of his quota, because of an unexpected order from a big builder in his territory, and, therefore, 300% of his bonus.

Managers also see quota setting as an annoyance. Although the company's yearly objective is rather easy to decide on, splitting it equitably among salespeople remains difficult at best. Even if the distribution looks fair in January, so many new facts take place during 12 months that, in the end, it is never equal.

Let us stop here to recall the objectives all managers are shooting for in a complex sales environment. First, they want to pay salesmen for their absolute sales volume. Second, they want to pay them for their effort, even if they are in tough areas where they will sell less. Third, they want good and fresh field information on market potential for planning and control purposes.

In the achievement system, salesmen are paid only according to actual sales volume. Since they are not paid extra if they achieve their quota, salesmen simply do not care and forecast poorly. The achievement system, therefore, satisfies only the first objective (volume), and works only in businesses where the second and third objectives (payment for effort and planning) are not pursued.

The objective-achievement system does not stress the first objective. Salesmen are paid by the percentage of their quota that they achieve and not by absolute results. Unfortunately, for payment to be based on quota achievement there must be good forecasting. This dependency is exactly what acts against the system. To ensure reaching their quota, salesmen try to provide the lowest possible forecast, which affects the company's overall plan and could eventually kill the chances for a perfect quota distribution.

In spite of this deficiency, however, this system can be used successfully in all cases where management has certain quota-fixing flexibility, and where the

Exhibit II
The OFA system grid and formulas

	F/O (Forecast divided by objective)										
A/O x 100 (Actual results divided by objective, then multiplied by 100)		0	0.5	1.0	1.5	2.0	2.5	3.0	3.5	4.0	4.5	5.0
	0	—	—	—	—	—	—	—	—	—	—	—
	50	30	60	30	—	—	—	—	—	—	—	—
	100	60	90	120	90	60	30	—	—	—	—	—
	150	90	120	150	180	150	120	90	60	30	—	—
	200	120	150	180	210	240	210	180	150	120	90	60
	250	150	180	210	240	270	300	270	240	210	180	150
	300	180	210	240	270	300	330	360	330	300	270	240
	350	210	240	270	300	330	360	390	420	390	360	330
	400	240	270	300	330	360	390	420	450	480	450	420
	450	270	300	330	360	390	420	450	480	510	540	510
	500	300	330	360	390	420	450	480	510	540	570	600

Calculation of grid numbers

If F equal to A then   OFA = 120 x F/O
If F smaller than A then   OFA = 60 x (A + F)/O
If F bigger than A then   OFA = 60 x (3A − F)/O

---

company's planning cycle does not depend deeply on the salesmen's forecast.

In any case, analysis of these two systems shows that there is still substantial room for improvement. This is why we at IBM Brazil have developed a system which includes all three objectives and which was successfully tested in a very important contest for salespeople.

Measuring the 'OFA' system

Through a new approach, which is known as the "OFA" system, earnings are based on a combination of three different measurements:

1
The objective, O, or quota the company chooses.
2
The forecast, F, the salesman provides.
3
The actual, A, results the salesman achieves.

Exhibit II displays the grid and formulas on which the OFA system is based. After receiving his objective, O, a salesman must turn in his forecast, F; F divided by O determines the column in which the salesman's bonus percentage will fall. For instance, the 1.0 column represents a forecast equal to the quota, the 0.5 column means the forecast is half the objective, and the 1.5 column indicates a forecast 50% larger than the objective. The letter "A" stands for actual sales results. Thus A divided by O and multiplied by 100 is the percentage of the objective that was actually achieved by the salesman; 100% means full achievement of the company's objective, not of the salesman's forecast.

Now let us see how it works. John sells photographic equipment. His quota is 500 cameras. Let us assume that John fully agrees to his quota and turns in a 500-units forecast. (On the grid, F/O equals 1.0.) If John sells 500 cameras, he makes 100% of his objective and is entitled to 120% of his bonus. In other words, he gets a 20% premium for his good planning capability. How much that represents in dollars depends on John's personal value, namely, his experience, time with the company, and merit.

If John sells 750 cameras, which is 150% of his objective, he is entitled to 150% of his bonus; the more he sells the more he earns. But now John realizes that if his forecast had been 750 instead of 500 units (1.5 on the grid), then he would have received 180% of his bonus instead of 150%. Bad planning on his part has deprived him of a good chunk of money. If John had sold 250 units, half of his objective, he would have earned just 30%

of his incentive. Here again, John sees that it would have been better to have forecasted 250 instead of 500 for his earnings would have been 60%.

In other words, the best earnings lie in the diagonal that goes down from left to right in the grid. For a given result, A, the more precise John's forecast is, the higher his earnings. But John will always earn most if his forecast is perfect.

After being introduced to the grid, John goes back to study his territory. This time he does not want to return a faulty forecast—his earnings are at stake. He may still complain that the objective set up by his manager is too high—there is no solution to that —but for the first time he can enhance his earnings through a good work plan. If he comes in with a low forecast, he may damage his earnings in exchange for safety. On the other hand, a high forecast may plunge him into trouble if his sales are too low. John understands that he must be precise. This is exactly what his manager is waiting for.

From that moment on, John becomes committed to the number he forecasts. The grid tells him that his sales should be equal to or higher than the forecast in order for his earnings to increase. Soon, John sees that, because of the new interactive approach, the headquarters staff begins to really understand the market and sets sales objectives that approach his own forecast. Total accuracy will never happen, but for practical purposes the three main objectives of the system—sales volume, payment for performance, and good field information for planning—will be brought about.

Putting the system to work

The OFA system is a new idea. IBM has tried it successfully two times in its Brazilian operations during 1975 and 1976. Both times the OFA supplemented IBM Brazil's regular incentive programs. (See the Appendix for a description of how IBM Brazil adopted the system. A description of how the system might be applied to accounts receivable is included in the ruled insert.)

Clearly, however, there will be hitches in actually using the system that do not appear when one considers it in the abstract. For instance, it is difficult for salesmen to present good forecasts one year in advance. Because of this, in most cases the bonus can be an average between the monthly and yearly objectives.

For example, Sherm sells tractors. His quota of 1,200 units a year means he must sell 100 a month. But Sherm knows the true opportunities of his territory and is shooting for higher gains. He forecasts 1,800 tractors for the coming year, that is, 150 for each month.

The company asks him also for a monthly forecast. Sherm thinks that 50 is a good number for January. Unfortunately, he sells only 25. With the help of the OFA grid, let us see how much he will earn, assuming his incentive bonus is $24,000 a year, or $2,000 a month.

Since F/O = 150/100 = 1.5, Sherm's yearly forecast falls in the 1.5 column of the grid. In January he sold 25 units. Therefore, according to the grid formula (see *Exhibit II*):

OFA = 60 x (3 x 25 − 150)/100.

The result is zero bonus. Since F/O = 50/100 = 0.5, Sherm's monthly forecast falls in the 0.5 column of the grid. F is still bigger than A, so the same formula applies:

OFA = 60 x (3 x 25 − 50)/100 = 15%.

The average between the yearly and the monthly calculation is 7.5%. Sherm receives $150 which is 7.5% of his monthly bonus.

In any traditional approach, forecasts would not have been considered, and Sherm would have received a quarter of his bonus, $500. Under the OFA system, Sherm was penalized for reaching only half of his forecast as well as for his low sales.

Let us keep in mind the whole concept. The company wants Sherm to sell 100 tractors a month as an average. He foresaw potential sales of 150 units by month, and decided to shoot for the 1.5 grid column which could give him 180% of his bonus. Because of his own choice, if he sells just 100, which *is* what the company wants, he gets only 90% of his bonus.

Sherm's January forecast and results did not help him. In February, however, Sherm forecasts that he will sell 200 tractors, which puts him in the 2.0

column of the grid, and he meets his forecast. Let us compute his earnings.

Sherm's yearly forecast, of 150 tractors a month, is smaller than his February achievement of 200. Therefore, he receives:

OFA = 60 x (150 + 200)/100 = 210%.

For the monthly bonus, Sherm's forecast, 200, was equal to sales, so he gets:

OFA = 120 x 200/100 = 240%.

Sherm's average is (210 + 240)/2 = 225%; his bonus value is $4,500.

For January *and* February, Sherm got 232.5% of his monthly incentive (7.5% + 225%). He sold a total of 225 tractors against a forecast of 300 and a company objective of 200. In any traditional system he would have received 225% of his bonus (225/100). With OFA, his February planning was so good that it compensated for January's failure and provided him with an additional premium.

Sherm's company decided to use a direct average between monthly and yearly forecasts. Say Company B decides to weight them differently, considering the yearly forecast two times more important than the monthly one. Working for Company B, Sherm would have received slightly less money in February since the weighted calculation would have been

2 x 210% + 1 x 240%)/3 = 220%.

Size, number of salesmen, and market type are some of the aspects to be taken into consideration when deciding the weighting factor.

Penalties for delays

No matter how rough the waves, the surfing expert will manage to find the best path. While the corporation is working out a compensation system that will pay for high quality work and foster precise forecasting, its salesmen will try to uncover the best way to earn the most out of, or beat, the system.

Sherm, our brightest tractor salesman, for instance, finds out that whenever he receives a customer order that is bigger than his monthly forecast, it pays to hold it for the next month. In March, Sherm forecasts 50 tractors but he gets an unexpected 100-unit

The OFA system for accounts receivable

Professional collectors and even branch office managers can work under the OFA incentive system. Because of cash flow problems, good forecasting is as vital in accounts receivable as it is for sales figures.

To start with, the objective should be divided into short periods, weeks if possible, and the collectors should visit customers before the actual collection in order to add pressure and improve their input to the accounts receivable department.

Sticking to the OFA concept that every objective must include a piece of the previous unfulfilled objective, the collector's weekly quota should equal the current debt, plus a percentage of the overdue at the beginning of the period under consideration.

A collector who turns back a low collection forecast is doing a good job by informing the company in advance of any problems in cash availability. But he is not free of his responsibility to improve that situation. The OFA system pays him a premium for his correct information, but it also penalizes him for staying under his objective. On the other hand, those that collect much more than they have forecasted cannot earn as much as those who really know what is going on in their territory.

order. By the grid, his bonus will by 90%. If he holds the order until April, and then forecasts 100, his payment will go up to 120%.

Clearly, this absurdity is not supposed to be part of the OFA system, but Sherm's cleverness allows me to introduce a major piece of the OFA concept: the tool for penalizing the salesman for any delay in achieving the objectives set up by the corporation.

The problem is not new. How can we make the sales uniform throughout the year instead of having the usual peaks and lows? How can we avoid the traditional downturn during the first months of a new year? How can we avoid intentional or unintentional delays? The OFA system provides a clue. Sherm's company set his objective at 1,200 units a year. *We* immediately assumed 100 tractors a month and started to measure Sherm's results against this standard. But that assumption was wrong.

In the OFA system *every objective must include a piece of the previous unfulfilled objective.* If Sherm sells 100 or more tractors in January, then his February objective would also be 100 units. But if his January sales fall short of 100 units, then his February objective should be immediately raised. Since Sherm sold only 25 tractors in January, his new monthly objective should be between 100 and 175 units, depending on how tough with sales delays his company wants to be.

With an 80% penalty factor, Sherm's February quota would be 160 (80% of 175) instead of 100. Since he forecasted and sold 200 tractors, Sherm's final monthly percentage would be

OFA = 120 x 200/160 = 150%.

At this point, Sherm will think twice before he holds up a customer order until the following month. Better than that, Sherm will rush ahead to reach his forecast as soon as possible.

Every objective must be attainable. The company ought to decide on a penalty that fits the type of business and not set up impossible goals for its sales force. A certain level of delays will always exist and should be accepted.

When preparing a sales incentive plan, the management team needs to understand that it will not be doing a good job if in the end the salesmen do not come out with a fair dollar share of the business.

Appendix: The IBM Brazil sales contest

In designing a special sales contest to achieve $7 million revenue from a certain product in 1975, the IBM Brazil headquarters' staff had a number of concerns. It wanted to reward salespeople for good performance, given different territories, and at the same time it wanted to make sure the company achieved its objectives.

Management divided the total sales potential into three segments— A, B, and C—each group representing a different customer size and, thus, different degrees of difficulty. The relationship among the groups as to sales effort was 1 to 2.5 to 4.0. Each branch office, and so every salesman in it, was then assigned to one of the three groups.

In addition to regular incentives, top management selected $20,000 as the bonus base for $7 million in sales.

Management assessed the overall marketing opportunities for the three groups, based on historical data, and made the following sales prognoses:

Group A (small) $ 500,000   (7% of the total objective)
Group B (medium)   2,800,000   (40% of the total objective)
Group C (large)   3,700,000   (53% of the total objective)

In addition to requiring four times less effort than Group A customers, Group C could also absorb over seven times more sales.

The salesmen were not given management's sales forecast by group. Yet it provided us with the major tool to compute the index or objective by salesman, as follows:

$500/1 + $2,800/2.5 + $3,700/4 = $2,545

Assuming that a salesman receives a $100 bonus for attaining his objective, then for a salesman in Group A, the objective would be figured as follows:

$100 × $2,545,000/$20,000 = $12,725 (rounded to $12,700)

The final figures for the objectives were:

For a Group A salesman: $12,700
For a Group B salesman: 12,700 × 2.5 = $31,750
For a Group C salesman: 12,700 × 4.0 = $50,800

When the contest and objectives were made public, not one salesman complained about the effort relationship and its effect on the objectives. The distribution was considered fair, a very uncommon reaction.

If actual results had been precisely as planned, the bonus payment would have been as shown in *Table A*. Since we expected salesmen to be 80% precise in their forecasting, we figured the final bonus should be $19,238 (0.8 × $24,048).

At the end of the year, we achieved $8 million in sales, almost 15% over plan. Of the total sales force, 33% provided forecasts, and 3% received orders which, on the average, amounted to 85% of their forecasts. These orders represented 35% of the $8 million. Nine other orders came from nonforecasted customers and represented the other 65% of the total achievement.

The actual results by market group are shown in *Table B*.

Sales by group, as projected by the headquarters staff, were extraordinarily precise for Groups A and C, but underestimated for Group B. On the whole, despite the $1 million extra revenue, IBM spent less in bonuses than expected ($16,760 against $19,238).

Satisfaction at the salesmen level was high. Over $5 million came from nonforecasted orders, which showed that the usual sales drive was not disturbed; quite possibly it was enhanced by the payment for performance concept. All salesmen who closed orders were clearly pleased with the level of their bonuses.

The fact that only 8% of the salesmen got any orders means that a traditional quota distribution system (where everyone receives a quota objective) would have upset over 90% of the salesmen. On the other hand, if we had used a pure objective system, assuming that the same results could have been achieved, which is questionable, we would have paid around $23,000 ($20,000 × 8/7), about 50% more.

In addition to the $8 million achieved in 1975, another $7 million of possible sales were identified, which represented significant revenue potential for 1976. The overall result of the program, therefore, totaled $15 million.

For 1976, however, a new objective of $16 million was set for the same product. Once again, the company decided to use the OFA system exclusively for this bonus, as well as the regular incentive program.

For 1976, 95% of all salesmen submitted forecasts, and 40% succeeded. The final achievement was $30 million, with the following distribution:

1976 sales from sales identified in 1975	$ 4.6 million
1976 sales never forecasted	6.7 million
1976 sales forecasted by salesmen	18.7 million
Total	$30.0 million

The most impressive fact was that in March 1976 (i.e., seven months before closing their orders), the salesmen who brought in those $18.7 million of forecasted orders had told the company that they expected to sell $18 million. They reached 104% of their forecast in only the second year of the experiment with the OFA system. This precision proved that a forecasting system with salesmen participation under the OFA grid would work and was efficient.

Once again, additional possible customers were identified and sales calls started. This time, a potential revenue of $18 million passed to 1977, and management felt that a new contest in 1977 was, therefore, not needed.

It is important to point out that IBM Brazil's success with OFA also has been dependent on other factors, such as strong central coordination, an effective education program, and accurate responses to customers' needs. The bonus was part of a complete marketing program.

The most important feature introduced by the system was undoubtedly the participation of the employees in creating their own objectives, which enhanced their overall motivation toward attaining the company's goals. The OFA system does not ignore the company's goals; on the contrary, it stresses their importance by setting them as the main objective in the bonus calculation.

Table A
Sales contest objectives by sales group

	Group A	Group B	Group C	Total
Objective by salesman	$ 12,700	31,750	50,800	—
Expected sales	$500,000	2,800,000	3,700,000	$7,000,000
Total objectives to sell	39.37	88.19	72.83	
Bonus by objectives	$ 100	100	100	
Bonus for perfect forecast	$ 4,725	10,583	8,740	$ 24,048
Bonus for no forecast	$ 2,362	5,292	4,370	$ 12,024

Table B
Result of sales contest by sales group

	Group A	Group B	Group C	Total
Plan	$500,000	2,800,000	3,700,000	$7,000,000
Actual results	$400,000	4,100,000	3,500,000	$8,000,000
Percentage of salesmen	36%	44	19	100%
Percentage of salesmen with orders	2%	4	2	8%
Total bonus paid	$ 2,350	$ 10,370	$ 4,040	$ 16,760

Confronting Comparable Worth

The term may be easy to dismiss, but the underlying problem — discriminatory pay disparities — will not go away

George P. Sape

Coping with comparable worth

Attacks on comparable worth come from every quarter these days. Government officials disparage the concept publicly. Business representatives charge that it will distort job markets, hamper competition, and unfairly redistribute wages. Even federal regulatory agencies seem to be backing away from any large-scale commitment to the idea of equal pay for comparable but dissimilar work.

Yet corporate executives who ignore comparable worth do a disservice to their companies and their employees. For one thing, basic questions of equity and fairness remain unresolved, however poorly the issue may be framed. And for another, the courts have made it clear that they will not tolerate sex-based wage discrimination by any employer, public or private.

Executives who see the logic of both law and equity will want to consider the course of action this author recommends. Drawing on both the judicial record and corporate experience, he urges managers to resist the temptation to view the problem as one that can be solved by raises alone. Instead they must examine all their company's compensation and employment practices to look for evidence of unsuspected discrimination.

A lawyer and former counsel to the U.S. Senate Subcommittee on Labor, Mr. Sape has written extensively about the effects of equal opportunity legislation on employment practices. He is vice president of Organization Resources Counselors, Inc. in New York, international consultants in human resources management.

Illustration by Karen Watson.

In December 1983 the Federal District Court for the state of Washington awarded damages of $800 million to $1 billion to female state employees for sex-based wage discrimination. This ruling, decided under the theory of comparable worth, represents the largest damage award ever handed down under the equal employment laws. It also dramatizes the potential liability this area of the law holds for all employers.

In this case, *AFSCME* v. *State of Washington*, decided under Title VII of the Civil Rights Act of 1964, the court found that the state had deliberately underpaid women in female-dominated state jobs compared with what they were paid in male-dominated state jobs. The damages assessed by the court in this ruling, which affected approximately 15,000 state workers, represented the amount the court thought necessary to correct the current effects of past discrimination in the state's pay system. In addition, the state may have to adjust the women's salaries upward by as much as 30% to counter future discrimination. Even while the decision is on appeal, the state has begun to distribute immediate pay raises to those jobs that are furthest below the "comparable worth measurement line."

Although the damages have not been as dramatic, private employers, too, have been held liable for pay disparities. In *Taylor* v. *Charley Brothers Company*, for example, the court found widespread evidence of sexual discrimination within the company. Accordingly, it ordered the employer to raise the wages of its women warehouse employees so that they would be more equivalent to those given the men who did similar work.

If the *State of Washington* ruling survives further legal challenges, and if employers lose other comparable worth cases awaiting decision by the courts, the pressure to correct male-female pay disparities or face damaging lawsuits will mount. Even now, we can reasonably expect other suits that may have been dormant or under consideration over the past few years to be activated with renewed enthusiasm. Recently, for example, the American Nurses' Association filed an action against the state of Illinois with allegations similar to those that led to the Washington ruling. And similar suits on behalf of women state employees have also begun in Michigan, Hawaii, and California.

In addition, at least one state has acted voluntarily to redress civil service wage disparities uncovered in the course of a 1979 pay-practices study. In 1982 the Minnesota legislature changed its personnel law to require pay equity, established a process for correcting existing disparities, and ordered continuing supervision of state jobs and wages. In 1983 it voted to put $21.8 million into a separate fund for general wage adjustments, benefiting some 8,200 employees. So far the state has paid out about $13.1 million from that fund.

The U.S. Equal Employment Opportunity Commission, the agency responsible for examining allegations of wage-based discrimination involving federal laws, has a large number of comparable worth cases pending. Severely criticized by the House Committee on Government Operations in 1984 for failing to move more quickly, the commission has established a task force to evaluate its role in this area.

It is unlikely, however, that major actions will be forthcoming given the strong opposition to comparable worth voiced by various members of the Reagan administration. (While the staff at the EEOC has not openly attacked the concept, officials at the Department of Justice and the Council of Economic Advisers have been sharply critical, as has the chairman of the U.S. Commission on Civil Rights.) Thus the issue is likely to evolve through state actions, similar to those mentioned, and through lawsuits where pay disparity is a concern.

Evolution of comparable worth

The forces that are shaping the comparable worth or pay disparity issue are both structural and legal. Over time, however, employers' primary concerns are more likely to be their own compensation practices and employee-relations administration than the details of specific court rulings.

Wage comparability surfaced as a discrete issue within the broader framework of EEO concerns when women's activist groups realized that "equal pay for equal work," the traditional standard for determining pay discrimination, left some important sources of pay disparity unaddressed. This standard is set forth in the 1963 Equal Pay Act, which predates Title VII, and addresses wage disparity not as a civil rights matter but merely as one of a series of pay administration questions embodied in the Fair Labor Standards Act. Moreover, in adopting the Equal Pay Act, Congress specifically rejected the comparison of men's salaries with women's salaries when the jobs could not be shown to be equal or substantially equivalent.

As women's understanding of workplace discrimination evolved, their attention shifted from the problems of equal pay to the issue of comparable pay. This shift was premised on the realization that even though the Equal Pay Act was correcting pay rates in substantially equivalent jobs held by both men and women, such jobs represented only a portion of those women held. Most women-dominated jobs, in fact, had no equivalent male comparisons and were thus outside the scope of the Equal Pay Act.

Accordingly, women began to concentrate on female-dominated jobs, which have no male-dominated equivalents against which direct salary comparisons can be made. So the issue of pay disparity widened from a focused concern with equal pay to an examination of job segregation in the workplace. This shift is critical because it means that the problem of wage disparity now potentially involves an organization's entire job structure, not just a few jobs that may be directly compared with each other. Discrimination remains an open question as long as certain jobs are held predominantly by women, and as long as those jobs are, by and large, lower paid.

By 1979 several studies had appeared suggesting that women continue to receive lower earnings because of a two-part act of discrimination: one, tacitly, if not overtly, employers support male-female job segregation, and two, they assign a lower value to jobs where women predominate. Women's advocates then began to focus on the way job worth is determined and to claim that the value given to female-dominated jobs does not represent their true worth, that it is not comparable to the value assigned other jobs in the organization filled predominantly by men.

Searching for standards

Following hearings on this issue in 1980, the EEOC concluded that there was reason to believe that discrimination could have caused the disparities in wages between male and female jobs. But the commission was unable to agree on standards for addressing the problem. Rather than promulgate rules and regulations, therefore, it asked the National Academy of Sciences to study the question and suggest an

HARVARD BUSINESS SCHOOL PRESS, BOSTON, MA 02163

THANK YOU FOR YOUR INTEREST IN THIS BOOK
We would like to know more about our readers. Please complete and return this card:

Book Title/Author _____
Purchased at _____
Comments _____
_____
_____

☐ **Please send me the Harvard Business School Press book catalog.**
☐ **Please send me information on forthcoming books in:**

☐ Accounting/Control
☐ Finance
☐ Manufacturing/Operations Mgt.
☐ Marketing
☐ Human Resource Management
☐ Information Technology

☐ General Management/Business Policy
☐ International Business
☐ Business and the Public Sector
☐ Business History
☐ Industry Studies – please specify:
_____

☐ **I am interested in academic adoption materials from Harvard Business School.**
☐ **I am interested in corporate training materials from Harvard Business School.**
☐ **I am interested in subscription information from the *Harvard Business Review*.**
☐ **My Job Title/Industry** _____

Your Name _____
Address _____
_____
City _____ State _____ Zip _____

Quantity discounts are available on corporate and institutional orders of HBS Press books.
For further information, call (617) 495-6700.   RRC6

HBS PRESS

Harvard Business School Press
Boston, Massachusetts 02163

NO POSTAGE
NECESSARY
IF MAILED
IN THE
UNITED STATES

BUSINESS REPLY MAIL
FIRST CLASS   PERMIT NO. 2725   BOSTON, MA

POSTAGE WILL BE PAID BY ADDRESSEE:

Harvard Business School Press
Harvard Business School
Boston, Massachusetts 02163

approach. The academy's findings are inconclusive, however, and the EEOC to date has not developed a unified approach to wage comparability. In fact, congressional criticism notwithstanding, the EEOC's case-by-case approach is probably the only responsible course available given the absence of a uniform standard.

In the meantime, pay disparity has taken on greater definition in the courts. In an important case before the Supreme Court, for example, employer groups argued that since the Equal Pay Act precludes the comparison of dissimilar jobs, comparable worth advocates have no legal authority to challenge the issue. In 1982 the Supreme Court rejected the argument, however, and ruled instead in *The County of Washington* v. *Gunther* that the later-adopted and broader protections contained in Title VII of the Civil Rights Act could include legal challenges to rates of pay for dissimilar jobs when discrimination was claimed as the reason for the disparity. The court did not, however, embrace comparable worth as an appropriate response in such instances. It appeared to suggest that traditional EEO remedies might be more appropriate, as determined on a case-by-case basis.

This decision demonstrated that employers cannot automatically insulate themselves from comparable worth challenges. But it said nothing about the kinds of standards to be applied in such cases. Rulings in parallel cases involving private employers, however, shed some light on this question.

In 1980 in *IUE* v. *Westinghouse Electric Corporation*, for example, the Federal Court of Appeals for the Third Judicial Circuit ruled that a union acting on behalf of its members could sue for pay adjustments if it could establish that an employer had knowingly set wage rates so that women were paid less than men for doing similar jobs. Because the dispute was settled out of court, the ruling never addressed the question of whether the company had underpaid women unlawfully. But it did establish an important legal principle that has yet to be fully developed in the courts, that is, the appropriate standard for proving the existence of a discriminatory pay disparity.

The burden of proof

In the *Westinghouse* decision the court concluded that the "disparate impact" standard, which places the burden of proof on the employer and has traditionally been used to establish violations under Title VII, could be used only as a starting point for a pay disparity inquiry. Establishing the existence of a violation would require some demonstration that the employer had acted intentionally: inferences of discrimination drawn from statistical findings would not constitute sufficient proof.

This modification suggests that good faith reliance on well-established, racially or sexually neutral practices to set wages and salaries may insulate an employer from subsequent liability for pay disparity. Whether the courts will apply this standard broadly cannot be known, given the paucity of rulings in this area. But the few cases that have addressed this issue indicate that the courts may be willing to use this more favorable standard in pay disparity suits.

While the *Westinghouse* decision raises important issues for the development of pay equity, it does not provide much guidance for those who want to know how an employer's liability for sex-based wage discrimination might be determined. At about the same time, however, the Federal District Court for the Western District of Pennsylvania handed down a ruling in *Taylor* v. *Charley Brothers Company* that bears directly on this question.

In this case the employer was accused of illegal wage discrimination for paying women warehouse workers less than their male counterparts. The allegation stemmed from the fact that the company classified its warehouse employees into two departments by sex and used a different wage scale for each, even though the employees performed similar tasks.

To explain these pay practices, the company presented a variety of data including a job evaluation study that appeared to justify the wage differentials. But the plaintiffs had also commissioned an evaluation study, and it painted a different picture. On the basis of this second study, which the court found more accurate, some of the warehouse jobs were judged to be equal under the Equal Pay Act standard, while others were deemed comparable though not equal. Accordingly, the court ordered the company to equalize wages where appropriate and to adjust others upward so that the women's pay would be more "equivalent" to that received by the men.

What makes the *Charley Brothers* decision important is not the fact that the court rejected the employer's job evaluation study but rather the reasons for its action. The record is full of evidence indicating widespread and blatant sex discrimination in the company. And even though this evidence had no direct connection with the company's wage rates, it was noted repeatedly by the court. We can safely assume that it colored the credibility of the company's job evaluation and contributed to the court's finding of significant sex-based discrimination, manifest in part by the pay disparities.

As the *Charley Brothers* decision emphasizes, none of these initial cases makes it clear whether the courts were applying a comparable worth standard or whether their decisions were based on more traditional legal principles that prohibit various acts of discrimination, including those arising out of compensation-based actions. It was also unclear how the courts would treat the existing standards by which discrimination could be proved in the context of the various components that make up the comparable worth issue. In 1984, however, the Ninth Circuit Court of Appeals handed down a ruling in *Spaulding* v. *University of Washington* that may signal an accepted judicial response to pay disparity issues. (This likelihood is enhanced by the fact that the Supreme Court denied review of the case and tacitly accepted the way in which it was resolved.)

The *Spaulding* case was brought by a group of nurses who claimed that they were the victims of illegal wage discrimination under both equal pay and comparable worth theories. To state their case, the plaintiffs compared various university jobs, including their own, in which women faculty members were paid less than men in different teaching posts. In addition, the plaintiffs claimed that the university's reliance on external market rates perpetuated historical sex-based discrimination.

In denying these arguments the appeals court seems to have accepted the loosely worded standard of proof set forth in the *Westinghouse* decision. The court rejected the plaintiffs' reliance on statistical evidence, ruling that the mere existence of a disparity does not establish discrimination. And it also rejected the plaintiffs' argument that the use of external market rates was a cause of discrimination, concluding instead that these rates were never meant to constitute a neutral employment policy. The court went on to state that the plaintiffs would have had to adduce more proof of discrimination than a disparity caused by external market forces. (As should be obvious, the court was not confronted with evidence of discrimination, such as that found in the *Charley Brothers* case, which would lead it to question the university's wage assignments.)

Thus both the *Spaulding* and *Westinghouse* decisions suggest that to prevail in a pay disparity allegation plaintiffs will have to demonstrate some specific and deliberate acts of discrimination and that the inference of discrimination drawn from the existence of disparities is not a sufficient meeting of that burden.

An unavoidable problem

Factors other than the law also ensure that pay disparity will be a key issue for corporate managers in the years ahead. Among them are certain critical workplace realities that affect most companies.

First, de facto segregation still exists in most workplace environments. The pressure for equal employment brought to bear during the last 15 years has significantly altered neither sex stereotyping nor women's continuing self-selection of "women's jobs."

Second, women's already large presence in the work force will continue to rise. Women accounted for the majority of the labor force's growth in the last ten years, and the Bureau of Labor Statistics (BLS) projects that they will make up two-thirds of the new entrants between 1985 and 1995. Under the most conservative estimates, women will account for some 47% of the total work force by 1995.

Third, women's earnings continue to lag behind those of men, even though they account for an ever-increasing share of the labor market. This earnings gap is cited by advocates of women's equality to demonstrate the continued existence of widespread wage discrimination.

BLS statistics, for example, show that in 1981 women earned 62 cents for every dollar earned by men, compared with 59 cents in 1970. Further, and more troubling, the gap in average starting salaries has widened over the past ten years, according to a study by Gordon W. Green, Jr., a labor economist with the Census Bureau. Whereas white women, on the average, could expect a starting salary that was 86% of a white male's in 1970, by 1980 the figure had dropped to 83%. Given the importance many compensation experts attach to starting salaries as a key determinant of future earnings, this finding may prove critical as the wage disparity issue evolves.

A rise in legal challenges is likewise inevitable as more and more women's advocacy groups come to believe that the current administration takes less interest in resolving EEO issues and that, as a consequence, employers are relaxing affirmative action efforts. Litigation in this area will also be spurred as some unions, seeking to expand their membership bases, assume an advocacy role on women's issues. (This factor is already evident in the *State of Washington* lawsuit and in recent actions by 9 to 5 Women Working, the public education and advocacy arm of the Service Employees International Union.)

Finally, with rising state-level litigation and interest in state government pay practices, pressure will continue to build for local legislation. Already, 15 states include some form of comparable worth standard in their pay statutes: Alaska, Arkansas, Georgia, Hawaii, Idaho, Kentucky, Maine, Maryland, Massachusetts, Nebraska, North Dakota, Oklahoma, South Dakota, Tennessee, and West Virginia. California, Montana, and Oregon have indicated that their fair employment practices laws allow them to inquire into comparable worth issues. And Minnesota has enacted legislation making equity compulsory for state employees' pay.

While much of this activity is haphazard and refers only to state payrolls, the questions and

Comparable worth 99

issues being debated are identical to those that confront private sector employers. So business executives must follow both the evolution of federal law and parallel developments at the state level.

What managers can do

Before management initiatives for coping with pay disparity can be developed, the interaction of the three basic components that underlie liability must be understood. These are job segregation, pay disparities, and the presence of discrimination.

Job segregation. Management must first ascertain whether any job segregation exists by identifying categories where women are in the large majority. While such job categories signal de facto segregation, they are not, by themselves, conclusive of any liability.

Pay disparity. Once job segregation has been identified, employers must determine whether the women's jobs are lower paid than similar, but not identical, jobs held by men. In making this determination, managers should be careful to choose jobs that can be reasonably compared. A data entry operator's salary grade should be compared with a programmer's (assuming that the latter is a male-dominated job), for example, rather than with a marketing manager's.

Other comparisons should likewise be made on the basis of common, though not identical, elements such as employment in the same department, plant, or other facility. Some observers recommend an even broader approach, such as analyzing all salaries within a certain "band" of pay in the company and then determining whether sex may have played a role in the placement of employees in those bands.

Presence of discrimination. Determining whether discrimination has caused pay disparities is the last and most difficult step in this process. Typically, some combination of history, the evolution of the job or job family, job evaluation (where used), and supply-and-demand considerations explains most salary differences. But none of these factors is immune to discrimination, and in the last analysis management may be able to ascribe only a portion of an existing wage gap to neutral sources that a court or outside agency would accept as nondiscriminatory. The remainder can therefore be presumed to be the result of discrimination and its elimination set as the attainment of comparable worth.

As the interaction of these three components demonstrates, the critical issue is not "comparable worth," as the term is commonly used, but rather the existence of unexplained pay disparity, with comparable worth the objective of any necessary corrective action. Second, and perhaps more important, analyzing and identifying the scope of the problem is more difficult than it may appear.

What the courts have said

The problem with eliminating pay disparity is that usually no one element accounts for all the causes of possible discrimination. As a result, the courts have sought to examine an employer's conduct in evaluating pay discrimination charges rather than establish a general standard by which illegal pay disparity can be judged. An employer's efforts to identify and correct perceived pay inequities in its work force, then, are an important factor when the courts determine liability.

For example, in the *State of Washington* ruling the court examined the employer's conduct as well as the existence of pay disparities. As it happened, the state had conducted several internal studies that seemed to show its pay scales for predominantly women's jobs to be undervalued by its own standards. After identifying the disparity attributable to discrimination, however, the state failed to act on its own findings. Faced with this fact, the court could only conclude that the state was engaging in willful discrimination.

In contrast, another federal court, examining similar pay disparities in *Briggs* v. *City of Madison*, found that the Wisconsin city had gone to great lengths to ferret out possible discrimination in its pay systems. Concluding that the market value established from salary surveys for key benchmark jobs was the only factor accounting for the continued existence of the disparities and that this factor was beyond the city's control, the court rejected a finding of illegal discrimination.

The court's reasoning in the *Spaulding* decision reinforces the *City of Madison* ruling. Although the decisions differ slightly, both conclude that the use of external market wage data does not, by itself, constitute discrimination under the law, even if it results in pay disparities. These rulings, along with earlier decisions on the use of market data, suggest that employers are protected from wage-disparity liability so long as the information comes from bona fide salary surveys and has not been manipulated. (This assumes, of course, that the court also finds no evidence of intentional discrimination in other aspects of the employer's conduct.)

Between these extremes lie a series of practical problems for managers grappling with this issue. Chief among them are the legal risks that can flow from a proactive posture. These risks will vary depending on the actions a company's management undertakes. But employers must recognize the fact that any initiative that calls attention to internal inequities can create a liability-producing situation.

The worst example of this is, of course, the *State of Washington* case in which the employer's liability was drawn from its own initiatives. Clearly, it is foolhardy to neglect taking corrective action once potential problems have been found.

Legal problems may persist even where management is committed to remedial action because there is no clear-cut standard for judging pay-rate comparability. Attempts to solve disparity problems through wage adjustments alone may only aggravate the situation by introducing new liability through ill-conceived or improperly executed pay realignments.

How one company coped

To understand how management can approach pay disparity from a broad-based perspective, let us consider what one large company in the chemical industry has done. Aware of pay disparity's growing prominence and the resolution of threshold legal issues in the Supreme Court's *Gunther* ruling, senior management concluded that it would be prudent to examine its internal pay relationships for areas that could lead to potential liability.

These managers believed that if such pay inequities existed, they would hurt employee morale and hamper employee relations and that the company probably had an implicit obligation under its affirmative action plan to address the issue. They were also concerned about the possibility of creating bigger problems down the line, given that the company's internal human resource projections showed a higher proportion of women workers at all levels during the next ten years.

The company ruled out massive wage readjustments from the start. Its managers doubted that an across-the-board adjustment would solve the problem in the long run, even though it might provide some short-term relief. Wage and salary administrators were concerned that a large wage-scale adjustment would distort the company's competitive position in the wage market and unjustifiably disrupt its wage and salary program.

Thus the company rejected single-factor thinking at the outset. Instead its management marked out three areas for its inquiry: (1) organizational questions, (2) specific compensation-administration issues, and (3) an evaluation of existing EEO principles as they would apply to pay disparity. It appointed a management task force to evaluate each area and tie the findings together into a comprehensive action plan.

It also concluded that the study should be initiated in response to a request from the company's legal department to protect the findings.

Task force members received assignments consistent with their area of expertise. Staff responsible for organizational issues, for example, were asked to identify female-dominated job groups and answer a series of questions about them: How long had the jobs been that way? Had their status or organizational placement changed over time? What were the conditions surrounding them?

The compensation staff was asked to conduct quantitative and qualitative evaluations of women's salaries across the entire company and within smaller units where meaningful comparisons between male- and female-dominant job groups could be made. It was asked to review job evaluation standards for bias and for inadvertent omissions that could be relevant to the women's jobs but would not apply to jobs held by men. And it was asked to examine salary policies and procedures, including the role of outside surveys in setting salaries, starting salary practices, and provisions for movement within and between salary grades.

The third segment of the task force studied some of the same factors as the other two, but it approached them from an EEO standpoint. It reviewed the job groups identified by the organization staff to determine whether rates of participation in these clusters had shifted over the years and what EEO-specific steps had been taken, consistent with the company's affirmative action plan, to change the make-up of both female-dominant and male-dominant job groups. The EEO staff also conducted an audit based on Equal Pay Act principles to ascertain whether pay disparities existed between men and women whose jobs involved substantially equivalent skills, effort, and responsibility.

By the time the task force completed its work, it had identified several potential problem areas:

1 Predominantly female job groups existed throughout the company, with particularly heavy concentrations in clerical work, electronic data processing, and some production jobs. In every instance these were the lower paying jobs in the organization, and all had been dominated by women since the passage of Title VII.

2 Modifications to the company's job evaluation plan, installed during the 1960s, had been small scale and few. Most involved adding new job titles and functions to keep up with technological advances. The task force felt that some of the determinants were outdated and that some could arguably be seen as discriminatory.

3 The pay audit revealed a significant number of women whose salaries were lower than the

company's statistical salary model predicted. Ironically, promotions created most of these discrepancies because corporate policy on merit increases limited raises to a fixed percentage of the employee's current salary. So the women continued to fall behind in pay as they moved ahead in grade.

4   Efforts to break up female-dominated job clusters, such as seniority and pay-rate protection, special training programs, and one-time incentive payments, had produced few changes. They had, however, changed the composition of some job categories.

5   The company was relying heavily on third-party surveys to set its entry-level salaries, using several simultaneously to ensure the best possible fit with its job structure.

On the basis of the task force findings, management adopted a five-year plan to address these areas. The plan established an immediate review process for all women whose salaries were below grade and set in motion a study of the total cost of amending the company's merit increase policy to eliminate salary lags for rapidly advancing women and minorities.

It also provided for a reexamination of the standards applied to women's jobs, authorized reevaluations where necessary, and instituted an organizationwide review to determine whether some jobs could be combined with allied male-dominated positions to expand their functions and achieve a better male-female balance. At the same time, the plan called for continuing efforts to speed the promotion of women into higher paying, male-dominated jobs through existing affirmative action procedures.

In addition to these carefully documented steps, the company set up a series of ongoing audit procedures to get better, more current data on a broad range of job issues. It decided not to alter its participation in existing salary surveys, choosing instead to broaden the survey population for female-dominated jobs by seeking out male job holders who could fit within the survey's parameters.

This company's approach reflects a positive and comprehensive view of pay disparity. Its initiatives are clearly in step with the law as it is evolving, yet they neither overstate corporate objectives nor overextend corporate resources. Moreover, while the plan commits the company to meaningful change, it does so in ways that are consistent with its established business practices.

Other executives may opt for different solutions consistent with their organizational needs. Managers bound by collective bargaining, for example, cannot initiate unilateral actions and will have to negotiate to get some changes they may want to make.

Nevertheless, there are several basic steps that all employers should consider given the direction of judicial decisions in this area.

Examine each element of the compensation system for controls on possible discrimination. Because pay systems contain many components that influence salary, the number of safeguards built into a compensation program to ensure EEO sensitivity will affect any subsequent findings of discrimination. Examples of safeguards include such items as EEO training on compensation issues for wage and salary administrators, periodic review by management of the salary decisions that affect male and female workers, and strong evidence that senior management oversees compensation programs with an eye toward their effect on corporate EEO policy. Management should also recognize that most compensation systems are neutral as they relate to discrimination and that their effects or application, therefore, are not self-correcting in areas where patterns of disparity may be found.

Review key job evaluation determinations for bias. Because many pay disparity cases can be traced to job evaluations, it is important to examine the factors considered relevant in a job's initial determination and in subsequent reevaluation. The focus of this examination should fall on those job elements in which "male values" were given more worth than "female values." Management should realize, however, that there is no perfect job evaluation plan and that it can probably more effectively audit and manipulate its current plan than try to install a new one.

Audit the impact of pay practices on men's and women's salaries on a regular basis. Most larger companies can accomplish this by developing a corporatewide statistical model of the pay program and running a regression against all incumbents. Management should examine any statistically significant findings to ensure that factors other than sex can account for the disparity. For smaller populations the same result can be obtained by examining the distribution of men and women within set salary bands without the aid of a computer.

Work to eliminate job segregation. Since this is a long-term proposition, employers should carefully document all attempts to move female incumbents to other, better paying, male-dominated jobs. Rejection by female incumbents of attempts by management to move them to male-dominated, better paying jobs is particularly important in this regard.

Take corrective action. Employers who identify potentially discrimination-based pay disparities should begin to take corrective action. This does not mean an immediate adjustment of 100 cents on the dollar for all employees affected, but rather a commitment over the longer term to eliminate unjustifiable disparities. Good-faith efforts to address internal disparity problems and work toward their elimination will not obviate the possibility of a lawsuit. But on the basis of the case law to date, they can reduce an employer's liability if a complaint reaches the courts.

Probing Opinions

Benson Rosen, Sara Rynes, and Thomas A. Mahoney

Compensation, jobs, and gender

Should a female nurse make as much as a male truck driver?

Female nurses in a Denver city hospital demanded pay equal to that of male employees doing outdoor maintenance and gardening work. Prison matrons in Oregon sued for the same pay scale as male guards. And in San Jose, California, municipal workers staged a nine-day strike when a city job evaluation study showed that female employees earned an average 15% less than males working in jobs of comparable worth.

Questions of what constitutes fair pay are surfacing with increasing frequency, maybe because women's advocacy groups and female employees have become more insistent on pay equity between men and women. Indeed, studies show that despite equal employment opportunity and affirmative action mandates, most working women continue to earn less than most working men. Some people say that women who want to earn more should choose higher paying careers. Others say that companies should value more highly the skills and responsibilities associated with typically female jobs. They support adoption of a "comparable worth" compensation policy, whereby companies would pay the same for jobs of equal value regardless of market wage rates and other factors.

Can and should jobs of equal value be compensated equally regardless of other factors? And what are the implications of setting pay according to objective criteria? In responding to a survey last summer, some 900 HBR readers answered these and other questions about compensation policy. The diversity of the responses reflects the complexity of the issues and the distance we have yet to go to arrive at a consensus. Men and women readers disagree, for example, about the causes of the earnings gap and about the likely consequences of closing it. While male readers focused on the problems that a comparable worth pay policy might create, female readers mentioned the potential gains in productivity and other positive aspects of adopting such a policy.

In light of these findings, companies may want to reconsider their compensation schemes. The authors outline some options and discuss the problems and benefits inherent in each stance.

Mr. Rosen is professor of business administration at the University of North Carolina. Ms. Rynes is assistant professor of human resources at the New York State School of Industrial and Labor Relations at Cornell University. Mr. Mahoney is Frances Hampton Currey Professor at the Owen Graduate School of Management, Vanderbilt University.

Can an employer justify paying auto mechanics more than the city pays librarians? Do prison guards deserve higher salaries than prison matrons? A recent National Academy of Science study reports that despite 20 years of antidiscrimination legislation, the earnings of working women in the United States average less than 60% of men's earnings. Moreover, in 1978 the average male high school dropout earned more than a female college graduate. Although people disagree about how much of the earnings disparity between men and women they should attribute to discrimination in pay-setting practices, economic and sociological studies indicate that even after adjusting for differences in education and work experience approximately half the gap remains.[1]

Since the defeat of the Equal Rights Amendment, women's activist groups have become far more vocal about their intentions to make pay equity a top priority for legislators and to work vigorously for the election of politicians who will support measures to bring women to economic parity with men. Additionally, a recent Harris poll of 600 executives representing 1,200 of the largest U.S. corporations revealed that managers perceive an increasing militancy in women's demands for strong enforcement of equal pay provisions. Eleanor Holmes Norton, former head of the Equal Employment Opportunity Commission, has billed pay equity as the foremost labor issue of the 1980s.

These developments have set the stage for a lively debate over whether jobs of equal value should be compensated equally regardless of variations in job content or differences in negotiated or market wage rates.[2] While one can trace the emergence of this "comparable worth" debate to the recognition of sex-based disparities in pay, the question of pay equity cuts

---

1 George T. Milkovich, "The Emerging Debate," *Comparable Worth: Issues and Alternatives*, ed. E. Robert Livernash (Washington, D.C.: Equal Employment Advisory Council, 1980).

2 For opposing views on this issue, see E. Robert Livernash, *Manual on Pay Equity*, ed. Joy A. Grune (Washington, D.C.: Conference on Alternative State and Local Policies).

Exhibit I	Profile of HBR survey participants						
Sex			**Kind of organization**			**Functional area**	
Male	45.2%		Manufacturing, consumer goods	11.3%		Accounting	5.3%
Female	54.8		Manufacturing, industrial goods	19.1		Engineering, R&D	4.5
Age			Advertising, media publishing	4.7		Finance	8.6
Under 25	2.4%		Banking, investment, insurance	13.8		General management	38.0
26 to 35	37.4		Construction, mining, oil	4.0		Marketing	13.4
36 to 45	32.9		Defense or space industry	3.3		Personnel or labor relations	12.4
46 to 55	18.9		Education, social service	8.1		Production	2.7
56 and over	8.4		Government	4.3		Public relations	1.9
Geographical area			Management consulting	4.5		Other	13.2
Northeast	33.1%		Retail or wholesale trade	4.8		**Size of company**	
Midwest	26.9		Personal consumer service	1.5		One of the largest in the industry	54.7%
Southeast	11.6		Transportation, public utility	5.0		About average in size	25.8
Mountain	3.6		Other	15.6		Small	19.5
Southwest	8.1					Average percentage of work force unionized	20.7%
Far West	16.7					Average percentage of work force males	55.4%

across all occupations, regardless of the incumbent's sex. Once nurses and secretaries begin publicly questioning how their pay compares with that of painters or mail deliverers, male attorneys or accountants will start comparing their pay with that of auto mechanics or construction workers. Thus with increasing frequency modern organizations may have to explain and justify their pay-setting practices.

What factors have contributed to the salary gap between the sexes? What, if anything, should organizations do to narrow the earnings gap between their male and female employees? How should companies determine job worth, and who should do it? What would be the consequences for women, employers, and society if workers were paid according to some standard other than market value?

To learn what managers think about these issues, we surveyed a sample of HBR readers. We found that:

☐ Male and female readers disagree dramatically about the causes of the earnings gap as well as about the probable effectiveness and consequences of requiring a comparable worth approach to pay.

☐ Women tend more than men to attribute the salary gap to biases in organizational selection and compensation processes. Men, on the other hand, are more likely to blame women for choosing low-paying jobs with restricted career opportunities.

☐ Readers of both sexes believe that women's advocacy groups are more likely than personnel specialists, unions, or the federal government to champion the cause of comparable worth. Respondents see women's groups, however, as lacking the necessary organizational skills and political clout to effect major changes in compensation policy.

☐ Readers are divided with respect to both the feasibility and the desirability of moving toward a comparable worth approach to compensation. Many readers are convinced that any reduction in the earnings gap is fraught with dangers to American business, such as a rise in labor costs and a concomitant decrease in our ability to match foreign competition. Other readers think that efforts to reduce the salary differential might boost U.S. business through gains in productivity and work quality in jobs held predominantly by women.

The survey

We mailed questionnaires to 5,000 randomly selected HBR subscribers; our sample was evenly divided between men and women. We received 910 completed questionnaires, for a return rate of 19% (corrected for nondeliverable questionnaires). The complexity of the compensation issues coupled with the fact that the survey was mailed during a peak vacation period may have contributed to the low response rate. *Exhibit I* shows a profile of HBR survey participants.

We grouped our questions into six categories: (1) how salaries ought to be determined; (2) factors contributing to the male-female earnings gap; (3) pressures and prospects for change; (4) effectiveness of proposed remedies; (5) consequences of attempts to reduce the salary gap; and (6) reactions to the comparable worth issue. On most questions we asked respondents to choose a value between "not at all important (effective or likely)" to "extremely important (effective or likely)" on a five-point scale. We also gave participants the opportunity to express their opinions in answering a variety of open-ended questions, which

Exhibit II Importance factors should have in setting salaries

■ Males ■ Females

Percentage* 0 20 40 60 80 100

Factor	Males	Females
Performance requirements in terms of skills, level of responsibility, and amount of effort necessary for success.	96%	96%
Overall estimate of how much each position contributes to the organization (in terms of profits, customer service, quality of production, and so on).	73%	76%
Pay rates of other organizations for similar work in the same region or industry.	74%	70%
Minimal qualifications required of applicants (education or experience).	62%	66%
Relative scarcity or abundance of applicants for the job.	56%	45%
Results of negotiation between union and management.	34%	35%

*Percentage of respondents who rated the factor very or extremely important.

Exhibit III Factors that contribute to the salary gap between men and women

■ Males ■ Females

Percentage* 0 20 40 60 80 100

Factor	Males	Females
Conscious or unconscious bias in hiring decisions.	46%	84%
Discrimination in setting wage rates: men earn more than women in similar jobs.	40%	83%
Shorter career ladders and fewer advancement opportunities in "female" occupations.	52%	71%
Women willing to work for lower wages than men.	40%	54%
Greater unionization in traditionally male occupations.	21%	33%
Women won't accept responsibility or relocate to further their careers.	35%	20%
A concentration of women in part-time jobs.	32%	16%
Excess labor in traditionally female occupations.	27%	19%
High turnover and absenteeism among women.	15%	4%
Women can't perform jobs that require physical or mental exertion.	11%	3%

*Percentage of respondents who rated the factor very or extremely important.

we analyzed and categorized by content.

Criteria for setting salaries

To get a picture of what respondents think is important in setting wages and salaries, we asked them to rate several criteria commonly used as the bases for pay determination. *Exhibit II* displays the findings.

Taken together, ratings and open-ended comments suggest general agreement as to what factors ought to be important in pay-setting practices. Most participants agreed, for instance, that the traditional criteria of skill, effort, and responsibility are important in setting wages. When considering organizational contribution, market wages and labor supplies, and collective bargaining, readers agreed less. Some people may have rejected a criterion because they saw difficulties in applying it rather than because they disagreed with the concept itself. For instance, many organizations claim to pay according to relative contribution; but skill, effort, and responsibility may be the defining criteria.

Men and women responded similarly to all criteria for pay except one: the relative scarcity or abundance of applicants for a job. People often cite the relative abundance of applicants for "female" jobs as one of the reasons for male-female pay differentials; considerably more men in the survey than women agreed that labor supply should be an important factor.

The fact that virtually all readers considered a variety of factors to be either very or extremely important suggests that optimal pay-setting practices stem from a workable balance between a number of factors. In addition, responses to open-ended questions stressed the need for management to incorporate into its compensation approach unique circumstances, such as civil service regulations, the company's financial condition, location, changes in the cost of living, and intangible job characteristics such as opportunities for advancement or unusually stringent requirements for loyalty, teamwork, or confidentiality.

Salary gaps & career traps

Men and women have strikingly different views on the cause of the earnings gap between the sexes (see *Exhibit III*). Overall, our results suggest that women are far more likely than men to attribute earnings disparities to organizational practices, while men tend to place most of the responsibility on women themselves.

More than four-fifths of our female respondents (compared with less than one-half of the men) believe that women earn less than men because of discrimination in organizational hiring and compensation systems. Women were also more likely than men to stress the scarcity of promotional opportunities in traditionally female occupations and the lesser tendency of women to organize for collective bargaining. Interestingly, women also view female willingness to work for low wages as a more important cause of the earnings gap than did men.

Responses to open-ended questions suggested that women attribute much of the problem to social norms and constraints that, from early childhood, limit women's aspirations for careers in nontraditional, high-paying occupations. In addition, women think that continued resistance by both male and female co-workers to women in nontraditional careers further dampens women's aspirations. While many women acknowledge that women's lower earnings are a direct consequence of their occupational choices, they nevertheless view those choices as heavily constrained by societal and organizational preferences and prejudices. Further, most female participants maintain that organizations could do more in the way of training, developing, and upgrading women and in promoting a more egalitarian distribution of the sexes across occupations.

While most of the written comments focused on job placement issues like hiring and promotion, other responses suggested the existence of widespread feelings that organizations seriously undervalue and unfairly compensate jobs traditionally held by women. Respondents raised objections to what they perceive as status differentials in job titles (e.g., male "managers" versus female "supervisors") as well as to the low weights attached to typically feminine skills in most job evaluation and compensation schemes. Finally, readers are considerably dissatisfied that compensation decisions tend to be made by male-dominated, if not exclusively male, compensation committees.

Although males were far more likely than females to attribute pay disparities to women themselves, a sizable proportion of men nevertheless think that biases in hiring and compensation are important contributors to earnings inequality. Indeed, men cited conscious or unconscious bias in organizational hiring or pay practices as sources of the earnings gap more often than they did any of the factors directly attributable to women themselves. Men were, however, more likely than women to believe that females are either unwilling or unable to accept responsibility, to relocate when the job requires it, to attend work regularly, to accumulate seniority, and to perform jobs requiring heavy physical or intense mental exertion.

In their written comments men elaborated on the theme that women are victims of their own educational and career-related decisions. Some men expressed the belief that most women are ill-equipped – in terms of education, attitude, and experience – to move into higher paying executive positions. Others responded that women are too willing to abandon their careers to be considered reliable sources of executive talent. Finally, many male respondents echoed the belief of one financial analyst who said that women are paid less because of their "unwillingness to push for equivalent wages, choosing instead not to make an issue of it."

Males and females agree that in the long run, equity will oblige women to make earlier and firmer commitments to establishing careers and working their way up the corporate ladder. Men in particular see the need for women to be more active and assertive in managing their careers. While women agree, they expect their employers to help by removing obstacles to advancement and providing career-planning assistance. In the meantime, however, a number of female respondents think that companies should upgrade salaries of women trapped in low-paying careers to match those received by men in positions of similar responsibility.

Prospects for change

Clearly, readers are concerned about women's earnings, but what are the prospects for change? Opinions are divided on the likelihood of a national movement aimed at revising compensation practices and redressing perceived salary inequities. As item A of *Exhibit IV* shows, 50% of the male respondents but only 39% of the women anticipate a nationwide movement to raise women's earnings.

The following comments of those who foresee pressure for change cite women's increasing political activism, coupled with their advance to positions of power in companies, as the driving force:

> "The ERA movement will regroup and resurge. Salary equity is the next target."

> "Women's groups are becoming more sophisticated and better organized. The ERA fight has taught them some hard-earned lessons."

> "Women will run for political office and champion the cause of comparable worth."

> "Women are moving into high-ranking corporate positions, positions with clout to challenge the establishment."

Comments of those less inclined to expect change in women's earnings cite lack of social support as well as lack of commitment by women and unfavorable current economic conditions:

> "The mood of the country, unlike in the 1960s and 1970s, seems to be against or at least apathetic to national movements."

Exhibit IV	Prospects and pressures for change in compensation policies		
A	In the next few years, do you see a major national movement to raise women's earnings relative to men's? Percentage responding "yes":	Male respondents 50%	Female respondents 39%

B. Rank these groups according to their likelihood to support efforts to reduce salary differentials. Rank as number 1 the group most likely to support efforts.

	Average rank	
	Male respondents	Female respondents
Women's political groups	1.5	1.4
The federal government	2.5	3.1
Compensation specialists and personnel administrators	3.0	3.1
Organized labor	3.4	3.2

C. Rank these groups according to their power to influence compensation policy. Rank as number 1 the group with the most clout.

	Average rank	
	Male respondents	Female respondents
The federal government	1.9	1.9
Organized labor	2.6	2.2
Compensation specialists and personnel administrators	2.8	2.9
Women's political groups	3.1	3.3

D. What is the most effective way to reduce the salary gap between the sexes?

	Percentages agree		
	Male	Female	Both
Government should issue standardized guidelines for all organizations.	24%	41%	33.5%
Organizations should design their own strategies.	76%	59%	66.5%

"Most women don't feel that they can effect change, and most who are getting ahead don't want to take the time to get involved."

"Due to the dismal economic picture, women will continue to be laid off first and paid less than men. There is little hope for change until the company regains its strength."

Male and female participants agree on where pressure for change will most likely originate in the next few years. Item B of *Exhibit IV* shows that respondents of both sexes ranked women's political groups as most likely to work for change. Readers think it unlikely that organized labor, corporate offices, or the federal government will push hard for change. Yet according to other responses (summarized in item C of that exhibit), both men and women perceive the government as possessing the greatest power to bring about change. Women's political groups, the force viewed as most likely to push for change, ranks as least capable of wielding the clout necessary to effect it.

Voluntary or legislative action? Assuming the nation becomes committed to eliminating the earnings gap, respondents generally favored voluntary action by employers (see item D of *Exhibit IV*). It is interesting, however, that although women are less inclined to expect government action, they see it as the most effective way to eliminate the gap: almost twice as many women as men (41% compared with 24%) favored federal guidelines.

Jobs and gender 107

Respondents' preference for either voluntary action or federal guidelines is based more on rejection of one strategy than on strong support of the other. Those who favor voluntary action, for example, cited past problems with EEOC guidelines, difficulties with enforcement, administrative waste, and inevitable loopholes. Those who prefer federal guidelines based their choice on lack of faith in voluntary action and lack of other incentives for employers to raise women's wages relative to men's.

Some of the respondents rejected federal action and any specific policy for employer voluntary action on the grounds that neither remedy was necessary. According to these readers, as women move into traditionally male occupations, earnings differentials will disappear as a matter of course. And one person with extreme faith in voluntary action observed that "business has the message" so any social action is unnecessary.

Effectiveness of remedies

In the fourth section of the questionnaire we asked readers to rate the effectiveness of each of four approaches to narrowing the earnings gap between men and women and to write the reasons for their evaluations. (See *Exhibit V.*)

Break the mold. Almost two-thirds of both the men and the women we surveyed said that the most effective strategy for reducing the earnings differential is for women to prepare themselves to enter nontraditional, and presumably higher paying, occupations. Readers' comments highlighted the importance to women of breaking out of traditional female career tracks and noted the career opportunities for women in engineering, architecture, and computer technology. They also noted entrepreneurship as an option.

Comments also reflect an understanding that these changes won't be accomplished overnight. One executive noted that the process must begin with family socialization patterns and school guidance programs. One reader stated that the process will

Exhibit V: Effectiveness of proposed remedies

Percentage* of respondents who rate the remedy very or extremely effective.

Remedy	Males	Females
Encourage women to prepare themselves to move into nontraditional occupations.	66%	64%
Require compliance with government-issued guidelines designed to reduce or eliminate average earnings discrepancy between men and women.	28%	52%
Encourage employers to reevaluate job worth with an eye to raising salaries for "women's jobs" so they correspond more closely to salaries for "men's jobs".	27%	46%
Expand collective bargaining to cover more "female" occupations.	21%	42%

*Percentage of respondents who rate the remedy very or extremely effective.

Exhibit VI: Likely consequences of attempts to reduce the salary gap

Consequence	Males	Females
Government regulations and enforcement would result in a sharp increase in the cost of doing business.	66%	42%
Fewer sex-typed jobs would exist because more men would be attracted to positions traditionally held by women.	31%	63%
Productivity and quality in predominantly female occupations would rise because, through higher wages, such jobs would attract higher quality employees.	30%	56%
Unions representing male workers would press for increases in wages to offset the gains accruing to female workers.	44%	38%
The U.S. would experience even more intense competition from foreign producers because of the wage gains in primarily female positions.	41%	24%
There would be problems attracting workers to jobs requiring physical effort or poor working conditions without current pay differences.	28%	11%
Voluntary changes in compensation policy by one organization would lead to competitive erosion because other organizations would not follow similar practices.	22%	12%
A number of U.S. industries staffed by women (e.g., textiles) would probably disappear.	19%	10%

*Percentage of respondents who rate the consequence very or extremely likely.

---

require two more generations of workers.

Men and women view quite differently the effectiveness of other proposed remedies for reducing the earnings gap. Considerably more women thought that government guidelines would be effective in raising women's earnings relative to men's. Those who endorsed such guidelines recommended tax incentives for compliance with and penalties for avoidance of pay equity guidelines. A male manager of a major Illinois corporation suggested that "mandating an individual plan designed by each company and subject to approval by a bipartisan board consisting of government and industry representatives would provide the mechanism for reducing the earnings differential."

Similarly, half the women but only one-fourth of the men think that encouraging employers to reevaluate job worth would be effective in closing the gap. This disparity reflects women's greater attribution of the salary gap to sex discrimination in wage setting.

More women than men judge expansion of collective bargaining to more female occupations to be effective in reducing salary differentials. Several readers, however, fearing a backlash among predominantly male unionists, cautioned against collective bargaining as a remedy.

A retired schoolteacher expressed the sentiments of many: "One approach will not apply to all levels of skill or to all sections of the United States. We need a variety of methods to address this issue."

Consequences of closing the gap

Because some people think that the consequences of raising salary levels for predominantly female jobs will be dramatic for employers and society as a whole, we asked respondents about the implications of reducing sex-based pay differentials (see *Exhibit VI*).

Results suggest that, just as there are wide differences in how male and female respondents perceive the causes of the earnings gap, so are there notable disagreements between the sexes as to the likely consequences of attempting to eradicate it. Perhaps not surprisingly, male readers tend to see mostly negative consequences while female respondents anticipate more positive effects.

Men are considerably more likely than women to see attempts to narrow earnings disparities as sharply increasing business costs and weakening the U.S. competitive position in world markets. They also worry more about potential difficulties in recruiting employees for difficult or unpleasant positions, and they tend to believe that organizations voluntarily reducing salary inequities will be hurt because other employers won't follow suit.

Women, on the other hand, expect less serious economic consequences and anticipate more positive effects. For example, nearly twice as many women as men believe that pay increases for women's jobs will draw more productive individuals to those occupations. Women are also more than twice as likely to see a narrowing of the earnings differential as leading to a reduction in the number of sex-typed jobs.

Nearly half the women acknowledge that they too would expect short-run increases in business costs to follow implementation of a comparable worth approach to compensation. Women, however, expect long-run benefits such as higher productivity and stronger commitment to offset those higher costs.

Reactions to comparable worth

The final section of the survey dealt with readers' opinions about a comparable worth approach to setting wages and salaries in which jobs judged to be of equal value to an organization are compensated equally even if the nature of the work differs greatly (see the insert for details). Respondents explained in their own words what they believe to be the major positive and negative consequences of determining pay according to comparable worth. Their reponses are summarized here.

Problems

Negative reactions to comparable worth sorted roughly into five categories:

1 Implementation. A majority of both sexes cited practical problems in administering a comparable worth scheme as a major obstacle to paying jobs on the basis of relative worth. As one respondent put it, "It sounds great philosophically, but how do you make it work?"

At least two factors make implementing a comparable worth strategy problematic. First is the lack of consensus on what criteria should be used to determine job value and how criteria should be weighted. This is a crucial issue, since shifts in criteria and weights have been shown to produce different orderings in the overall "worth" of jobs.[3]

Readers we surveyed expressed concern that moving away from traditional criteria—such as skill, effort, responsibility, and working conditions—might indeed resolve some inequities but only at the risk of creating new ones. Some participants questioned how universal criteria could be defined so as to be equally relevant to such diverse jobs as secretary, molder, chemist, and operations manager. Also, as jobs become more complex and interdependent, it becomes harder to define common criteria of worth and to assess the unique contribution any given position makes to the organization.

The second troublesome aspect of implementation is the question of who is to be responsible for selecting and applying these job-worth criteria. Women in particular noted that men have traditionally taken responsibility for evaluating jobs and argued that this would have to change if job evaluation is to be fair and credible. Other respondents, however, expressed fear that mixed-sex compensation committees might get embroiled in political tugs-of-war and fail to evaluate jobs objectively through careful comparisons of job content. In any event, most of our participants seem to agree with the reader

---

3 Donald J. Treiman, *Job Evaluation: An Analytic Review* (Washington, D.C.: National Academy of Sciences, 1979).

who said, "You would need the wisdom of Solomon to make the necessary judgments."

2 Costs. The second serious concern with respect to comparable worth centers on the costs it might impose on U.S. businesses and consumers, such as reduced competitiveness in foreign markets. Since most of our participants take a dim view of attempting to narrow the earnings gap through a reduction in men's wages, the question seems to be by how much (rather than if) comparable worth would raise costs to U.S. employers. Readers also argued that insensitivity to market wages runs counter to our free enterprise system and that upgrading salaries inevitably leads to inflation, loss of competitive position, and reduced sales.

3 Resistance. Survey participants are also wary that attempts to tamper with long-standing, customary pay differentials could lead to unrest among male workers, who would see their relative advantage erode in the face of new standards for determining job worth. Some respondents saw lower morale and productivity, increased difficulty in attracting people to physically demanding or otherwise unpleasant work, and the emergence of efforts to reestablish customary differentials through such means as collective bargaining as potential problems.

4 The law. Respondents expressed concern that attempts to enforce a comparable worth approach to pay would become a legal nightmare. Given the inherent subjectivity in all pay-setting procedures and the unpredictability of the courts, participants worry that a shift toward a comparable worth philosophy would open a Pandora's box of discrimination litigation.

5 Social concerns. Finally, some participants worry about the social implications of adopting a comparable worth pay policy. Comparable worth might, some respondents wrote, intensify competition among the sexes, lower male self-esteem, and further change American family structures and child-rearing practices. One pessimistic Arizona attorney predicted

The legal history of comparable worth

In 1963 Congress passed the Equal Pay Act (EPA) requiring that men and women performing work of equal skill, effort, and responsibility under similar working conditions be paid equally, unless an employer could show that pay differentials were attributable to merit, incentive, or seniority systems or any factor other than sex. Over the years, courts have interpreted the equal work provisions of the act very narrowly; for the EPA to apply, jobs had to be virtually identical in terms of skill, effort, responsibility, and working conditions.

The 1964 Civil Rights Act contained a far broader antidiscrimination mandate than did the EPA. To clarify the relationship between the EPA and the CRA on matters of sex discrimination in compensation, Congress hastily passed an amendment by Senator Wallace F. Bennett stating that "it shall not be an unlawful employment practice...for any employer to differentiate upon the basis of sex in determining the amount of wages or compensation paid or to be paid to employees if such differentiation is authorized by the provisions of...the Equal Pay Act."

In the first 15 years of judicial rulings following enactment of the CRA, courts uniformly dismissed cases of women claiming pay discrimination if a man and a woman could not be shown to be performing equal work. Pay differentials in such cases were therefore insulated from litigation under both the EPA and the CRA. This pattern was disrupted in 1979 by the Third and Ninth Circuit Courts of Appeal, both of which held that the Bennett Amendment did not preclude women from pursuing pay discrimination claims simply because no male happened to perform identical work.

In 1981 in its most direct examination of the issue to date, the Supreme Court ruled in *County of Washington, Oregon* v. *Gunther* that, consistent with findings of the Third and Ninth Circuits, the Bennett Amendment does not restrict pay discrimination claims under the CRA to the "equal work" standard of the EPA. At the same time, however, the Court stressed the narrowness of its decision, noting that the women's claim in *Washington* v. *Gunther* was "not based on the controversial concept of comparable worth, under which plaintiffs might claim increased compensation on the basis of a comparison of the intrinsic worth or difficulty of their job with that of other jobs in the same organization or community. Rather, respondents seek to prove, by direct evidence, that their wages were depressed because of intentional sex discrimination, consisting of setting the wage scale for female guards, but not for male guards, at a level lower than its own survey of outside markets and the worth of the jobs warranted."

So although the Supreme Court holds that employees in completely sex-segregated jobs are not precluded from bringing pay discrimination claims under the CRA, it is not likely to find in favor of any claim in which the sole basis for bringing suit is that a particular job held by women is of worth comparable to better-paying jobs held by men. In cases of unequal work, the claimant will likely have to prove the employer's *intent* to discriminate; unfortunately, however, the Court has not delineated types of practices that reflect discriminatory intent.

Also unclear at this time are the probable actions of lower courts with respect to claims of pay discrimination. With a clear trend toward less frequent judicial review at the Supreme Court level, the outcomes of lower court decisions bear close scrutiny.

---

that "society would be so shaken up, men could never stand it."

Benefits

Respondents cited a number of positive effects on women, their employers, and society for moving in the direction of a comparable worth compensation policy. Survey participants viewed corporate efforts to upgrade pay levels in predominantly female jobs as having important symbolic as well as economic value in women's struggle for equal rights. A comparable worth compensation policy promises a higher standard of living and greater financial independence for U.S. women and their families. As one woman put it, "In a society where dollars symbolize the primary measure of success, women have been shortchanged for too long."

Supporters of comparable worth argued that greater pay equity will reduce competition and hostility among the sexes and will free women to direct more of their creative energies toward corporate goals. According to one male respondent, setting job rates on the basis of worth to the organization "will ultimately allow greater freedom of life-styles for both men and women."

Other participants commented on what they perceive to be the economic necessity of comparable worth compensation schemes because of the growing numbers of single parents, working widows, and wives whose spouses are unemployed.

Although most respondents are concerned that comparable worth pay practices may put employers in a precarious financial situation, at least some are optimistic that the benefits to employers of such a policy may more than offset the increased costs of upgrading women's jobs. These people think that by increasing salaries for previously undervalued jobs, companies could attract better workers of both sexes.

Strategic options

The strong emotions the comparable worth controversy provokes and the diverse opinions regarding its probable consequences leave top management wondering what strategies to pursue. Alternatives range from adoption of a passive "wait and see" approach to complete revision of corporate pay policies and practices. In the following paragraphs, we outline three strategic options.

Wait, watch, and worry. Employers may choose not to take any steps to reduce or eliminate the earnings gap. Under current legal precedents, they are not obligated to assign equal wages or salaries to positions differing in skill, effort, responsibility, or working conditions even if those positions are judged equivalent in overall worth to the organization. Moreover, government trends toward deregulation suggest that passage of a "Comparable Worth Act" is unlikely. Further, in times of uncertain economic conditions and surplus labor, it is risky to modify pay practices in a way likely to increase average unit labor costs.

Employers must be careful, however, to keep abreast of lobbying, legislative, and collective bargaining developments so that such a conservative position does not become outmoded or illegal.

Take affirmative action. A second approach to reducing the earnings gap between males and females focuses on speeding up the selection, training, career counseling, and promotion of women to higher level positions. This approach raises women's earnings without disrupting established methods of salary determination but it also requires a much longer time horizon than direct manipulation of current compensation policies.

In an affirmative action approach, the company must first identify job classifications with disproportionate numbers of male or female employees. The organization can then take steps to correct any imbalances. Such steps might include aggressive recruiting of women for nontraditional entry-level positions, development of novel lines of transfer and promotion, and intensification of training, development, and counseling efforts to prepare women for a range of nontraditional career tracks.

Advocates of this approach note that once women become employed in positions now held exclusively by men, salary differences between the sexes will disappear. Women's advocacy groups argue, however, that affirmative action efforts must be supplemented with a third corporate strategy: modification of conventional pay procedures.

Review, revise, reevaluate.
Several corporations and a number of state and municipal governments have started to reexamine their entire compensation systems. Their motivations for undertaking such self-study vary. Some employers, particularly in the public sector, act out of a strong sense of social responsibility to set an example of fair compensation policy. Other employers have learned from experience that failure to take aggressive voluntary action on politically volatile issues often leads to strong government regulation. Still other employers enjoy the prestige and challenge of being at the cutting edge of human resource management. Finally, as our survey results suggest, many managers act in anticipation of growing pressure from employees, unions, and women's advocacy groups.

Companies that choose to address the comparable worth controversy must decide precisely which of their compensation practices require revision, and they must assess the economic feasibility of moving toward a comparable worth philosophy. They might start by searching for possible bias in the naming of positions and in the description of job duties. For example, jobs requiring equivalent levels of skill, effort, or responsibility should not have titles that imply differences in difficulty or status. As one of our respondents observed, male jobs designated "manager" or "account executive" are often quite similar to, yet paid considerably more than, female jobs entitled "supervisor" or "sales representative."

Efforts are also needed to eliminate sex-biased language in job descriptions. Experts have suggested using standardized procedures, such as the Position Analysis Questionnaire or the Management Position Description Questionnaire, for objectively describing position duties and responsibilities.[4]

A second important step in the review of compensation policies is reexamination of the nature and number of factors used to assess a job's value to the organization. Critics of conventional job evaluations contend that the compensable factors often incorporate subtle biases favoring predominantly male occupations. This view is supported by a recent National Academy of Science study, which concluded: "Perhaps because job evaluation was initially developed largely in an industrial context, the factors actually measured appear to be oriented to predominantly male jobs.…For example, effort is usually measured by strength requirements rather than fatigue levels.…Manual skill factors stress ability to handle tools rather than manual dexterity."[5]

A broader range of compensable factors might make ranking of an occupation's worth more accurate.

---

4 See Ernest J. McCormick, P.R. Jeanneret, and Robert C. Mecham, "A Study of Job Characteristics and Job Dimensions as Based on the Position Analysis Questionnaire (PAQ)," Journal of Applied Psychology, vol. 56, p. 347; and Walter W. Tornow and Patrick R. Pinto, "The Development of a Managerial Job Taxonomy: A System for Describing, Classifying, and Evaluating Executive Positions," Journal of Applied Psychology, vol. 61, p. 410.

5 D.J. Treiman, Job Evaluation: An Analytic Review (Washington, D.C.: National Academy of Sciences, 1979).

Based on research it recently conducted, a Michigan civil service task force on comparable worth endorses the use of an expanded set of compensable factors for measuring job worth in state government.

Using one evaluation system for setting administrative wages and another evaluation system for setting wages for technical specialties frustrates attempts to compare relative worth across male- and female-dominated job classes and is therefore another important area for review. In 1981 municipal workers in San Jose, California staged a strike to get the city to agree to use a single evaluation system and to eventually eliminate market wage information in the determination of municipal salaries.

To assess the consequences of revising compensation policies, corporate planners can undertake a simulation. Following the guidelines we have discussed, planners can develop a single, comprehensive job evaluation system and apply it to all positions for a ranking of jobs in the organization. Setting salaries based exclusively on internal equity considerations would simulate an idealized comparable worth compensation method. Comparisons of present practices with the idealized comparable worth system would then show how much of the salary differential between men and women would be reduced by adopting a comparable worth policy.

Further comparisons can approximate the effects on payroll expenditures. On the basis of these projected benefits and costs, corporate decision makers can better judge the kind and extent of compensation policy revisions that are practical in their organizations. Open-minded efforts on the part of managers to examine the issues and explore the alternatives represent an important first step toward creating fair and equitable reward systems for all employees.

YOU SAID: AND WE SAID:

"Give us training tools that are relevant to our business...ones we can use *now*."

"We need new cases that stimulate meaningful discussion."

"It can't be a catalog of canned programs... everything we do is custom."

"Make it a single source for up-to-date materials ...on the most current business topics."

"Better yet if it's from a reputable business school. That adds credibility."

"Introducing the Harvard Business School Corporate Training and Development Catalog."

You asked for it. And now it's here.

The new Harvard Business School Corporate Training and Development Catalog is created exclusively for those who design and develop custom training programs.

It's filled cover-to-cover with valuable materials you can put to work on the spot. You'll find a comprehensive selection of cases, *Harvard Business Review* articles, videos, Special Collections, books, and more.

Our new catalog covers the critical management topics affecting corporations today, like Leadership, Quality, Global Business, Marketing, and Strategy, to name a few. And it's all organized, indexed, and cross-referenced to make it easy for you to find precisely what you need.

HOW TO ORDER

To order by FAX, dial 617-495-6985. Or call 617-495-6192. Please mention telephone order code 132A. Or send a check for $10 payable to HBS Publishing Division, or credit card information to: HBS Corporate Training and Development Catalog, Harvard Business School Publishing Division, Operations Department, Boston, MA 02163. **All orders must be prepaid.**

Order No.	Title	Qty. ×	Price +	Shipping* =	Total
39001	Catalog		$10		

*U.S. and Canada: 5% for UPS or first class mail. *Foreign Surface Mail*: 15% for parcel post registered; allow 3–6 mos. *Express Deliveries* (credit card orders only): billed at cost; all foreign orders not designating express delivery will be sent by registered surface mail.

☐ Check enclosed (in U.S. funds drawn on U.S. bank)
☐ VISA ☐ American Express ☐ MasterCard

Card Number_____ Exp. Date_____

Signature_____

Telephone_____ FAX_____

Name_____

Organization_____

Street_____

City_____ State/Zip_____

Country_____ ☐ Home Address ☐ Organization Address

Please Reference Telephone Order Source Code 132A

Harvard Business School Publishing